Praise for

An Accident of Geography

"*An Accident of Geography* offers a rousing, uplifting, high-octane tour of an extraordinary life. Although Dick Blum has made an indelible mark in many spheres, I know him primarily as the driving force behind the amazing American Himalayan Foundation. Over the past twenty years I have witnessed Dick's visionary leadership and irrepressible energy transform hundreds of thousands of lives in Nepal, Tibet, and India. If you're wondering how to make the world a better place, this book will inspire you."

—**Jon Krakauer,** author of *Into the Wild, Into Thin Air,* and *Missoula: Rape and the Justice System in a College Town*

"*An Accident of Geography* could also be called *An Accident of Birth.* Where we are born determines so much about our chances to fulfill our potential on earth. This inspiring book describes the work being done by people who want to make sure that this accident does not turn into a punishment, even a life sentence. It is a book about innovation but above all, compassion."

—**Fareed Zakaria,** author and CNN anchor

"Dick Blum is an American original. His chapter on reviving two moribund financial institutions in Asia, generating $4 billion for investors by 2010, is destined to become required reading in courses on business strategy and international management."

—**Walter Isaacson,** president and CEO of The Aspen Institute, and *New York Times* best-selling author

"Richard Blum has been engaged in philanthropic work in Nepal, Bhutan, Tibet, and the Himalayan regions of India. He has generously helped many poor people find new opportunities, enabling threatened communities and cultures to thrive. *An Accident of Geography* is a moving account of what he and his colleagues have achieved in their efforts to promote development and happiness for all. There is much in the pages of this book to emulate and admire."

—**His Holiness the Dalai Lama**

"*An Accident of Geography* abounds with life lessons, showing us Richard Blum's fascinating and, at times, surprising journey as a leader in business and finance, education, politics both domestic and international, global economic development, religion, spirituality, and philanthropy. The book includes, close-up, some of the most significant figures of his era, from Sir Edmund Hillary to Jimmy Carter; the Dalai Lama; Bill Clinton; Barack Obama; and Blum's wife, Senator Dianne Feinstein. His book shows how an optimistic, talented, and energetic American made himself into what Isaiah Berlin might have called both hedgehog and fox."

—Michael Beschloss, presidential historian

"Dick Blum's passion to make the world a better place, particularly for those born in the world's poorest regions, is evident on every page of this important and moving book."

—George P. Shultz, former US Secretary of State

"This timely call to action begs us to consider how we can turn privilege and good fortune into positive action to reduce poverty and suffering in a world of increasingly limited resources. Dick has made it his life's work to share his success by fostering programs which provide education, healthcare, food, and access to clean water in needy communities around the world. The seeds he has sown will continue to grow and bear fruit for generations to come."

—Richard Gere, actor and humanitarian

"The friendship between Dick Blum and my father, Ed Hillary, came from time shared in the Himalayas. But, unlike most expeditionaries, their focus moved from the mountains to the people who lived among them. Dick's book is about how these people in turn became good friends. Once you have friendship and trust, it is a short climb to empowerment and from there the climb ascends the arête of innovation to the summit spur of actualization. This is the story of that climb."

—Peter Hillary, mountaineer, philanthropist, and writer

"Dick Blum has worked for more than forty years to fight poverty, strengthen democratic institutions, and promote education. He has written a timely, engaging book about the promise and challenges of today's global development work—and one person's focused determination to make a difference. I urge you to read *An Accident of Geography*."

—**Madeleine Albright,** former US Secretary of State

"*An Accident of Geography* is the well-told story of one man's fight against global poverty. The book abounds with energy, innovative ideas, and impatience with existing governments and bureaucracies. After reading it, you will ask yourself what you have done to improve the lives of others. On this score, Blum's record will be hard to beat."

—**Janet Napolitano,** president of the University of California and former US Secretary of Homeland Security

"Deeply troubling at times, this absorbing, fast-paced personal journey is also affectionate, humorous, instructive, and, ultimately, uplifting. Dick Blum makes a compelling case that the best response to today's urgent challenge of avoiding deadly regional conflicts is fighting poverty with compassion *and* disciplined management that gets results."

—**Walter F. Mondale,** former Vice President of the United States

"As a successful investor, Richard demonstrated that smart strategic thinking and analysis coupled with persistent, focused leadership could build market value for companies in the United States and around the world. This same approach can transform global poverty and expand the reach of justice, especially for the world's poorest people. *An Accident of Geography* is a must-read for all young people and especially those with that important inner desire to do something special for the world."

—**Rajiv Shah,** distinguished fellow, Georgetown University, and former administrator of the US Agency for International Development

"Dick's philanthropic generosity makes the world a far better place . . . and inspires me every day. *An Accident of Geography* gave me even more insight into Dick's extraordinary contributions to mankind. For anyone wishing to give back to society, this book will serve as a template for how to do so effectively, and with great passion and humility."

—**Sherry Lansing,** founder and CEO of
The Sherry Lansing Foundation

"An adventurer–philanthropist's lively, passionate combination of memoir, manifesto, and manual for anyone who wants to improve the world."

—**Strobe Talbott,** president of the Brookings Institution

"In this thoughtful and inspiring book, Richard Blum offers his personal journey as a model for how to improve the lives of others. He shows us through example that although one person cannot defeat poverty, one person can make a profound difference."

—**Robert B. Reich,** Chancellor's Professor of Public Policy,
University of California, Berkeley

COMPASSION, INNOVATION,

AND THE FIGHT AGAINST POVERTY

An Accident
of Geography

FOREWORD BY JIMMY CARTER

RICHARD C. BLUM

with Thomas C. Hayes

GREENLEAF
BOOK GROUP PRESS

This publication is designed to provide accurate and authoritative information in regard to the subject matter covered. It is sold with the understanding that the publisher and author are not engaged in rendering legal, accounting, or other professional services. If legal advice or other expert assistance is required, the services of a competent professional should be sought.

Published by Greenleaf Book Group Press
Austin, Texas
www.gbgpress.com

Distributed by Greenleaf Book Group

For ordering information or special discounts for bulk purchases, please contact Greenleaf Book Group at PO Box 91869, Austin, TX 78709, 512.891.6100.

Design and composition by Greenleaf Book Group
Cover design by Greenleaf Book Group
Cover photo by Luigi Fieni

Cataloging-in-Publication data is available.

Print ISBN: 978-1-62634-334-4

eBook ISBN: 978-1-62634-335-1

Part of the Tree Neutral® program, which offsets the number of trees consumed in the production and printing of this book by taking proactive steps, such as planting trees in direct proportion to the number of trees used: www.treeneutral.com

TreeNeutral®

Printed in the United States of America on acid-free paper

16 17 18 19 20 21   10 9 8 7 6 5 4 3

First Edition

For Dianne
Annette, Heidi, Eileen, and Katherine,
and my seven grandchildren, that each in their own way
I hope will advance the work of global development

Contents

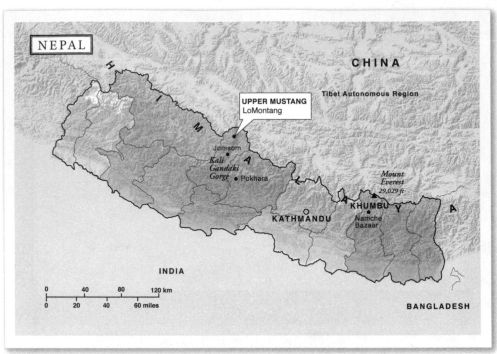

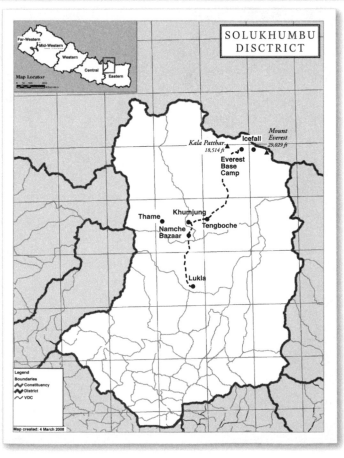

Foreword

I first met Dick Blum in the 1970s because of politics. He became
a friend and advisor to Walter "Fritz" Mondale not long before
Fritz became my running mate in our victorious 1976 campaign
for the White House, and he then aided Fritz after the election in
crafting our administration's urban policies. But it was trekking
with my wife, Rosalynn, and Dick in the rugged mountains near
Mount Everest ten years later that first opened my eyes to Dick
Blum's expansive humanitarian commitment.

His initial acts of generosity in Nepal had accelerated, as I
learned, through his friendship and work with Sir Edmund Hillary. Both men loved and admired the loyal, hardworking Sherpa
people. These two Westerners—one the world-famous con-
queror of Everest and former beekeeper from New Zealand, the
other a private-equity investor from San Francisco with a long-
held fascination for the Himalaya and an eye on Asia's growing
middle class—wanted to help the families and communities of
their Sherpa guides.

It was the Sherpas who not only accompanied and cared for
them but in fact made possible their personal adventures across

the Himalaya and, in the case of Sir Edmund's world-captivating achievement years before, to the very peak of Everest. So Sir Edmund and Dick asked the Sherpas, *How can* we *help* you? What they learned set their agenda for the next few decades: build schools and health clinics; restore Tibetan Buddhist monasteries, the wellspring of Tibetans' cultural identity; and introduce hydroelectric power, airplane access, and simple modern conveniences. All this became part of initial development work by Sir Edmund, Dick, and their mountaineering colleagues in Nepal's northeastern Khumbu, in the mountains and valleys beneath Mount Everest.

Following Sir Edmund's philanthropic lead, Dick and a few of his trekking buddies made a long-term commitment to helping the poorest people of Nepal, Tibet, and northern India when they established in 1981 a nonprofit organization, the American Himalayan Foundation. They and their growing roster of donors and volunteers have kept that commitment, often in extraordinary ways and especially in the months following the devastating earthquakes that killed more than nine thousand people and left nearly three million homeless in Nepal in the spring of 2015. Perhaps the foundation's most important work, however, is confronting the scourge of sex slavery by supporting the full-time education of 14,800 vulnerable girls, from early grades through high school.

Dick's American Himalayan Foundation and The Carter Center, our nonprofit organizations focused on improving human rights and health care and founded around the same time, share many principles regarding global development and how to combat poverty. The most important may be putting local people at the center of any project. If people have the right knowledge, encouragement, and skills, and if they have reason to hope, they can change their own lives. We know from more than seventy-five years of combined experience in confronting poverty in Asia, Africa, and Latin America that focused, disciplined, science-led efforts do work.

Dick is a longtime trustee of The Carter Center. We often have traveled together over the past thirty years, with hours of opportunities to discuss our goals and share ideas. Dick has for many years helped guide our financing at the center. He has journeyed with me often to countries such as Nepal, Burma, Sudan, Nigeria, and Ghana to advocate for democracy, and to Sudan, Ghana, Ethiopia, and elsewhere in Africa as an advisor and funding partner in the center's projects to fight preventable diseases such as Guinea worm, trachoma, and river blindness.

Beyond our work at The Carter Center, Dick is a prominent activist and supporter of public policy organizations and institutions such as The Brookings Institution; the National Democratic Institute for International Affairs; the President's Global Development Council; George Soros's Central European University in Budapest; and the University of California, where he is a longtime member of the governing board of regents and served more than two years as its chairman.

Through many vivid and often surprising accounts, Dick masterfully describes in this book guiding principles and examples of what we know works best in the field in the fight against poverty. Dick and his staff have a hands-on attitude. They know what's happening in these remote villages and communities among the people who are in need. They are efficient. There is minimal bureaucracy and waste. They concentrate, as we do at The Carter Center, on helping the people who are most deprived and neglected, and who suffer from the most correctable problems. I don't believe any nongovernment organization (NGO) can possibly do more with available funds than the American Himalayan Foundation does.

It's no accident that, in addition to serving on the board of the American Himalayan Foundation, I am one of the advisors of the interdisciplinary academic and research center on combating global poverty that Dick helped establish in 2006. The Blum Center for Developing Economies on the University of California's ten campuses may well be the finest program of its kind in the world. It turns out legions of young graduates who are well prepared with expertise, humility, purpose, and a pragmatic optimism for combating poverty in the United States and globally.

The breadth of Dick's interests, knowledge, experience, and influence in practically every area of life in which he's involved is remarkable. He has been an impressively principled and successful investor. He is a prominent activist in several public policy institutions supporting global development and the spread of democracy. He and his wife of more than thirty-five years, Senator Dianne Feinstein, are longtime supporters of the Tibetan campaign for autonomy within China, with close ties to His Holiness the Fourteenth Dalai Lama.

Dick Blum helps improve the policies of each organization, agency, or program in which he's engaged. The heart of our humanitarian work together has always been helping poor people figure out how they're going to get out of poverty.

An Accident of Geography is a book you should read to learn more about progress in and pathways for fighting poverty. You will find many moving stories and concrete examples in the pages that follow. I hope they inspire you to find your place alongside Dick, me, and millions of other activists around the globe who are dedicated to making the developing world work better for its people.

—Jimmy Carter

Introduction

I wrote this book over the past few years with an increasing sense of urgency. While we continue to make progress in fighting poverty, significant challenges remain to raise living standards in the world's poorest communities.

Overcoming those challenges and winning this fight are crucial. Wherever poverty and ignorance continue to exist—and access to dangerous weapons is unchecked—the risk of more conflict and a more dangerous world will continue to threaten us all. Wherever we can help people improve their access to basic health care, food, clean water, and education, we will advance the cause of world peace.

* * *

When I was a University of California undergrad at Berkeley in the 1950s, I traveled by train and hitchhiked across much of Western Europe and northern Africa the summer before my senior year. I didn't really know much about the world. I'd hardly been outside the United States, and not often beyond the San Francisco Bay Area where I grew up.

I never realized how difficult life was for so many. From Vienna to Casablanca, I saw deplorable living conditions for millions of people. Years later, trekking through remote villages of the Himalaya in Nepal, I realized even more clearly how fortunate I was: the random assignment of family, culture, and basic resources necessary to live a happy life is an accident of geography.

You can do the math in different ways, but the facts are billions of people alive today were born in villages, cities, or countries where they have had little access to the simplest necessities.

What has made my pursuits in business, public policy, and philanthropy deeply interesting *to me*—what I care about most—is the experience of joining with others to study and fight the causes of global poverty.

This book comes out of that cumulative experience.

It's organized in four parts. My particular passion has been helping people in the Himalaya, especially the Sherpa and Tibetan people, and in part 1 I introduce you to people I met in the mountains of Nepal more than thirty years ago who inspired me and my climbing buddies to found the American Himalayan Foundation. We were very lucky—a handful of scruffy climbers with a dream to do good—to have one of the best partners possible, our dear friend the late Sir Edmund Hillary, whose respect for the Sherpas combined with his intensely hands-on and practical way of working still informs our operating style.

AHF now touches the lives of more than three hundred thousand people each year, people throughout the Himalaya who are in need and have no one else—the poorest children, young girls in danger of being sold, destitute elders, refugees adrift, marginalized communities losing their culture.

In part 2, we turn to the importance of the private sector and finance in building scale for ideas and innovations, and building wealth. As a young private equity investor, I began to understand how to manage the dangers and rewards of risk, the importance of investing for the long term, the role of innovation in growing companies (and economies), and the importance of capital, often foreign capital, in developing economies.

I was curious about why things are as they are, how they might be made better, and what I could do about it. I applied the essential lessons I learned as an investor to our philanthropic mission about how organizations operate best, and how they can spot trends for future growth and focus on core strengths to deliver the best products and services.

Those same essential lessons guided my experiences volunteering in local and national government, as well as multinational think tanks and policy advocacy groups, the focus of part 3. How can public institutions and public policy be better managed to improve the lives of everyday people? How can we better allocate resources? How can we build stronger partnerships?

You can't talk about development and poverty without talking about public policy. And you need to understand how these institutions actually work—and how basic business disciplines can improve them—if you want to develop informed opinions and build valuable partnerships. Understanding improves through action.

Finally, in part 4, we turn to the work that is now the most important in my life in taking on the challenges of reducing global poverty: The Blum Center for Developing Economies at the University of California.

The Center has tapped into a huge unmet, even unanticipated, demand. Our Global Poverty and Practice minor is the most popular on the Berkeley campus. Our multidisciplinary model has influenced unrelated departments at Berkeley and across the UC system in breaking down the infamous silos of academia. The students and faculty are an inspiration to me, tackling and solving real-world problems.

* * *

I'm a realist, and this book certainly covers some grim topics. But I'm also an optimist. Everywhere I look I see progress being made, with people participating at every level of society to solve our biggest problems. That is one message that I hope you will take away from reading this book: everyone has something they can contribute; everyone has something they can do to actively help others less fortunate.

The main point is to keep marching on. As Nelson Mandela said, "After climbing a great hill, one only finds that there are many more hills to climb."

Part 1

The Passionate and Inspired

Chapter 1

Life's Inspiration

*"Nothing for me has been more rewarding in life
than the result of our climb on Everest, when we have
devoted ourselves to the welfare of our Sherpa friends."*

—Sir Edmund Hillary

When I was a boy, one of my most treasured possessions was Richard Halliburton's *Book of Marvels*. I read and reread his stories—of riding an elephant across the Alps like Hannibal, of swimming the fifty-mile length of the Panama Canal, of flying in a small aircraft close to Mount Everest in 120-mile-an-hour winds. Halliburton wrote with awe about the three attempts by George Mallory to scale Everest and the mystery surrounding the disappearance of Mallory and his partner, Andrew Irvine, on the third try. I pored over the pages again and again, until the book's large black-and-white photographs and drawings of the world's great wonders were smudged by years of fingerprints.

So you might imagine how I felt when, in my final year at Lowell High School in San Francisco, I heard the news that

Edmund Hillary and Tenzing Norgay had reached the summit of Mount Everest.

It was May 29, 1953. The impact was stunning—a mix of awe and astonishment around the world. For at least thirty years, millions of people like me had wondered, *If someone ever reached the top of the world, what would they see? Would they be able to breathe, to survive? How would they get there, and how would they get back?* I read some of the answers in the morning *San Francisco Chronicle.*

I was thrilled these two men had made it to the summit, but I was also a little jealous—my opportunity to get there first was gone. Nearly thirty years after their triumph, though, I was excited to lead the first foreign expedition on the only side of Everest that had yet to be climbed, the forbidding Kangshung Face on the east, in Tibet. Sir Ed was with our team, a great honor for me and the last time he ever was on Everest. (Bad weather forced our lead climbers to abandon this historic attempt, as I describe in chapter 11, but two years later six members of that team completed the ascent, aided by the same rope lines they had secured before on Kangshung and by warmer El Niño wind currents.)

When you carry a deep passion, what might seem like magical thinking can lead to something very real. My passion as a young man was trekking in the beautiful lands of the Himalaya. As the years passed, inspired by Sir Ed; my Sherpa guide, Pasang Kami; and other people I met on my journeys there, that passion evolved into finding ways to help the people of Nepal, Tibet, and elsewhere in those mountain ranges improve their lives. Now those activities have expanded dramatically into a much wider ambition and joining with legions of others in the fight against poverty.

Poverty problems are complex. They have to be addressed on multiple fronts to make a lasting impact. Ours include developing multidisciplinary studies with a strong connection to engineering; helping fund and advise on scores of local projects for poor people in isolated towns and villages in South Asia, such as keeping fifteen thousand Nepali girls in school and safe from sex traffickers, and supporting Tibetan refugees; and assisting former presidents Bill Clinton and Jimmy Carter in the work of their nonprofit organizations. We also fund policy research on poverty and development at the Brookings Institution and advise government organizations such as the US Agency for International Development (USAID) and the President's Global Development Council, which I helped design and initiate.

Pasang Kami

After that astonishing news of Sir Ed and Tenzing's success, it took me fifteen years to make my first trip to the Himalaya, in 1968—and it was exactly the kind of life-changing experience I expected it would be.

Still carrying my dream of seeing Mount Everest and the breathtaking surrounds, I found a way to extend my first business trip in Asia to include Nepal. At the time, it was far from a common destination. When I asked a travel agent in San Francisco about flights to Kathmandu, he replied, "I'm sorry. Our expert on Africa is out to lunch."

In the four weeks I spent backpacking through rhododendron forests, giant bamboo ranges, and otherworldly vistas to reach Annapurna (the tenth-highest peak in the world) and beyond, I never saw another Westerner (other than the two friends who joined me for the first two weeks). It would take another decade for Nepal's reputation as a prized destination for trekkers and climbers to grow.

Our head Sherpa, or *sirdar*, was a polite, generous man named Pasang Kami. He was short and wore glasses but was also strong. He spoke only when he needed to. On our journey, he looked after everyone, paying careful attention to how I labored through some of the narrow trails, high passes, and deep valleys. He was motivated not by the money we were paying but by the dedication of a devout Buddhist to show compassion for another human being. I liked him immediately.

We shared an obvious desire to learn what we could about each other. Everyone called him P. K.—including his wife, I discovered. He had first worked on trekking expeditions as a cook boy, rising in time to porter, guide, and finally *sirdar*. Trekking or climbing with foreigners offered a better opportunity to support his family than being an assistant cook in the Indian army, where he had earned a pittance of less than fifty cents a day. There were no schools in the mountains where he grew up, so he never had any formal education. But he had ambition and was a hard worker. He had taught himself to read, speak, and write in Nepali and English.

I didn't realize at the time that he would become one of the most important people in my life.

An Epiphany about Destiny, Opportunity

We started our trek from Pokhara, then a quiet town and today a tourist hub with a population of more than 250,000. We spent our first night at a Tibetan refugee camp called Hyangja. People living there and in many similar settlements in Nepal and northern India were among the many thousands who had fled Tibet with little money and few possessions after troops sent by the Chinese government mounted an increasingly ruthless invasion starting in 1950.

The camp resembled a small Tibetan village, with stone buildings, flat roofs, and a small temple. People were incredibly friendly, in a way that, especially given their circumstances, was spellbinding for a Westerner like me. Small children came and sat in our laps. Some even spoke to us in English. Many had been born in Hyangja or carried there over the mountains on somebody's back. Beneath the smiles and laughter that night, I felt uneasy, inadequate. Here in this isolated encampment was stark evidence of how the hand of fate works randomly across the human race, especially in shaping the lives of the very rich and the very poor, with absolutely no respect for innate talent or potential.

These bright, cheerful kids and their parents seemed trapped in the most forbidding circumstances. In contrast, I had had opportunities for a strong public education and career success, all within twenty miles of the middle-class neighborhood in southwest San Francisco where I had grown up. Barely scratching out an existence as subsistence farmers, the families here often were denied even the most basic needs—access to health care, education, clean water, and especially the wisdom that had passed down through their ancient Tibetan Buddhist traditions. Of course, I had never had to worry about any of these issues. I had accumulated many resources and other advantages by the young age of thirty-two. These children had been born into a place where poverty and isolation from the post-Renaissance world were simply a way of life.

This is all just an accident of geography, I thought. I was certain of that as Scot Macbeth, Ron Lawrence, and I stretched out for the night in our sleeping bags. I was tired after the day's trek from Pokhara and in need of some serious, restful sleep, but restful sleep was not in the cards that night. Many questions raced through my mind: *How can I possibly help these people? How soon can I get started? Who might join me?*

This simple altruistic reflex had been ingrained in me from a young age by two strong-minded women: my mother and my grandmother. Both were good women who were active with local charities. Donating our time and sharing what we could was always a given in our house. My mother, Louise, known to most everyone as "Lou," was our Cub Scout den mother when my brother, Bob, and I were young. When we were grown, she volunteered at various art museums and ran the gift shop at the local hospital.

During World War II, my grandmother, Cleveland Heil Hirsch, decided to do her duty and joined the American Women's Voluntary Services. She was assigned to repairing airplane instruments at McClellan Air Force Base in Sacramento. I can just imagine my five-foot-tall, highly proper grandmother wearing blue jeans or coveralls, lying on her back under an instrument panel for hours every day. She was sixty years old. The grandmother Cleve I knew had never worked outside the home, yet once she signed up for the war effort, it wasn't long before she won an award for suggesting how a cockpit instrument could be improved.

To me, that first night of the Himalaya trek, "signing up" seemed the obvious thing to do.

My understanding of the situation in the Himalaya was primitive, though. I couldn't even speculate about plausible answers or solutions. This was the first of many, many fitful nights thinking about these people and their struggles. The injustices were baffling to me. I could not accept them. I do not accept them now.

Khumbu, Land of the Sherpas

I was enthralled by what I saw of Nepal on that first trip and anxious to return to the Himalaya. I had always wanted to see the Everest area, where most Sherpas live—in the Khumbu part, within what is known as the Solukhumbu District—even more so now because of our new connection with P. K.

The Sherpas originally migrated from eastern Tibet—the name

in Tibetan literally means "people of the east"—several hundred years ago through what is known as the Nangpa La, a pass at an elevation of more than nineteen thousand feet into Solukhumbu.[1] They share the Tibetan heritage in language, clothing, and Tibetan Buddhism. Sherpa guides and porters were vital to the success of the early Western explorers in the Himalaya. Their mountaineering skills and ability to tolerate extreme altitudes are emblematic traits of the singular Sherpa culture. So is their adaptability.[2]

In 1970, two years after our first trip, Scot Macbeth and I found ourselves hiking up the mountainside from tiny Lukla Airport toward P. K.'s village, an ancient trading center known as Namche Bazaar. We trekked along the fast-flowing Dudh Kosi River and through the Himalayan forest, passing small Sherpa huts and villages, each with dome-shaped Buddhist meditation and worship houses known as *gompas*. We saw prayer wheels—small cylinders bearing sacred written prayers that, when spun, are believed to bring the same benefits as prayers recited orally, and strings of colorful prayer flags rippling and snapping in the breeze.

Himalayan Buddhists believe spiritual beneficences etched on the prayer flags, known as *lungtas* or "wind horses," are received by all who are touched by the winds that animate the flags. The most important mantra in Buddhism, *Om Mani Padme Hum*, is a prayer for protection from danger and a call to compassion, "the Jewel in the Heart of the Lotus." You see it in Tibetan script adorning prayer flags, prayer wheels, and mani stones—large, smooth stones with this or other mantras etched into the surface—wherever you go in the Himalaya, but especially in the Khumbu. His Holiness the Dalai Lama tells us the mantra is best understood as six syllables embodying Buddha's teachings on the six realms of existence in suffering.[3]

As we neared Namche Bazaar, we could see Mount Everest for the first time through the trees. Chomolungma, "Mother

Goddess of the World" in Tibetan, or "Sagarmatha," as Nepalis have called it for centuries, was more exciting than I had anticipated. We stood on a ridge above the village, enthralled by the wonderful vistas before us. Everest was in the distance; closer at hand were the soaring, snow-covered peaks of Thamserku, Kangtega, Ama Dablam, and Lhotse, the world's fourth-highest mountain at nearly twenty-eight thousand feet. Glancing downward, we saw verdant forests and, thousands of feet below, rivers in the deep gorges of two canyons.

For us, arriving in Namche Bazaar was like traveling into the past. The tableau was rough and rustic. There were no hotels then. Most people lived in little huts—sheds, really—with holes in the ceiling for smoke to rise from fires lighted daily for cooking and heat. The rooms were smoky. Tuberculosis was widespread. Food was scarce.

P. K. invited us to stay with him, his wife, Namdu, and the four children they had at that time. As I came to learn, P. K. was known around the Khumbu villages as ambitious, even a bit wily, when it came to latching on to foreign trekkers. He was eager for the business at a time when there weren't many Western visitors. Maybe that is why his homestead was better than most.

The family lived in a two-story house made of stone and coated with a plaster of mud and dung to fill in the cracks for warmth. The door was about five feet high and nearly as wide, making it easy for their livestock—a cross between yaks and cattle—to enter. The animals spent their nights downstairs; the family used the living area upstairs. Typical of the Sherpas and other Himalayan mountain dwellers, the family cooked indoors over an open fire. There was no chimney. Smoke filled the house, not to mention our nostrils, clothing, and hair. We retrieved water from a nearby stream and used the outhouse outside the front door.

Everything used in Namche Bazaar was either grown nearby or carried by yaks or porters long distances through the mountains. P. K.'s house was constructed in Bhutanese style without a single nail, and the two windows had no glass. Instead, a wooden lattice holding two dozen small squares of thin paper filled each opening. These paper "windows" softened the wind and the cold, and allowed a little light in. The walls were built from rough, dark wood secured by jute rope. There was no electricity or interior lighting. We went to bed soon after dark fell, on Tibetan carpets rolled out in the main room. And we were deeply grateful for the hospitality.

During my early treks in the Himalaya, I quickly came to appreciate, as many Westerners have before and since, that Sherpas are exceptional people. Generosity and kindness are revered in their Buddhist tradition—essential conduct for ever-higher rebirth on the spiritual journey toward nirvana. The sacred nature of these traits no doubt is closely linked to, and magnified by, the harsh conditions of the high mountains. Years later, recalling our journeys in the Khumbu, Jimmy Carter said to me, "I have never met any people as admirable in their friendship, their unselfishness, and their eagerness to do what is right than the Sherpas who helped us in the Himalayan region."

Your Daughters Are My Daughters

Over the years, P. K. was my guide on many trips in Nepal. More than that, he was my close friend, and I was welcomed always as a member of his extended family.

P. K. eventually had six children—one son and five daughters—in an era when it was rare for any Sherpa girl, or Sherpani, to have an education beyond grammar school. The odds were not much better for Sherpa boys. One day in the early '70s, about to board a plane back to Nepal after a trip to the United States, P. K. said to me, "Dick, if my daughters don't get an education, and they don't get married, they'll spend their lives carrying loads up and down their mountain." For P. K., enrolling his children in school would mean having to send them to boarding school in Kathmandu. This was not something he could afford.

"P. K., from today on, your daughters are my daughters," I promised him. "You get them into school. We'll help educate them."

When some of my climbing buddies heard of my promise to P. K., they wanted to do the same for the children of their Sherpa guides. It seemed the least we could, and should, do: an expression of thanks to these men who not only risked their lives to support our dreams, but were such soulful companions amid what were, for us, extraordinarily challenging physical conditions.

Thus was born my first charitable organization: the Sherpa Scholarship Fund. We helped support the education of hundreds of Sherpa children. I kept my pledge to P. K., helping to educate his children and grandchildren. All of his children attended schools in Kathmandu, three attended college in the United States, and one of his grandsons was a straight-A student at the University of San Francisco.

For me, the success of P. K.'s children shows so clearly that when children anywhere in the world are given the right resources, under the right conditions, many will thrive, and some will accomplish wonders. Poor kids are no less smart or capable than any kid with better access to education and opportunity. P. K.'s oldest daughter, Nawang Doka, is a shining example.

One year, we took a family vacation to Hawaii, and Nawang was with us. It was the first time Nawang had ever seen an ocean. She didn't know how to swim. Annette, the eldest of my three daughters, remembers her leaping agilely across some nearby rocks, "like a mountain goat," avoiding a shallow pool of water near the beach. I gave her a mask and snorkel and said, "Come on, you've got to see this! Just let me hold on to you." As she floated face down, breathing through a snorkel, I expected her to stiffen from fear, but she was completely relaxed—that Sherpa adaptability at work.

Nawang hoped to study dentistry after graduating college in Kathmandu, but she needed a program that was adapted for a cold-weather climate like the Khumbu. The only suitable training was at a small academy in Saskatchewan, 250 miles north of the Montana border. At times, Nawang's life there was difficult. She felt isolated, lonesome, a cultural misfit. Yet she persevered.

When she returned to Nepal, diploma in hand, she opened the first dental clinic in the Sherpa village, along the Everest mountain trail where she was raised. For nearly thirty years, she has been the only practicing dental technician Namche Bazaar has ever had. I am delighted that Nawang took her triumph in the Saskatchewan classrooms back to the Khumbu community she loved. She returned well-prepared, and has given hundreds of people the comfort of better health care—and more radiant, pain-free smiles—with advanced, modern techniques. That makes me smile, too.

Sir Ed and the Push for Schools

I was trekking once again in the Everest region in 1978 when I came across a tall, lanky New Zealander. I recognized him instantly. It was Sir Edmund Hillary. I introduced myself and told him I was a great admirer. He was gracious and humble even though strangers came up to him all the time to shake his hand and share favorite stories. I told mine—how thrilling and motivating his and Tenzing's achievement on Everest had been for me—and mentioned my modest efforts to help Sherpa children with the scholarship fund, and we continued on our separate ways.

At that point in his life, Sir Ed had dedicated himself to the Sherpas for nearly two decades. He was determined to improve their living conditions and opportunities, and he often remarked that what he did after climbing Mount Everest—giving back to the people who had helped him and Tenzing—was more important than reaching the top. The Sherpas came to regard Sir Ed as their greatest modern benefactor.

The spark that started it all was the answer he got from a Sherpa friend when Sir Ed asked what he could do to help. "Our children have eyes but they cannot see," the friend replied. They needed schools, he said, to open their eyes to the world. Sir Ed immediately went to work with local Sherpas to build a school in Khumjung, a village above Namche Bazaar.

At the time, in 1961, most people in Khumjung and the neighboring villages were illiterate, and the local agricultural economy was barely at subsistence level. More than fifty years later, there are sixty-three schools in Solukhumbu, with over six thousand students in classes from nursery school through tenth grade. The flagship, Khumjung Secondary School, has 317 students, mostly from surrounding villages and some from farther away who live in a hostel. Khumjung's students are remarkably successful: 97 percent pass their school leaving exams—double the national average for public schools.

In recent years, there have been changes in the Khumbu as many Sherpas, now much more prosperous, have moved to Kathmandu and beyond, and other Nepali ethnic groups have come to make the Everest area home. As a result, the student population is more diverse, and schools are merging as enrollment has declined. Once again there is a push to improve the quality of education.

Access to education is crucial for all Sherpas and Nepalis who dream of lives beyond subsistence farming or bearing heavy loads for neighbors, tourists, trekkers, or others. The country's population is fast-growing, now at twenty-eight million, and as Internet access improves, most young people understand more clearly than ever that education is critical for their future. They increasingly have role models who show what can be accomplished. Many students from remote Nepali villages have become foresters, engineers, and teachers.

Building the Khumjung school was just the beginning for Sir Ed. The Himalayan Trust he founded in 1960 in Nepal pulsated with his energy and commitment. He believed the climbing community owed a large debt to the Sherpas, who made their mountaineering expeditions possible at great risk to their own lives. The Himalayan Trust went on to develop not only schools but also clinics and clean-water projects all over the Everest region.

"To many Western eyes, the Everest region is a place of great beauty and high mountains to be conquered," Sir Ed said when the Himalayan Trust was created. "For the Sherpas who live there, however, life has few privileges. Medicine and education are scarce, bridges and paths are often destroyed, and the forests on which they depend are rapidly depleting." Later, he told an interviewer, "I suddenly decided that instead of just talking about it, why didn't I try and do something . . . I was brought up to believe that if you had a chance to help people worse off than you, then you should do it. Plus I really enjoyed the work."[4]

LIKE DRIVING INTO A PARKING GARAGE AT 80 MILES AN HOUR

Sir Ed had scouted the area below Namche Bazaar for a landing strip before his 1953 expedition, but came up short in finding a suitable field or pasture where he might be able to fly in loads of equipment. He knew after the expedition that if he were going to build schools and clinics, the Khumbu would need an airport. Airlifting construction materials and equipment in a matter of hours instead of having them ferried up narrow mountain trails on the backs of Sherpa porters for eighteen days would sharply reduce the cost of and time required for any project.

This time he spotted a place that seemed right, but the Sherpas misunderstood him and started building along a moderately sloping hillside at a place known as Lukla. Lukla was not even large enough to be called a village. There were a few herders' huts and potato fields. That was it.

Landing at Lukla today is like driving into a parking garage at eighty miles an hour. The airstrip is one of the highest, most dangerous in the world. The paved runway is just fifteen hundred feet long (or one-fourth the length of typical runways in US airports) and slopes upward for incoming flights at an unusually steep grade of 12 percent. On their approach, pilots first must fly across a canyon, avoid a steep left-to-right hillside where the ground is so close that you can see trekkers' footprints in the dirt as you pass above, and then nearly stall the aircraft to descend rapidly.

Once on the ground, the pilots can't relax. In the trekking season, up to forty small plane flights arrive each morning from Kathmandu, all within a few hours. Each aircraft has only a few minutes to disembark incoming passengers, load outgoing passengers on board, and get airborne again. The sequence has to be rapidly, carefully choreographed. Flying in and out of Lukla is always hair-raising.

Sir Ed's main motivation for building the airport was to better connect the Sherpas to the outside world and aid local development. In reality, the airport's largest impact was in luring many thousands of tourists, most of whom arrived after a thirty-minute flight from Kathmandu. By the 1990s, tourism had easily become the biggest contributor to the Khumbu's economy.

P. K. was early to spot the economic opportunities that tourism would bring to the region. He founded a trekking company and participated in expeditions to Everest, Dhaulagiri, and Annapurna, among other places. He helped introduce hydroelectric power to Namche Bazaar and built one of the first travelers' lodges in the area: the Khumbu Lodge, now managed by P. K.'s son, who studied business in Australia. Nearly fifty of these inns now stand where dozens of Sherpa huts once dotted the terrace farmlands near Namche Bazaar. P. K. and Namdu's original house is the only one that remains.

Partners for Impact

Sir Ed was an inspirational figure and a tremendous organizer, but not a fund-raiser. Some months after our chance encounter in the Himalaya in 1978, we arranged to meet in San Francisco. Over lunch at the Fairmont Hotel, we explored how we might collaborate to do more for the Sherpas.

Sir Ed remembered my brief mention of our Sherpa Scholarship Fund, which, he said, was why he wanted to follow up in person. He needed money to pay villagers in Khumjung who could provide room and board and other help for kids who lived too far away to walk every day to and from his school. He wondered if I could help. If those kids' families didn't have the money to cover room and board (and most did not, he told me), the school would never reach its potential. Nor would those kids.

"Sure," I said, "I'll be glad to provide funding for room and board." And I had a request to make of him in return.

Those scholarships my friends and I were funding were going to the kids of fathers who had been our guides, but not necessarily to the most deserving or motivated students in their communities. But we had been mulling over doing something bigger and more organized. We wanted to get our funds to where they would do the most good, but we needed someone near Namche Bazaar, someone who knew the families and the kids who might benefit most, not just Sherpas we had befriended. I said, "We'd like to do more, but we want to do it in a fair way."

Sir Ed immediately signed up to be our agent. He would tap the most promising kids in the Khumbu to receive help from the Sherpa Scholarship Fund. In turn, climbers in our group had the option to continue supporting their guides' children on their own, which is what I did for P. K. and others. A win–win.

And that is how, in 1981, I joined with several friends and colleagues to establish the American Himalayan Foundation. Over the years, we have been quiet partners continuously with the Himalayan Trust. The handshake agreement with Sir Ed at the Fairmont laid the groundwork for what I consider a classic model of effective partnerships in philanthropy. (I'll come back to this in chapter 3.) The tally of infrastructure and environmental support overseen through the Himalayan Trust, as of mid-2014, after more than three decades, was twenty-seven schools built; thirteen medical clinics and two hospitals established; numerous monasteries restored; clean-water systems provided to villages; and two million trees planted to reforest the mountains.

Nearly a quarter century after he and Tenzing Norgay summited Everest, Sir Edmund Hillary became one of my closest friends and a true mentor. Even after his passing in 2008, he remains one of my great inspirations. Tenzing Norgay's eldest son, Norbu Tenzing, has been a friend and valued colleague as vice president of the American Himalayan Foundation for more than twenty years.

Every year, the American Himalayan Foundation (AHF) touches the lives of three hundred thousand Sherpas, Nepalis, Tibetans, and others throughout the Himalayan range. From our headquarters in San Francisco and our regional office in Kathmandu, we have raised tens of millions of dollars, and join with local partners on more than 175 projects that we help fund in this part of the world. You'll find AHF projects in the remotest far west of Nepal, throughout the ancient kingdom of Mustang, with the Sherpas in the Khumbu at the foot of Mount Everest, and throughout the Kathmandu Valley down to the jungles in the Terai region bordering India. AHF also supports many Tibetan refugee communities in India.

There are more than 2.3 million charitable organizations operating in the United States, and more than 1.5 million registered with the Internal Revenue Service, according to the National Center for Charitable Statistics,[5] but we have not come across another charitable organization with a profile quite like ours. We work in a country—Nepal—where government has little ability to assist in what we do. We consult with a government in exile: the Central Tibet Administration in Dharamsala, India. And we work in Tibet, which has been ruled by the Chinese since the 1950s takeover.

We help people who have nowhere else to turn with education, care for the aged, surgeries and rehabilitation for children, restoring deforested lands, and reclaiming monasteries or building nunneries, which are important Tibetan Buddhist cultural centers. We know the territory and work closely with local partners to create the greatest impact with the least possible cost. And we have succeeded in ways we never imagined when we started more than thirty years ago. Over the next few chapters I'll describe our approach in greater detail, as well as the wide impact of the work of our partners—proof that progress is possible.

P. K. and Sir Ed's Tremendous Influence

In 2003, at the American Himalayan Foundation's annual dinner in San Francisco, we celebrated the fiftieth anniversary of Sir Ed and Tenzing reaching the summit of Mount Everest. Looking out on the faces of hundreds of people gathered before him, and reflecting on four decades of service that had helped improve the lives of many thousands, Sir Ed spoke with characteristic grace and humility:

> I have been fortunate enough to be involved in many exciting adventures. But when I look back over my life, I have little doubt that the most worthwhile things I have done have not been standing on the summits of mountains or at the North and South Poles, great experiences though they were. My most important projects have been the building and maintaining of schools and medical clinics for my good friends in the Himalaya—and helping with their beautiful monasteries, too. These are the things I will always remember.[6]

Pasang Kami and Sir Ed Hillary were role models for me, each in their own way. P. K. taught me many things both subtle and sublime about compassion, kindness, and courage. When he visited us in San Francisco in the early 1970s, he carved a mani stone in our yard, and that stirred me to build a meditation center nearby. He was more than a friend; our lives were bound together in many ways. Sadly, in 2000, he was diagnosed with a liver ailment. I brought him to the United States for treatment, but there was nothing doctors could do. He passed away a few years after the millennium at the age of sixty-two.

These two men changed the course of my life, inspiring me first to do whatever I could to help poor people across the Himalaya and then to broaden our efforts to reduce global poverty. This work has been so rewarding to me personally that I can't conceive of letting up. Roughly half of the world's population still lives on $2 a day or less. I know that if each of us will choose to play a role in fighting poverty—wherever we are, however we can, whatever our age or station in life—there is no doubt we will cut that ratio dramatically over the next twenty years. What ratio will reporters be citing then?

My motivation as a young man in going to Nepal was the mountains, but in the end it was P. K. and Sir Ed who inspired me to serve others.

Chapter 2

Respecting Culture, Reviving Community

"Our main concern is preservation of our identity."

—His Holiness the Fourteenth Dalai Lama[1]

Centuries ago, the Kali Gandaki Gorge in northwest Nepal was a main route for traders carrying goods between Tibet and India, on yaks or Tibetan ponies. It was a navigable passage through the highest mountain range in the world. It also was—and remains—one of the most stunning. When I first trekked along the gorge in 1968, on trails carved into the steep, pastel-hued hillsides looking down on the Kali Gandaki River, I was mesmerized.

Born from the massive tectonic forces that created the Himalaya hundreds of millions of years ago, Annapurna and Dhaulagiri, two of the highest mountains on earth, rise majestically on opposite sides of the gorge. The gorge itself is the deepest on earth by some measures—more than three times as deep as the Grand Canyon. The snow-covered peaks soar nearly three and a half miles skyward from the river bed. Looking out (and mostly up) beyond those 26,000-foot summits and listening to the Kali Gandaki waters nearby, you know the experience will be unforgettable.

In 1968, if you followed the trail north along the Kali Gandaki, it eventually led you to a military checkpoint at the border of the Mustang District. For close to four decades, that was as far as most foreigners could go, despite the growing influx of Westerners attracted by Annapurna. If you were caught anywhere inside the Mustang borders, you were arrested and deported. Of course, I wanted in.

My pursuit of Mustang, the Forbidden Kingdom of Lo, led to some of the most important work the American Himalayan Foundation has done to revive a community: restoring temples and a monastery, and the monastic school within.

Many nonprofit organizations are reluctant to take on projects associated with religious practices. Some of our board members questioned why we would spend money to restore fifteenth-century temples and revive monastic institutions for Buddhist monks and nuns. To me, it was not a question of supporting religious institutions. This was a truly rare opportunity to help preserve a splendid culture that was barely hanging on, only a few miles beyond the reach of the Chinese government's decades-long campaign to destroy that culture.

In life, we can become so obsessed with the most immediate, urgent needs—food, safe living conditions, basic medical care—that we lose sight of the fact that healthy, self-sustaining communities need more than just the basics of survival. What our efforts would help prove is that respect and focus on culture can be essential to successful development, and can help us access and build trust in the poorest, most isolated communities in the world.

Mustang, the Forbidden Kingdom of Lo

In 1951, the ruling Ranas of Nepal were banished to India during a revolt, and slowly the country began accepting foreigners. In 1964 Michel Peissel, a French adventurer and ethnologist with a fascination for Tibet, became the first European to reach Mustang. He even lived for several weeks in LoMontang—the old, walled capital city of Lo—despite orders by Nepal's reigning monarch that no foreigners be allowed anywhere in Lo. I was familiar with Peissel's 1967 book about his time in the region: *Mustang, The Forbidden Kingdom.*

I also had heard stories while trekking from Tibetan *khampas* about the Forbidden Kingdom of Lo, their sanctuary during that time. The CIA had trained members of this ethnic Tibetan group in Colorado and had supported them secretly years earlier in raids against the Chinese army inside Tibet, at a clandestine military base just south of the Tibetan border. The US government would abandon support a few years later, in advance of President Nixon's 1972 meeting with Mao Zedong in Beijing.[2]

Over time, with each trip to Nepal, my fascination with Mustang, and especially with LoMontang, intensified. I was hooked. I could only imagine what it would be like to be there. I had to see these places for myself.

Mustang is remote—an appealing feature on its own. LoMontang is even more so, situated near the north end of the Kali Gandaki River, near the border of Tibet. This earthen-walled city had been the capital of the Forbidden Kingdom of Lo since the fifteenth century. I could only imagine the adventures that might await me there.

But I also wanted to go simply because it was off-limits.

I've never been good at accepting orders or arbitrary displays of authority. One day during World War II, when we were seven or eight years old, my best friend Phil Fehlen and I decided to visit Fort Funston. The fort was on a cliff overlooking the Pacific and had a pair of sixteen-inch guns that could shoot thirty miles to protect the entrance to San Francisco Bay.[3] Phil and I thought it would be fun to sneak onto the base and see those guns up close. We had just cleared a couple of barbed-wire fences when we saw two MPs in a jeep barreling toward us. We tried to run away—Phil made it back over the first fence, but my pants got stuck on the wire and I couldn't get free.

One of the MPs called out, "Halt! Who goes there?" as if he were in a movie. He pulled out his .45-caliber pistol and pointed it at us. They put us in the jeep and took us to see their sergeant. My recollection is a bit hazy, but in Phil's version of the story I yelled, "Keep your hands off me!" and added there was no need for the MP to pull a gun on a couple of kids.

It was an early sign of the rebellious streak that has stayed with me all my life, not to be driven out even by the couple of years I spent at a military boarding school. I was ten when my father, Herbert Blum, died of breast cancer and my mother took over his job as the State-O-Maine's western representative selling robes and raincoats. Because this required a fair amount of travel, and possibly because she feared what might become of us without a male role model in our daily lives, she sent Bob and me to the San Rafael Military Academy. I was in fifth grade, and Bob was in second.

I detested the place—wearing the wool uniforms, standing at attention, parading in the hot sun, saluting upperclassmen who treated us despicably. Warren Hellman, a lifelong friend whom I first met at San Rafael, said to me years later, "Maybe it was a reform school."

I replied, "Well, if it was, it didn't take."

* * *

My desire to get into Mustang only intensified as I learned more about the local people whose culture, village patterns, architecture, and religion on the ground were, and remain, distinctively Tibetan Buddhist. The roughly five thousand Lobas and Tibetans living there at the time were very poor. In winter, when the weather turns bitterly cold, most able-bodied people headed south, as their ancestors had for centuries, to buy sweaters from wholesalers and sell them across India. In warmer months, Lobas in Mustang scratched out a living as best they could by subsistence farming in thin, rocky soil, the fate of most nomads of the Himalaya.

Maybe we could help.

It Only Took Twenty Years . . .

By the mid-1970s, I had become friendly with Prabhakar Rana, a prominent Nepali business leader who was dedicated to improving the lives of his people. Then managing director of the diversified Soaltee Group, he became an AHF board member and was very helpful with our projects for many years. During several trips to Kathmandu in the '80s, he arranged meetings with the new Nepali king, Birendra Bir Bikram Shah.

Prabhakar and I covered a lot of topics in our meetings, but I made sure to petition the king often to be allowed officially into LoMontang. These conversations went on for at least five years. King Birendra told me that I would be the first Westerner allowed in—but he didn't say when.

We continued building our relationship as AHF collaborated with an NGO sponsored by the king's wife, Queen Aishwarya, to support several clinics, or "health posts," in Upper Mustang. Finally, around the time King Birendra and his advisors yielded to public pressure to end Nepal's isolation and embrace democracy and a constitutional monarchy, he agreed the time had come.

In late 1991, a few months before the Nepali government

officially opened the Forbidden Kingdom to foreigners, I was heading at last into Mustang and on to LoMontang.

After a short flight from Pokhara to Jomsom, I set out on a journey of about two weeks alongside my frequent business partner, David Bonderman; David's wife, Laurie Michaels; my youngest daughter, Eileen; and P. K. We trekked or rode on horseback along fifty miles of steep, narrow trails, back and forth across the Kali Gandaki River several times and through mountain passes as high as fourteen thousand feet.

Sometimes, strolling along a wide path in the river valley, we found ourselves in thrall to the majestic vistas in every direction. At other times we would be edging along a cliff next to a three-thousand-foot drop, wondering if we had lost our senses. Today you can travel by jeep or truck for about six hours along a hazardous dirt road, but in those days you either walked or rode on a sturdy Tibetan pony.[4] For my money, walking is still the best way to go if you have the time.

RUPEES FROM THE MASTER

If you want to see a Buddhist ritual on the wisdom of finding inner peace in our disorderly world, a Kalachakra Initiation would be an excellent choice. The twelve-day teaching tradition is held most every year, usually led by His Holiness the Dalai Lama and attended by hundreds of monks, from most erudite to ordinary, of Buddhism's Sakya sect. More than a hundred thousand people make the pilgrimage from all over the world, including remote parts of the Himalaya.

Monks and others students take vows of compassion and helping others. The multitudes attending receive blessings for long life from holy teachers. Intricate sand mandalas, seven feet in diameter, are crafted over eight days then left only to memory as the sands are poured into a nearby stream or river, releasing "positive energy" before the crowds return home.

On very rare occasions, once every twenty years, this sacred gathering is held for people in remote areas. By sheer coincidence, we came upon one during our first trek into Mustang. It was at Ghar Gompa, one of the oldest monasteries in Mustang. Hundreds of people had converged. Tents were being pitched everywhere. In one, we were introduced to a thin, elderly man with a stringy white goatee and a gentle nature.

"He looked like a sage from an old western movie," my daughter Eileen remembered.

This, as we soon learned, was one of the great living masters of Tibetan Buddhism, Chogye Trichen Rinpoche. He had been one of the Dalai Lama's teachers, also escaping Tibet in 1959, and helped reestablish Tibetan Buddhism in Nepal. He was the classic lovely, sweet lama. As our visit ended, he gave us an old Tibetan carpet and absolutely insisted we take 30 rupees for buying tea along the rest of our journey to LoMontang.

"No, no," I said. "We're fine." But he insisted.

Fifteen years later, while in Kathmandu and again totally by chance, we had a second unplanned audience with the Rinpoche. He was very frail now, in his late eighties, but, amazingly, still remembered our meeting in Ghar Gompa.

"Here," he motioned gently, as we were leaving, "take this with you," thrusting a currency note for 100 rupees in my direction.

I smiled and tried to wave him off. But he insisted, and, with admiration and respect, I tucked the rupee note into a pocket.

I still have that old Tibetan carpet, too. I would never think of parting with it.

When we first entered the walled city of LoMontang, the few people we saw were either quite old or very young. The population, then as today, was no more than a thousand during the spring and summer seasons. In the winter, then as today, more than three-quarters of the people migrated south—many trading sweaters in India or Nepal, and a few studying in Kathmandu or Jomsom.

As a foreigner traveling with the permission of King Birendra, I had a chance to meet the king of Mustang, Raja Jigme Bista. The raja was about sixty years old then and had sovereignty over the Forbidden Kingdom under the wider authority of the Nepali king. He seemed sincere as he described what had happened to his people over the generations. The community was dying, he explained, and he saw himself as another in a long line of monarchs who had allowed things to deteriorate.

As with anything else in life, you've got to judge people as you see them. Raja Jigme Bista, the twenty-sixth in an unbroken line of reigning monarchs, was authentic and believable, and I wanted to help. Our foundation had been building and supporting schools, hospitals, and sacred sites in the Himalaya for nearly a decade, including those several health posts in Upper Mustang. I described this work and asked what the raja thought we could do for him and his people in LoMontang. He replied, "We've got to restore the monastic school. If we are going to bring this area back to life, it has to start with the temples, the monasteries, and the monastic school."

It was not the answer I was expecting.

Crumbling Temples, Crumbling Community

The temples of Thubchen and Jampa, the two great monastic assembly halls within the whitewashed city walls of LoMontang, had been built in the fifteenth century, during a golden era for Buddhism in Lo.

The kingdom was prospering as a trading center, with a bustling trade in salt from the dead lakes in Tibet exchanged for wool, grain, and spices primarily from India. Merchants tapped their growing wealth to build the elaborate monasteries, or *gompas*, in appreciation of their good fortune. They hired the best artisans, Newaris living in the Kathmandu Valley, who filled the monasteries with sculptures and exquisite, vibrant paintings of deities and mandalas, the geometric art form that Buddhists believe express the nature of the cosmos.[5] Thubchen and Jampa were architectural triumphs. Both were windowless. Thubchen rose twenty feet above the ground floor; Jampa, nearly sixty feet. They had anchored the traditions and culture of the people of LoMontang for several centuries, and Thubchen endured as the spiritual heart of the Loba culture.

But beginning in the eighteenth century, Upper Mustang's fortunes began a slow decline, and its position as a trading and cultural center waned due to shifting trade routes, hostilities with neighboring fiefdoms, and superior trading practices of better-educated tribes living downriver. Mustang became even further isolated along its northern border after China invaded Tibet in the 1950s.

Decades later, the neglected temples were crumbling. A few ceiling timbers in Thubchen had sunk to within inches of the head of the beaten copper image of Shakyamuni Buddha within. In both gompas, tantric mandala paintings of the Buddha and Bodhisattvas were covered by soot, grime, and grease released from the burning butter lamps used in many centuries of daily rituals. Earthquakes over the years had damaged the gompa structures, with roof supports threatening to collapse, and rainwater and snowmelt had defaced much of the art. Rats were rampant and spreading filth.

I thought it would be a shame to lose such priceless cultural treasures, but we had no experience in restorations. Our focus up to that point had been on what we considered essential to life: schools, health care, and elder care.

Yet Raja Jigme Bista understood, correctly, that without cultural identity, a community has nothing to hold it together, nothing to build upon. He told me he had asked the government of Nepal for financial assistance, but received nothing. His Holiness the Dalai Lama later confirmed this for me, sadly explaining that Buddhist traditions decline as monastic institutions are destroyed. I began to see why His Holiness believed the conservation of religious art, artifacts, and monasteries was critical to continuing the tradition of Tibetan Buddhism.[6]

Though the raja had heard stories passed down from ancestors about fabulous paintings on the earthen walls, he really didn't know what we would find if we mounted a conservation program. Neither did we. AHF had never been involved in such a program. Plus, as David Bonderman remembered, "It was so dark in the temples, you couldn't see anything except when we took photos using a flash."

Laurie Michaels added, "It wasn't until we had the film developed when we got back to the United States that we could see what was there."

It was obvious that a restoration would require a focused effort of several years, and we didn't even know if the restoration was going to work. We were doing it because the raja wanted to revive that little kingdom and the soul of its community. And, after giving it some thought, it made sense to me: Starting with monasteries would be a wellspring for reviving Buddhist traditions and cultural identity in Mustang. Yes, I told the raja, we would help.

He was taking a calculated risk on us—and we, on him.

WHEN FLAMES DESTROY A SACRED MONASTERY

Although AHF had never been involved in an architectural or artistic restoration project, at the time of our first LoMontang visit we were in the process of helping rebuild the Tengboche Monastery in the Khumbu, one of the most important Tibetan Buddhist centers in the Everest area.

Perched high on a mountain ridge overlooking the Dudh Kosi, with a rhododendron forest cascading down the mountain slope to the river, Tengboche is a symbol of peace and serenity for trekkers and climbers. At an elevation of 12,800 feet, it is surrounded by snow-covered peaks, with Everest rising in the distance on clear days. Those who come to rest at the monastery can hear the monks chanting ancient Buddhist prayers in the morning and evening to the ritual sounds of their cymbals, drums, and Tibetan long trumpets.

I have spent much time there over the years. Jimmy and Rosalynn Carter and I were guests there when we trekked together in the region in 1985. Lama Nawang Tenzing Jangpo, the *rinpoche* (abbot) of the monastery, conducted a Buddhist prayer service for us. At one point, the former president noticed Rinpoche reading from some very old, handmade prayer sheets covered by Tibetan script. The sheets were about a foot long and four inches wide, with gold lettering. Knowing that some of the monastery's sacred texts and relics dated from the seventeenth century, Carter asked Rinpoche if he knew who had written the texts.

"I did," Rinpoche replied.

Carter looked puzzled, until P. K. leaned over and whispered, "He did it in a previous life."

One of the first projects Sir Ed and I developed together, outside of schools and health clinics, was bringing electricity to Tengboche in 1979 by funding construction of a small hydroelectric power station on the river below the monastery. The goal was twofold: to ease life at the monastery and to save the surrounding forests. It is bitterly cold in the winter, and the monks would spend much of their time cutting trees for fuel.

At that elevation, however, trees grow very slowly, and their firewood harvesting was destroying the forest in the area—an ecological disaster in the making.

The monks (and the forest) enjoyed these new comforts for almost ten years. Then, in the late 1980s, a fire broke out when most of the monks were away. The four-story wooden structure burned to the ground, destroying precious relics, scrolls, murals, ancient texts, and more. The monks and the entire community were in a state of shock.

Sir Ed and I immediately went to work, doing the only thing we could think to do: We raised almost $450,000 for the monastery to be reconstructed exactly as it had originally been built. It was a monumental job and was still ongoing when I first traveled to LoMontang. The new Tengboche was completed and reconsecrated in 1993, in a ceremony with monks and rinpoches from several monasteries across Nepal. The restoration was a privilege for us and worth every effort, despite those many years, but it was just a warm-up for the marathon we were getting into in LoMontang.

Slow Process of Restoration

Our progress in LoMontang was slow in the first years. Some bureaucrats in Kathmandu blocked and then delayed the permits we needed, and we had to keep a close eye on the money we put into local charities to make sure it didn't end up in the wrong bank accounts.

Within a few years, though, we were able to sign a new project director—the world-renowned conservator John Sanday. His remarkable projects were all gems of historic and cultural preservation that included work on several Asian masterpieces, such as Angkor Wat in Cambodia; palaces in India and Kathmandu; and the Forbidden City in China. We could not have completed the work on the Mustang temples without Sanday's guiding hand. These restorations, he wrote years later in our 2006 anthology, *Himalaya: Personal Stories of Grandeur, Challenge, and Hope*, would become "the most daunting, and rewarding, challenges of my professional career."[7]

Sanday saw that the rafters supporting Thubchen's three-foot-thick earthen roof were unstable, meaning the roof could collapse at the slightest provocation. He and his team of experts, training and working with local craftsmen, replaced the decaying beams and columns with some sixty timbers, all of which had to be cut, hoisted, and carried on foot, eight people per timber, for many days from a forest in Tibet, beyond the Chinese border. Raja Jigme Bista himself traveled to the Tibetan village on horseback to arrange the deal.

There was a lot of skepticism. Communications were problematic, as cell phones didn't function in Mustang. Then, too, the well-intentioned local folks were thinking too small. They would send us skimpy budgets for patchwork ideas. I knew from my business experience that when framing a venture for long-term success, the really hard work is in the design and preparation.

It took four years to make the buildings structurally sound and seal them from the wind and rain so they would be safe for the restorers and painters doing the actual restoration work. In 1998, Luigi Fieni, a young Italian art conservator, spent his first summer restoring wall-paintings in LoMontang. "It was one of my first trips out of Italy," he later recalled. "We were literally in the Middle Ages. There was no electricity, no means of communication, and no means of transportation."[8] Yet every April since then, Luigi has returned to Mustang to work into October, when the weather becomes too cold and conditions too severe for the work to continue.

Unfortunately, more than half of the original murals had been damaged too severely over the years for restoration. So Luigi and his team focused all their efforts on those that could be saved. After a few years, the great cultural and historical significance of these paintings became clear. By then you could see a fair amount of artwork through the dirt and grime. When I saw with my own eyes what those first restorations revealed, I recognized an astonishing example of pure Tibetan culture and art, essentially untouched. It was captivating, beyond belief. Everyone who saw it was astounded. Journalist Saransh Sehgal, reporting for *The Independent* from LoMontang in 2013, wrote that the artwork restored in Mustang is believed to be among the most valuable across the Himalaya, "the best-surviving examples of classical Tibetan monastic architecture of the Sakya-pa, one of four major schools of Tibetan Buddhism."[9]

Since 2004, Luigi and a few of his expert colleagues from Italy and elsewhere have led the training of roughly thirty-five local people, including twenty women and two former monks, who carry on the quietly exhilarating work of restoring the art. "I could have never imagined that we could have gone so far," Luigi told *The Independent*. "Literally, we had to turn farmers into restorers . . . working directly on masterpieces."

AHF wants to see the LoMontang restorations endure as a striking cultural statement of Tibetan Buddhism for current and future generations.[10] That remains our goal despite two devastating earthquakes that shook Nepal in the spring of 2015. The first, a 7.8-magnitude quake, caused wide portions of wall paintings in Thubchen to separate from the wall. In Jampa, walls on the upper level separated from the floor, and some sections of wall paintings on other levels either fell or were detached. Luigi's team knows it could have been much worse. Once they complete the Thubchen repairs, they'll shift to Jampa. We originally estimated the gompa restorations would be completed by 2017. That goal has not changed.

Ripple Effects of a Focus on Culture

As the wall paintings, wood carvings, and clay statues in Thubchen and Jampa have come back to life, more members of the Loba community have embraced their cultural heritage. It is not an exaggeration to say AHF is in a large sense responsible for a spiritual and community reawakening across the kingdom of Mustang. As vivid images of the deities emerged from the restorers' handiwork in LoMontang, villagers returned to performing daily prayers. The monks reconsecrated the temples of Thubchen and Jampa. And across Mustang, monasteries have been revived as linchpin cultural institutions for their communities. About one hundred monks, including students from as far away as India, live in LoMontang. In all, there are four monastic institutions in Lo, including a nunnery teaching hundreds of young students. In an era when so much of Tibetan Buddhist culture has been systematically, and at times brutally, eradicated by the Chinese army, the Mustang restoration may prove to be of even greater historic and cultural significance than we expected.

We are incredibly happy to have been a part of it. And the broader effects on the community have been equally rewarding. More than sixty artisans have been trained—some in art restoration, others in structural restoration—for work in monasteries and temples. "Learning these new skills means a lot to me," said one of the local artisans, Tsewang Jigme, thirty years old and father of three children between the ages of five and eleven. Known as Jojo by his family and friends, he worked for two years as an unskilled laborer on the Sanday team rebuilding the gompa and then was selected to join the Fieni team. "Had I not been trained and employed on the project," he has said, "I would be either a farmer or a migrant laborer working overseas."

Jojo has said that the work in the monastery and temple is "spiritually more fulfilling." He explained, "When people come to the gompa now, they say it is more *chi lap chay* [blessed and sanctified]. We have a great amount of respect in the community. They say of us that we are the ones who 'paint God.'"

Another LoMontang artisan, Tashi Wangyal, said the work made him "heart happy"—a familiar Tibetan expression that translates roughly to being happy and, as a result of this happiness, being kindhearted.

The restoration work took us beyond the sacred scenes within Thubchen and Jampa. We had to expand our repertoire to embrace what I can only describe as "artful" plumbing techniques called for to upgrade the town's drainage system. Without the repairs, runoff water would have continued to weaken the *dzagri*, the original high earthen wall of LoMontang constructed in the fifteenth century. Our next steps were paving public areas both inside and outside of the wall. This work also took years to complete, an unavoidable concession to LoMontang's isolation and its lack of materials and skilled craftsmen. But now the *dzagri* is secure and muddy plazas are part of the past.

Other projects beyond the temple and monastery walls helped deepen our appreciation of traditional Tibetan culture in Mustang, and the villagers' trust in us. We developed a child-care center in 1999 in LoMontang to help support parents who were working on the site. Through the Lo Gyalpo Jigme Foundation, we funded seven Tibetan language and culture teachers in local government schools. The raja's son, Crown Prince Jigme Singi Palabar Bista, established this nonprofit foundation so we could work more effectively with the raja and his family in managing projects. Our collaboration will mark its twenty-fifth anniversary in 2017, making it the longest of dozens of partnerships AHF nurtures with local organizations.

We were already beginning to organize development projects in Mustang before I first visited LoMontang, and that support has continued. We back youth groups in eleven communities, which take the lead in village improvement projects to build bridges, paths, and irrigation and water systems, and since 2007 we have funded six health clinics that provide year-round staffing and medicines, mobile health camps, and vaccinations. Since 2004, we have provided funding for Loba students who live and study together in Jomsom until they graduate from high school. The first Loba studying to be a doctor, Wangdi Sangpo BK, passed his final medical exams in 2016. After completing an internship, he hopes to qualify for a two-year residency at a medical facility in Mustang. We actively help fifteen day-care centers across Mustang that give 250 kids a safe place to play, sing, dance, learn their alphabets in three languages, and brush their teeth. We also have built flood-control systems in these villages, sharply reducing threats to children who might be crossing or near sites where runoff from melting snows or heavy rains once spawned lethal rapids.

In every case, these programs were requested by the local communities, either directly from us or through one of our local partners in providing social services. They have improved basic living conditions and opportunities for current and future generations.[11]

Persistence Is Always Your Friend

It is hard to describe how scraggly and dispirited Mustang was in the early 1990s when we first met the raja, yet within his lifetime the district has been transformed into a living microcosm of Tibetan Buddhist culture within the borders of Nepal.

We continue to visit Mustang and the raja, now in his eighties, every year. It remains one of the poorest, most isolated regions in one of the world's poorest countries, but life has improved. Families in many villages, including LoMontang, have access to day-care facilities, elder care, job training, health services, and instruction in traditional Tibetan culture in primary schools that didn't exist a quarter century ago. We stepped in to provide many functions that in the developed world, governments are expected to deliver.[12]

It is quite possible that even greater treasures of Tibetan Buddhist art exist in other parts of Mustang. We've supported some preliminary conservation work at the oldest known temple in the area, which dates to the eighth century, and at another temple in Charang, a half-day's walk from LoMontang. Many other fascinating possibilities have come to our attention, such as ancient Buddhist paintings discovered over the past two decades, carved into cliffs in caves high above the Kali Gandaki River as many as three thousand years ago.[13]

We have heard that other organizations, including government agencies, want to follow our lead, but so far none has done so. For our part, we have had to draw the line somewhere. You can't do everything. That said, persistence is always your friend. If I had ever let go of my fascination to enter the Forbidden Kingdom, none of what has been accomplished with our help in LoMontang and beyond in Mustang would have happened. "You saved the kingdom," said my old trekking companion, Scot Macbeth.

If we had been a typical top-down NGO or government agency—if we had arrived on our own schedule and told the local people what we wanted to do, without a care for what they thought—we wouldn't have achieved any of these successes. Instead, we simply did what the raja asked us to do—because we trusted his instincts and, over time, came to see that what he asked of us was the right thing to do. The Mustang stories carry two simple lessons. The first is that effective development requires walking the village, respecting local culture, and helping provide basic resources people need to improve their lives. The second is that these actions offer the potential of wondrous human connections, connections that can touch your soul.

Chapter 3

To Protect, Educate, and Heal Children

"Because of strong motivation, you keep plugging on."

—Sir Edmund Hillary

When we were ten, my best friend, Phil Fehlen, and I staged The Blum and Fehlen Magic Show. With some basic tricks (not very well done), we put on two performances in our garage on consecutive Saturdays. We grossed $12—not bad for a couple of ten-year-olds in 1945.

After our second show, Phil and I rode the streetcar to the old Shriners Hospital on Nineteenth Avenue in San Francisco and donated our proceeds to help children who were being treated there. This was a time when the polio virus was rampant in the United States. It was a scary, paralyzing disease that seemed to strike down children at random, afflicting forty thousand people (mostly children) a year and resulting in more than two thousand deaths. We could relate to kids our age with polio who would be trapped for the rest of their lives in an iron lung.

That trip across town with Phil was my very modest start in helping children receive health care, education, and other necessities they couldn't afford. Supporting schools, medical care programs, clinics, and water supplies in some of the world's most isolated areas has become a major focus of the American Himalayan Foundation. The work is critical. In poor countries and communities, each generation bearing stronger confidence and a higher sense of self-worth has a better chance to escape poverty.

AHF aims to create these possibilities for children in many projects in the Himalaya. Two that I'll describe in this chapter that have had the greatest impact in Nepal are Stop Girl Trafficking (SGT) and the Hospital and Rehabilitation Center for Disabled Children (HRDC).

Aruna, Erica, and a Staggering Crisis

In 2014, UNICEF estimated that seven thousand Nepali women and girls are trafficked into India annually and as many as two hundred thousand may work in India's brothels. Although accurate figures are hard to assemble, the US State Department estimated in 2009 that 7,500 children each year end up in Nepal's growing domestic sex trade. This is a staggering humanitarian crisis.

"Of all the children suffering in the brothels of India, perhaps none suffer more frequently than the daughters of Nepal," wrote Siddharth Kara in his landmark 2009 book, *Sex Trafficking: Inside the Business of Modern Slavery*. "Up to thirty thousand of the one hundred thousand prostitutes in Mumbai are Nepalese." Why Nepali girls? Brothel operators believe they are more compliant, speaking little Hindi and being stranded so far from home. Moreover, customers prefer them because of their small, thin figures and because they have a reputation for not trying to hustle men who enter their rooms.[1]

Nepali girls in these brothels, often as young as twelve, are forced to have sex fifteen or twenty times a day with adult men, occasionally even more. Most are beaten into submission, and are scarred physically and mentally from repeated daily raping. With the added threats of unwanted, life-threatening pregnancies and HIV/AIDS, and only the most basic medical treatment provided to keep them working, many die before they turn twenty.

At a breakfast meeting in Kathmandu in 1993, Erica Stone, the imaginative, tough-minded, and compassionate executive who by then had led the American Himalayan Foundation for a decade, brought together eighteen people with knowledge of human trafficking in Nepal. Nearly all were women. One was Dr. Aruna Uprety, and, for Erica, she was an unforgettable presence.

Aruna had been helping colleagues with a safe house for girls who were rescued from traffickers in India and returned home to Nepal. What was really needed to keep girls from being sold to sex traffickers, Aruna explained (and we soon agreed), was pre-vention—education. Keep girls safe from traffickers by helping them stay in school. An education would make them more valu-able to their communities, open their eyes to the wider world and opportunities, and help them understand their intrinsic worth.

Nobody else was doing this. Aruna had already started an NGO in Nepal called the Rural Health Education Services Trust (RHEST), and was keeping a steely yet maternal watch on a few dozen girls in rural schools. That small-scale commit-ment soon became the inspiration for RHEST's biggest pro-gram and what is now, under Erica's ardent direction, AHF's largest funding effort: Stop Girl Trafficking. It's an important story of how people in local communities, with access to suf-ficient resources and the vision of a dedicated leader, can tackle socioeconomic and cultural issues in order to protect the most vulnerable among them.

Nepali Girls' Nightmare

As a young doctor in 1992, Aruna Uprety was attending a medical conference in Mumbai when a colleague asked her to see one of his patients, a young woman from Nepal. The woman, in her midtwenties, had been lured years before from her village in Nepal, the Indian doctor said, and forced into a life of slavery in Mumbai. She was dying from AIDS in a time and place where all but the medical community's most committed people shunned AIDS victims. This young woman was so mortally ill that she could not speak, but her ghastly appearance left a powerful impression. "I still remember her face," Aruna said. "She was very, very thin with white hair, a long nose, and sunken eyes."

Aruna learned a few days later that the woman had died. Saddened and outraged, she was determined to learn more about the abuse of women in the sex trade. How many more Nepalese girls might be living a nightmare in Mumbai's brothels, already suffering from or in imminent danger of being exposed to AIDS?

The red-light districts of Mumbai, such as the still-notorious Falkland Road, were filled with Nepali girls who had been enslaved. Most were isolated, without hope. Some told Aruna they had no desire to return home to Nepal because they would be stigmatized, rejected by their families and society. Once these girls become trapped in a life of slavery, it is nearly impossible to escape. Some are told they are not free to go until they pay back the amount of their purchase, but just as in times of bonded labor, they can never work enough to erase their ever-increasing debt.

Even parents who know the risks will commonly send their daughters off in hope of receiving income from abroad; at the least, they will have one less child to feed. Occasionally, a handsome young *dalal*—one of the deceitful, smooth-talking traders who comb the countryside for girls they can lure into the sex trade or domestic servitude—arrives in a village posing as a man seeking a wife. He marries a young girl and takes her off to what he promises will be a better life. Soon after crossing into India, however, he sells her to a brothel.

"It's too late for us," Aruna heard again and again from the girls she met. "If we had known anything, if we had been able to go to school and learn and work, we would never have landed here. Please, keep this from happening to other girls."

Heartbroken by despair, Aruna began to understand that for these women and girls, education could have made a huge difference. Maiti Nepal, an NGO that rescues and repatriates young victims of sex slavery, reported for example in 2010 that 15 percent of 221 girls rescued in the prior two years had received only informal or elementary school education, and nearly 80 percent had never attended school.[2] An optimist by nature, Aruna was gripped by the horror of these girls' lives. As a social activist, she urgently began thinking about what could be done. The answer, she found, was in her own life experience.

A Source of Salvation

Born in 1960, Aruna is one of the few women of her generation in Nepal to complete an advanced education and pursue a medical career. Her mother had been married when only ten years old to a man who became a prominent lawyer. However, she was not allowed to go to school and remained illiterate. One of her dreams was to give Aruna and her sister and brother a good education.

Aruna's grades were outstanding in high school, and when she graduated in 1979 she qualified for a premed university scholarship. Nepal had no medical school at the time, but the Soviet Union did and welcomed students—both men and women—from across South Asia. Aruna won more scholarships for medical studies and other advanced training, and started out in 1986 with a fresh medical school diploma in hand. She worked for several years in India, near the Nepal border, on public health issues. Later, she had postings in some of the poorest regions of the world: Afghanistan, Laos, Sri Lanka, Tibet, Iran, and Sudan.

The fear and desperation Aruna witnessed among women in the many villages she served pushed her to this vision: "If we can educate girls in these remote areas, they will have greater value to their families, not be easily tricked by traffickers and their lies of high-paying jobs overseas. They will have a chance to build their own independent lives." Aruna knew from her own life that extending the rare "privilege" of education to these over-looked girls could make all the difference.

Social Ills Often Strike Girls Hardest

The trafficking of Nepali girls was a little-understood issue that caught my attention by 1993. I had been traveling to Asia for more than a decade by then, to keep up with my growing port-folio of business investments, get a closer look at the operations and results of our foundation's activities in the Himalaya, and hear directly from the Dalai Lama and other senior officials of the Tibetan government in exile in Dharamsala about the press-ing humanitarian needs of his people.

Nepal was a feudal state until 1950 and has a long history of social injustice. Human trafficking wasn't banned by law until 1986, yet today only a few cases are prosecuted each year in Nepal or India.[3] As in much of the world, the hardships in rural Nepal are greatest for women and girls. Traditionally, the role of a village girl is to work in the household and fields until she is old enough to wed. Her parents arrange for her marriage, and she is sent off to live with her new husband's family, rarely to return home. In homes with many mouths to feed, girls too often are seen as a burden and are valued less than cattle by their families.

In the late 1990s, widening poverty and political instability fed into a Maoist insurgency that became a civil war in Nepal. Amid this social upheaval, the *dalal* continued to prey upon village girls. Many rural people had fled to the cities to escape the violence, providing traffickers there with new targets. Nepal's National Human Rights Commission reported in 2014 that approximately fifty thousand women and girls work in Kathmandu's restaurants, bars, and massage parlors, and as many as one-third of them are exploited sexually.[4]

The victims overwhelmingly were the helpless children of mostly ignorant, destitute parents. As we learned, however, the explanation for these tragedies occasionally was far worse: Some fathers or older brothers sold girls in the family to traffickers, often for the equivalent of $500 or even much less, with no hint of remorse. (Annual per capita income in Nepal is roughly $500.) For them, the sex trade is simply a ready and reliable source of much-needed cash.

AHF regional field director Bruce Moore once met such a man while making the rounds to update our SGT reports in the isolated Sindhupalchok District, a three-hour drive northeast of Kathmandu:

> This man said he had seven daughters, and was very happy about this. I asked him why, since having seven daughters typically was considered a curse, and he said, "You know, girls are worth money." I didn't quite get it, but a school principal explained as we walked away that when some guy had come along and said he bought girls to sell them to brothels, this man had sold his sister for fifty dollars.

This chance encounter occurred in an area where, from age nine, some girls are given herbal or plant hormone supplements so they develop breasts and start menstruating earlier. The men find it easier to persuade government officials that the girls are close enough to the legal age of eighteen to be given an adult passport. "So here is this man raising seven daughters to sell each of them into brothels or bonded labor," Bruce lamented. "I had been looking into the eyes of a devil."

Even when girls weren't actively sold off like cattle, they often were seen as not valuable enough to educate. According to Nepal's Central Bureau of Statistics report for 2011, about half of the girls and one-third of the boys in the lowest two of five income groups nationally have never studied in schools. As Jimmy Carter observed in his book *A Call to Action: Women, Religion, Violence, and Power*, "Every effort is made to educate boys, but fewer than 5 percent of women are literate in some poorer communities."[5]

Too many fathers still pass along an old Nepalese saying: *Educating your daughter is like watering a flower in another man's garden.*

The SGT Formula

By 2016, more than seventeen thousand Nepali girls from the poorest families had been educated through Stop Girl Trafficking. Not one girl in the SGT program has been lost to traffickers over a twenty-year period when perhaps more than two hundred thousand girls from Nepal have been forced into sex slavery or bonded labor. Not one.

Aruna's goal is to build a cooperative relationship with the community. She sees education of a child as the responsibility of three entities: the parent, the government that operates the schools, and Stop Girl Trafficking, which provides the $100 needed to fund a child's entire year in school. That's right: SGT can keep one poor girl in school in Nepal for a year for only $100.

When possible, RHEST works closely with school officials;

in districts where administrators aren't enthusiastic about promoting the enrollment of girls, Aruna recruits local advisors. With the help of teachers, principals, and the local advisors, each January RHEST identifies the girls most at risk and suggests to SGT staff which ones to select for funding.

But SGT offers more than scholarships. Staff from RHEST's central office visit each school with girls in the SGT program four times a year: twice to distribute required materials and to hold counseling sessions with students and parents, and twice for monitoring and evaluation of the girls. For girls in grades eight through ten, the counseling sessions include talks with them and their parents about the lives of bonded laborers, cases of women and girls who were trafficked, and real stories about dangers girls and women face when they go to India or the Middle East to work without proper identification and education.

We have found that within five years of the start of our work in a community, overall school enrollment goes up. SGT changes the way girls are valued in a family, and once a girl's standing rises in her own family, it can affect an entire village. The women understand this all too well. One of them told Bruce, "We are changing society one girl at a time."

By paying for these girls' education expenses, making them and their families aware of the dangers they may face, and keeping a close eye on them, Aruna's team has taken big steps to ensure that the girls no longer are at risk of being sold or tricked into slavery.

Aruna's most courageous work may well be in Sindhupalchok. When she first came to the area, it was truly a heart of darkness where many girls and women were denigrated, horribly abused, and delivered into the underworld of modern sex trafficking in South Asia. This cross-border sex trade has prospered for more than sixty years and may even be expanding, as Siddharth Kara wrote in *Sex Trafficking,* despite increased government, law enforcement, and media attention. "The reason for this persistence is simple: immense profitability with minimal risk," he added. "Until the market force of risk is increased radically, and as long as sex trafficking remains immensely profitable, the industry will flourish."[6]

In late April and early May 2015, two horrific earthquakes, the most destructive and lethal in Nepal in eighty years, killed nearly nine thousand people and laid waste to entire villages. Nine hundred thousand homes collapsed, becoming useless against the elements. Sindhupalchok, the site of a landslide disaster that had claimed more than 150 lives following heavy rains the previous summer, was the epicenter of the second earthquake, and locus of the majority of four-hundred-plus aftershocks that continued to rock the country into 2016.

After the quakes, traffickers soon were spotted in rising numbers around makeshift camps in Nepal's Central Hills. Within the first week, a bus carrying forty-two girls from Sindhupalchok was about to cross into India when it was stopped by Nepali officials. "The girls' families had been promised, presumably by traffickers, that the girls would find jobs and a better life," Bruce Moore later explained. "The families were desperate and emotionally vulnerable as tremors continued, and they had been too eager to agree. Fortunately, the girls were taken off the bus."

Our response to the heightened dangers was to get these girls quickly back to school. Teams fanning out across the remote villages built fifty-four temporary learning centers, some made of tin and others simply large tents, to protect both the girls and the teachers from the summer heat and monsoon rains as well as to get classes going again. Villagers had alerted us quickly to lurking traffickers, often posing as aid workers. By summer's end, SGT was preparing to add with AHF's financial support another 3,800 girls from seven quake-ravaged areas, bringing total enrollment in the fall of 2015 to 14,800. More than five thousand of these girls and young women were from the Central Hills, nearly twice the number before the quakes.

Pushing for Growth

I first met Aruna in Kathmandu in 1997, when the RHEST program was in its second year and had fifty-two girls in school. She is diminutive, extremely smart, determined, and high energy. After getting acquainted, I urged her to envision a future with thousands of girls in the SGT programs, not hundreds. When I said we should aim for fifteen thousand, adding at the rate of about a thousand girls a year, I thought she was going to faint.

In those early years, Aruna didn't want the program to get too big because she feared it would become too difficult to manage. But I knew that with the dynamo we had found in Aruna, we were staring at an opportunity to make an immediate impact. "Clone yourself, Aruna," I said. After a few years of our coaching and nudging, she began to train others to work with the girls, their families, and their villages. Whole villages were coming to Aruna and saying, "Please educate our girls."

Assessing realities, challenges, and opportunities, and then helping our partners grow appropriately to meet them, is some of AHF's most important work. Many local leaders we discover and then lock arms with have shown striking commitment to improving the lives of people, often against staggering odds. Most began like Aruna: with big ideas but little in the way of financial resources or management experience.

We emphasize accountability. The leaders of every program are expected to give us regular reports on the number of people they are serving and any challenges they encounter, as well as budgets detailing how funding is used. To help them do this, where possible, we expand or introduce capabilities to improve efficiency and effectiveness. We help with basic accounting,

budgeting, planning, training, and other skills these social entrepreneurs need to build their organizations. If something goes
wrong, unlike many NGOs, we don't abandon the entire partner
organization. We help its leaders learn what went wrong, how
to make it right, and how to keep it from happening again. We
don't give up on our good partners.

Basic management skills are, in many ways, more essential
than funding. I've met so many well-meaning activists working
in nonprofits all over Nepal with little or no idea of how to
run an organization. It's sad. Their potential to help many more
people is never realized—squandered, actually.

Even Sir Ed faced this challenge when we worked with him
as leader of the Himalayan Trust. It was funny at times. Each
year, especially as he got older, I had to go through a process of
reverse negotiations with him. He would outline budgets for the
Himalayan Trust that were heading lower. He'd actually bargain
for *less* money from us. He would say, "I need $150,000," and I
would reply, "We're going to give you $200,000."

After reciting our lines again one year, I finally said, "Ed, I
get it. You're tired of running around the world with your tin
cup. But you've got all these important things to do. Make your
annual budget as high as you want. Whatever you don't have,
we'll pay the difference."

This humble manner was quintessential Sir Ed. He was a very
down-to-earth guy who never acted like one of the most famous
men on earth. In fact, one of the last times we flew to Auckland
to see him, we noticed billboards advertising a brand of scotch,
with Ed's face and a headline blaring ED HILLARY DRINKS XYZ
SCOTCH! When we got to his house, I needled him about it.

"Yeah, they're really nice to me!" he said with a big smile. He
pointed across the room. "They gave me those two cases—free!"
And that was his total payment for the deal.

Girls, Now Seeing Endless Possibilities

When Bruce Moore talks with mothers of SGT girls, he often asks them to compare their lives with those of their daughters. "The answer is inevitably the same," Bruce has said: The girls have hope, something their mothers never had as children.

When Bruce asks the schoolgirls what their own daughters' futures might be one day, the girls' answers are much more varied: teachers, doctors, other health care professionals, social workers, scientists. In other words, they anticipate endless possibilities—mostly in the educated professions.

This generational shift in attitudes means we and our many allies are making progress against sex slavery. It has happened in little more than twenty years, since Erica first met Aruna in Kathmandu. As Bruce reported back to us in San Francisco, "Changing these dark practices is not going to be easy or quick . . . But we will do it. We have to." Why? As my stepdaughter Katherine Feinstein, a former presiding judge of San Francisco Superior Court, said, "Because no one else will."[7] We are doing it, with each child we are able to help Aruna educate at every step, from early grades through high school, until each girl has earned her diploma.

Aruna Uprety's stirring achievement in continuing to expand the reach of Stop Girl Trafficking with AHF's support demonstrates that staying passionate and focused on your core purpose are vital to advance your cause.

Changing Grim Futures through Medicine

The American Himalayan Foundation wouldn't have gotten much accomplished in the past thirty-five years if leaders of our local partners, especially in Nepal, had not had similar extraordinary values and instincts.

Nepal presented extremely challenging, even precarious, political and governmental turmoil during the fall of the monarchy, the Marxist insurgency, and the nation's slow evolution toward democracy.

It is also true that Nepal's mountainous terrain, ruggedly beautiful though it is, often presents an enormous obstacle to people who urgently need medical care. Travel in the Himalaya happens mostly on foot, especially in the northern tier of the country. Furthermore, the rural parts of the country are chronically short on doctors, nurses, and modern hospitals. According to the World Health Organization, as recently as 2011, Nepal had only two physicians, and fewer than five nurses and midwives, for every ten thousand people. By comparison, China had fourteen physicians for every ten thousand people. One of five births in Nepal was attended by a skilled health professional. In the United States, the comparable figure was more than nine doctors for every ten births.[8]

One reason Nepal has so few physicians outside Kathmandu is that until recently many of its medical students had to study overseas. Medical training was not available in Nepal. Once the students saw clearly that they had little professional opportunity back home, many decided not to return from the industrialized countries in which they studied medicine.

This was certainly true in 1972, when Dr. Ashok Banskota finished his medical studies at the prestigious All India Institute of Medical Sciences in New Delhi and was accepted into a five-year residency program at the Albert Einstein College of Medicine at Yeshiva University in New York City. Yet Ashok would return and become one of our partners in delivering critical health care to tens of thousands of Nepali children.

Encouraged directly by the Swiss humanitarian group Terre des hommes,[9] Ashok opened an orthopedic clinic in a converted section of a small private hospital in Jorpati, a suburb of Kathmandu, called the Hospital and Rehabilitation Center for Disabled Children.[10] His sole focus was treating children with disabilities. These children weren't just invisible to the medical community. Often they were invisible to their entire communities, or worse: shunned and consigned to a beggar's misery.

Ashok's story is a powerful illustration of how one child born into modest circumstances can grow up to make a huge impact. In his case, it was committing to a life in medicine to help the poorest, most disadvantaged children of Nepal. Once burdened with grim futures as beggars, outcasts, or worse, thousands of his former patients now contribute as adults to better lives for their families and to social and economic progress in their communities. And Ashok has never taken a penny in compensation for his work. He has done this all for free. "The patients who came for help and treatment stole my heart. The enormous difficulties they faced to receive very basic and primitive care were hard to stomach," he has explained. "The immense satisfaction of helping these needy children spurred me on."

Treating Kids Nobody Would See

We first heard of Ashok a few years after his Jorpati clinic opened, through one of the early Western doctors who settled in Kathmandu in the 1980s. Dr. David Shlim was a friend of Erica Stone and her husband, emergency room physician and mountaineer Dr. Gil Roberts. "You've got to meet this young orthopedist," Dr. Shlim told Erica and Gil when they visited him in Kathmandu in 1988. "He's taking care of these kids with orthopedic conditions that nobody else will see. He's just incredible."

We were convinced by what he had already accomplished that Ashok could make a huge difference if he had more funding and administrative support. AHF wanted to help, as we did with many other determined, visionary people we found in the Himalaya. On a visit in 1992 to the rented, five-story house Ashok had converted into a rudimentary hospital, Erica posed a simple question: "When are you going to get a real hospital?" He was doing so much with so little, and had the capacity to do much more if only he had the resources and support.

The pair were racing up concrete stairs to respond to an urgent case. Ashok paused midstride and said, "When you help me build one."

Erica didn't hesitate. "OK," she replied. "We'll do that."

My wife, Senator Dianne Feinstein, was enthusiastic as well after she met Ashok and toured the clinic with Erica and me the next year. Observing the children in rows of beds recovering from surgery or with fearsome metal braces on their legs, she said with a mix of awe and surprise, "These children are smiling, even with all that is happening here. Richard, this is really good. You have to keep supporting this." And then she signed and handed me a traveler's check and told me to go buy the kids some toys. It was an instinctive response to the question that I believe all humans ask themselves, at some level, when we encounter people who are suffering: *How can I help?*

Ashok had been talking with Terre des hommes about building a hospital where children could receive comprehensive orthopedic care regardless of their ability to pay. AHF joined the conversation. A foundation event to mark my sixtieth birthday raised all the funds required to build a modern surgical suite in the new hospital. I am honored and humbled to say that the surgical suite bears my name.

In 2016 HRDC was on track to reach a milestone by year-end: more than *seventy thousand* children treated with medical, surgical, and rehabilitation services since Ashok opened his tiny clinic in Jorpati. I have always been driven in my business investments and philanthropy to build scale and make an impact. By those measures, HRDC certainly has more than delivered on its mission for the disabled children and local communities of Nepal.

The new hospital in Banepa, a town a few miles east of Kathmandu, has modern operating theaters, large wards, facilities for physical therapy, and an extensive workshop for handmade prosthetics and orthotic devices. In 2013, an operating theater annex, a new intensive care facility, and a medical conference room opened. Equipment upgrades and a new solar-energy system began generating 80 percent of the hospital's energy requirements. And the location, away from the noise and traffic of Kathmandu, offers fresh air and a quiet, pleasant setting for children to recover.

Changing Lives by Healing a Common Affliction

Many disabilities treated by Ashok and his colleagues are congenital. The most common problem among children who come to HRDC is clubfoot. A baby with clubfoot is born somewhere in the world every three minutes, and the rate of incidence, although twice as common in boys than girls, varies little by country.

If you are born with clubfoot in the United States, the condition is identified quickly after birth—or often in utero, thanks to ultrasound images—and typically is corrected by the age of five through a series of manipulations, special shoes, and plaster castings. Children can go on to a completely normal life and even pursue careers in sports at the highest levels. A number of famous American athletes were born with clubfoot, such as Mia Hamm, seventeen-year member of the US women's national soccer team and two-time Olympic gold medalist; Troy Aikman, the football quarterback who led the Dallas Cowboys to three Super Bowl championships in the 1990s; and Kristi Yamaguchi, an Olympic figure-skating champion.

"In the mountains, there is not much understanding of clubfoot even among nurses. So it goes undiagnosed," said Eileen Mariano, the eldest of my seven grandchildren and a 2015

Stanford University graduate in human biology who was an intern at HRDC in her junior year. "As these little kids begin walking, with no corrective shoes, the feet turn inward and downward, and over time they are walking on their ankles. As you can imagine, this just kills the foot. Huge callous stubs develop on the outside of the ankle."

Some Nepali parents don't realize clubfoot can be corrected, and their children suffer needlessly for years. The lucky ones eventually find their way to Ashok's door. HRDC embraces a nonsurgical approach to treating clubfoot, known as the Ponseti Method, which has been proven to be very effective and to reduce both the costs and the psychological trauma of surgery.

Jivan, one of the patients treated for clubfoot, has seen both sides of the coin. His uncle had the same condition but was never treated. "He couldn't walk properly and ended up having his foot amputated. He couldn't earn a living as a farmer or a laborer. I can walk now and my leg looks normal," Jivan explained in 2014, when he was in tenth grade. "But life would have been very different for me if I had not been treated at HRDC."

Why Working with Partners Works

From the beginning of our work at AHF, we have rejected the idea that anyone sitting in the United States, leading a very different life under very different conditions, would necessarily have better ideas for real, lasting impact on the ground than would the people we work with in Nepal, Tibetan refugee camps across the region, and India. As Warren Buffett told *Fortune* magazine in 2006 when he committed much of his wealth to the Bill & Melinda Gates Foundation, "What can be more logical, in whatever you want done, than finding someone better equipped than you are to do it?"

We have just seven people in our Kathmandu office—Bruce

Moore, who directs all the projects we support in Nepal and India, and his six staff members. Bruce is absolutely essential for us in our capacity as agents for thousands of supporters. His work illustrates the AHF approach in oversight and support for local champions like Ashok. We rarely place workers or volunteers directly with our programs in the Himalaya. Our project partners in these communities use local talent: teachers, doctors, nurses, builders, artisans, community leaders. It has proven to be the most effective and efficient way to work.

Here is the key point: The programs AHF supports have to be rooted in local communities. We're trying to educate people, open doors to greater opportunity, and help as many individuals as possible. And the best ideas for achieving these goals come from local people.

We work closely with people on the ground so we can match the local realities and can plan, forecast, and respond capably. Many people come to our foundation or to our field directors and say, "We need schools," or "Help us create scholarships," or "We want to provide health care," or "We want to save girls." In eight out of ten cases, the stories don't check out. However, if we do think they have a good idea and can make life a little better for people in these communities, we try to get them the resources they need to succeed. We work with them. We make suggestions.

Those original programs with Sir Ed to educate Sherpas in the Khumbu were our model and our testing ground, yet we've gone much further in the past thirty-five years. Local leaders of these mostly modest, small-scale efforts supported through AHF are inspiring. We have observed two common traits in nearly all: fierce resilience and dedication to people in their communities. We continue to scan local communities for other visionary change makers, other rock stars we could support who are selfless and heroic in making life a little easier for people who are struggling. They are out there.

Chapter 4

Partnering with Jimmy

*"We can choose to alleviate suffering.
We can choose to work together for peace.
We can make these changes—and we must."*

—Jimmy Carter

Trekking in the Himalaya is a true test of friendship. This was especially the case, I've noticed, in the 1970s and '80s. The hardships then were greater than those of today. You stayed in tents or primitive lodges. Trails were rutted and poorly maintained. Cold-weather gear was not as warm or waterproof. And of course there were the ever-present risks of altitude sickness.

When you spend a couple weeks in the mountains with someone, one of two things happens: You never want to see them again or they become one of your best friends. I can tell you I never had a better time in the Himalaya than I did with Jimmy and Rosalynn Carter in 1985.

Although I had met him a few times when he was president, I didn't get to know President Carter well until we trekked together that year, five years after he lost the White House to Ronald

Reagan. Our connection was made through Walter "Fritz" Mondale, Carter's vice president and the aspiring candidate I had backed in the early going for the Democratic nomination in 1976. That had been my first experience in national politics and one of my first efforts to have a positive impact on public policy. But our trip didn't come until a decade later, three years after Jimmy had started The Carter Center in Atlanta, Georgia, and four years after my other trekking buddies and I organized the American Himalayan Foundation, and it helped cement a relationship of support and partnership between our organizations.

When you consider all the NGOs in the world—and there are more than forty thousand—you will be hard-pressed to find many that equal The Carter Center and its remarkable record in helping the poorest people in the poorest countries, especially by improving food security, eradicating illness, and advancing the quest for peace and democracy. These were the goals Jimmy and Rosalynn laid out when they founded The Carter Center in 1982, the year after they left the White House. Their purpose as private citizens, they felt, was to continue efforts made during Jimmy's presidency to advance the cause for human rights and take actions to alleviate human suffering.

I have been a Carter Center trustee since 2000, including three years as vice chair, and I have great admiration for the center's work and Jimmy and Rosalynn's leadership. The Carters have been remarkably focused, determined, and persistent in building this humanitarian organization.

Our American Himalayan Foundation and The Carter Center share many principles, ideas, resources, and best practices in global development and combating poverty. In my mind, these principles are the bedrock of both organizations. They are why we succeed often in getting aid to the poorest of the poor, despite the many daunting challenges.

Getting to Know the President

When you trek in the Khumbu today, even after thirty years, you'll still see framed photos of Jimmy Carter in lodges and restaurants up and down the trail. In P. K.'s Khumbu Lodge in Namche Bazaar, there is a small room with a brass sign above the door: JIMMY CARTER SLEPT HERE. I had the sign made for P. K. People in the Khumbu appreciated Jimmy not simply because he was a former president of the United States. Our trip there showed him to be gracious, compassionate, kind, and persistent—all traits of Sherpa character.

We trekked for close to two weeks through beautiful hills and valleys in the Khumbu—surrounded, of course, by some of the world's tallest mountains. We joked that Jimmy had reached the peak of his career—18,500 feet above sea level. The higher we trekked, the more people in the party fell prey to altitude sickness. Three people (including a young Secret Service agent who ran ultra-marathons) had to be evacuated by helicopter. Then Rosalynn and another agent had to turn back. "The size of our party was steadily decreasing," Jimmy wrote a few years later about the trip in his book *An Outdoor Journal.* "We began to feel as if we were in an Agatha Christie novel."[1] The former navy submarine officer himself seemed to be doing just fine. He had recently turned sixty-one. The farther we went up the mountain, the happier he was to climb higher.

Instead of sticking to the original plan that had us finishing our trek in Lobuche, a small settlement on the route to the base camp of Mount Everest, we agreed that going up another thousand feet to Kala Patthar was a great idea. Our thinking was: If you have gotten as far as Lobuche and you are still feeling OK, it's definitely worth the extra few hours of hiking for the breathtaking visual feast that awaits trekkers atop Kala Patthar. It offers a spectacular, sweeping view of Mount Everest, Lhotse, and other summits nearby.

The night before we planned to head out, the lead Secret Service agent said he was too ill and couldn't go higher; the other remaining agent was weakening too. With this final agent's status in doubt, I learned that it could well be up to me to ensure the thirty-ninth president was protected and safe. "We'll give you the shortwave radio," he said, "and swear you in as a temporary member of the Secret Service," to which Jimmy joyfully replied, "This will be the first day since I was nominated for president that I will be without the Secret Service!" As exhilarating as that prospect was for both of us, the hiatus didn't materialize. The agent felt stronger by dawn, and we headed out as planned.

The former president, his agent, and Ang Tsering, our guide, made it all the way to the summit of Kala Patthar, which required navigating a tricky, rugged slope, without rope or crampons. The experience must have left Carter a bit shaken. "At first I was more angry with my lack of judgment than pleased with our accomplishment," he wrote in *An Outdoor Journal*.[2]

On the way back down, on the ridge of Kala Patthar, they came upon an unfolding tragedy. Two Indian men, one looking through a telescope and the other holding a radio transmitter, were frantically scanning the South Col route toward Mount Everest. They had just spotted surviving members of a star-crossed expedition. Five mountaineers in the group had been swept off the mountain the night before by high winds.

"When these two men saw me, they almost fainted, because I'm very well known in India," Jimmy said years later. "They asked if I would talk to the survivors."

Carter told them that we were praying for them to be careful and that we admired their heroism. None of the five bodies of the lost climbers was ever found, but those survivors eventually made their way down the mountain to safety. "That was the most memorable part of the trip for me," Jimmy said.

I believe that President Carter felt he had helped, if only in a small way, by offering a bit of a morale boost for the survivors. And for Jimmy, empathy and altruism are at the core of who he is—his reasons for being.

Scale of Achievement, Height of Aspiration

It is acknowledged widely that what Jimmy and Rosalynn created in The Carter Center is a well-managed NGO that continues to work effectively on an ever-larger scale in global development, helping those who need it most. If anyone questions why so many contemporary historians consider Jimmy's accomplishments since leaving the White House the greatest of any ex-president, The Carter Center story alone offers abundant proof.

It is no exaggeration to state that tens or perhaps even hundreds of millions of needy people today have greater hope for their future because of The Carter Center's work. About 90 percent of the center's annual budget, including in-kind contributions such as medicines and water-filtering supplies, supports health care projects, mainly in Africa and Latin America. The center also promotes fair and democratic elections and economic growth in the developing world, and talks between nations and groups to prevent or resolve conflicts.

Founded in partnership with Emory University, The Carter Center has worked in more than eighty countries over the past three decades and operates more than a dozen field offices. Through the years, Jimmy, Rosalynn, and center staff have taught Emory students, and Emory faculty and students have participated in many of the center's health and peace programs. It's a good relationship.

Most people don't appreciate how well this organization is run, or the scale of its achievements and the heights of its aspirations. In 2002, when Jimmy won the Nobel Peace Prize, the Norwegian Nobel Committee cited The Carter Center for its efforts in conflict resolution, human rights, and observing elections around the world, and for its "hard work on many fronts to fight tropical diseases and to bring about growth and progress in developing countries."[3]

The three words health professionals use to describe the preventable diseases in The Carter Center's crosshairs—*neglected tropical diseases*—tell you the basics about how the center views its mission: *Do what others have not done. Go to the poorest places. Alleviate human suffering.*

Another of the center's vital roles has been monitoring nearly a hundred elections in more than three dozen countries. Jimmy personally has been on hand for about thirty-five of these events, and I was with Jimmy and his team in 1999 to monitor elections in Nigeria and Indonesia, two of the world's most fragile democracies. It was an education. The center sends monitors months in advance to observe the way campaigns are planned and conducted, and later to determine whether the balloting and the vote count are carried out properly on election day. Nigeria was rife with fraud; the picture in Indonesia was more favorable. The Carter Center's postelection assessments have a well-earned reputation worldwide as authoritative and nonpartisan.

Norman Borlaug, perhaps the most famous agriculture scientist of modern times—he was credited with saving hundreds of millions of people from starvation—was a senior advisor with The Carter Center for more than twenty years. Their project helped more than eight million small-scale farmers in fifteen sub-Saharan African countries increase crop production.[4]

Like our foundation, The Carter Center tries hard not to duplicate what other organizations are doing. It is not in either of our organizations' DNA to trumpet our brands in the field. However, we won't pass up opportunities to pitch in and enhance what other NGOs or governments are doing. And we'll take note of what services are available and what gaps we might be able to fill. Just as AHF does, the Carters and their staff of 175 people work quietly with politicians, health ministers, and especially local people leading programs in cities and villages. The key principle, as I emphasized in chapter 3, is that both organizations put local people at the center of a project.

An important Carter Center goal is to help create self-sufficiency. "You can't give somebody money and expect that it will alleviate their poverty," said Dr. John Hardman, a close friend, longtime trustee of the Blum Center for Developing Economies at UC Berkeley, and The Carter Center's administrative leader for more than twenty years before he retired in 2014. "They have a much better chance of sustaining success over the long term" if they identify problems and implement solutions themselves, with some training and advice. "We have this firm belief that if people are just given a little bit of knowledge, encouragement, and skills, they can change their lives," John continued. "All they need is the hope that they can do it, not that somebody is going to do it for them . . . Hope is the critical part."

Disciplined Conquests of Horrific Plagues

The Carter Center has played a massive role in sharply reducing outbreaks of preventable diseases in poor, rural areas with little formal health care. The center effectively has prevented the suffering of millions of people because Jimmy and his teams travel to Africa and other stricken areas all the time, talking with everyone from heads of state to local leaders to the very people afflicted with preventable tropical diseases. Jimmy, John Hardman, and I have walked the dirt roads in villages in Ethiopia, Mali, South Sudan, and other desperately poor countries where The Carter Center has been a respected force in curtailing these plagues. President Carter has generously acknowledged my contributions as having "been an integral part of it all." To be sure, we have been like-minded in our focus on global development for many, many years.

The center leads the international campaign to eradicate Guinea worm disease; works to eliminate river blindness throughout the Americas and regions of Africa; and helps treat and prevent lymphatic filariasis, blinding trachoma, malaria, and schistosomiasis, a parasitic disease that infects the kidneys or intestines and afflicts some 240 million people, mostly children. By 2014, the center had treated about twenty million people for river blindness, or "more than the number of people who live in the state of New York," Jimmy told reporters.[5]

As a summer intern, my granddaughter Eileen traveled twice to Hispaniola with members of The Carter Center's international public health team to research how far Haiti and the Dominican Republic had progressed toward eliminating two of the world's most widespread tropical diseases: malaria and lymphatic filariasis. The latter disease is transmitted by mosquito bites and can cause irreversible, disfiguring enlargement of arms, legs, and genitals, known as elephantiasis. More than 120 million people are afflicted by it—needlessly in every case. As with many neglected tropical diseases, we know how to prevent and eliminate lymphatic filariasis. With the support of Carter Center teams and others, two states in Nigeria already have achieved this goal. Eileen learned that the Dominican Republic is getting very close to doing so.[6]

But health conditions in Haiti remain much worse than in the Dominican Republic, partially because of the devastating 2010 earthquake near Port-au-Prince that killed at least 220,000 people, injured three hundred thousand, and displaced more than one million, according to UN estimates. Perhaps three million people were affected.[7] "The sickness in Haiti is worse—just tragic," Eileen said. "Tropical diseases are rampant." There is still much work to be done.

"Before The Carter Center began its work, diseases like Guinea worm and river blindness were seen as intractable—a fact of life in the world's poorest countries," said Dr. Nils Daulaire, leader of the Global Health Council, when the 2006 Gates Award went to the center. "The Carter Center has turned conventional wisdom on its head and reminded the world that seemingly impossible obstacles can be overcome with the right combination of innovation, dedication, and community involvement."[8]

The center's critical work in some of the world's poorest areas has brought hope and healing to millions. Two of the finest examples are its enlightened, relentless campaigns to eradicate Guinea worm disease and to prevent blindness as a result of trachoma.

Guinea Worm Countdown

One of The Carter Center's most amazing achievements in collaboration with many health ministries and other NGOs is the effort lasting nearly three decades to eradicate Guinea worm disease. During the same news conference when he first described his brain cancer diagnosis, Jimmy talked optimistically about an approaching, complete triumph. He said, grinning broadly, "I'd like to have the last Guinea worm die before I do."[9]

It is very possible that within a few years Guinea worm will become the second human disease (after smallpox in 1978) to be wiped from the face of the earth,[10] and the first to be defeated fully without the use of vaccine or medicine. For the millions of people now living who ever suffered from this debilitating, excruciating plague, and for their families and communities, those statements are cause for celebration.

"Even though Guinea worm disease does not usually kill people, its effect on communities is devastating," said Dr. Donald R. Hopkins, vice president for The Carter Center's health programs. "In the past, we saw entire villages unable to work or go to school because of a Guinea worm outbreak. That is why we must get rid of this disease."[11]

Guinea worm spreads to humans who drink water contaminated with larvae of the worm. Once inside the body, a worm can grow to three feet in length before it emerges from someplace on the person's skin. It then may take several weeks of excruciating pain before the worm can be completely removed, typically by being wrapped around a stick or piece of gauze as it slowly exits.

Nearly all progress in wiping out Guinea worm disease has been achieved through health education programs led by The Carter Center. No vaccines or medicines exist that can treat Guinea worm disease, so teaching people to filter all drinking water and stay out of contaminated areas when larvae are most likely present have been key factors.[12] At least thirteen million small "pipe filters," worn around the neck and used for drinking possibly contaminated water, have been donated through the center.

The Carter Center identified an estimated 3.5 million cases of Guinea worm disease worldwide in 1986. That figure was down to just over ten thousand in 2005 and then to just twenty-two cases at the end of 2015. In 1991, Guinea worm disease was endemic in 23,735 villages in twenty-one countries in Africa and Asia.[13] By the end of 2015, according to The Carter Center, the twenty-two cases of the disease were transmitted in only twenty villages, all in Africa—nine cases in Chad, five each in South Sudan and Mali, and three in Ethiopia. Guinea worm has been wiped out everywhere else.

The center estimated a few years ago that the eradication campaign had prevented nearly eighty million cases overall. It's almost impossible to fathom the ripple effects within communities struggling just to meet the daily needs of their people. Anywhere I go in Africa, Jimmy Carter is very well liked. Millions of people appreciate how they, their families, and their neighbors have become healthier and more productive because of The Carter Center's work.

Among the campaign's biggest donors in recent years, a testament to Jimmy Carter's vision, leadership, and results, are the Bill & Melinda Gates Foundation, the United Arab Emirates, the Children's Investment Fund Foundation, and the United Kingdom.

Trachoma, Ground Zero

I was not expecting what John Hardman showed me on my first visit to Ethiopia in the late 1990s. I thought I had seen the worst of the world's extreme poverty in Tibet and Nepal, but the people in Ethiopian villages and across the western border in South Sudan were emaciated, lacking food and the most basic health care.

Malaria, malnutrition, Guinea worm, diarrhea, river blindness, and infant mortality were among the many debilitating health problems at the turn of the century. Yet trachoma may have been Ethiopia's most feared plague at the time. Its people had the highest rates of infection in the world—two hundred times above what the World Health Organization has said is the threshold for concern. Yet trachoma was accepted in the villages as a way of life, a curse.

Trachoma, a bacterial infection spread by flies that breed on human feces or by simple contact between one person and another, is the leading cause of preventable blindness worldwide. Once an upper eyelid is infected, the eyelid turns inward, causing the lashes to scratch the cornea—painfully, with every blink of the eye—and leading to scarring, diminished vision, and eventually (after repeated infections) blindness. The infection almost always occurs in both eyes. Effective prevention involves nothing more than rudimentary infrastructure and basic hygiene.

Building pit latrines with covers and small anterooms is necessary to curb the fly population. Teaching villagers and schoolchildren to wash their hands and faces helps prevent infections. Surgery and antibiotics are simple ways to correct damaged eyelids and restore a patient's vision. By teaching basic hygiene, building latrine pits, administering antibiotics, and performing simple surgeries on infected upper eyelids, agents of The Carter Center and its many allies have again demonstrated how a disease that has plagued humankind for thousands of years can now be prevented.

Jimmy already was marshaling funds and teams to tackle Guinea worm, river blindness, and other preventable diseases near the horn of Africa when he added trachoma to The Carter Center agenda. He knew quite well that trachoma could be corralled and stopped, because he had watched as a boy when his mother, Lillian Carter, a nurse, treated trachoma victims in southern Georgia.

The front lines of The Carter Center's battle to eradicate trachoma stretched from the center of Ethiopia southwest to the Sudanese border. John took me there on my second trip to Ethiopia, in the late '90s when the center and other health organizations were just beginning programs to eradicate the disease. The scenes were shocking to me. I was standing at ground zero of the world's worst trachoma outbreaks. The corneas of people with advancing trachoma were cloudy white, ghostly. Trachoma presents the greatest risk to children: More than half of the children I saw were infected, which is catastrophic because children often spread the disease to mothers or other family members trying to care for or comfort them. Partially because of that maternal instinct, experts say, women are twice as likely as men to contract the disease.[14]

Back at The Carter Center's health office in Ethiopia, John Hardman arranged for the lead technical experts in the trachoma program to brief me and John Moores on the elimination plan. A brilliant technology entrepreneur and investor who owned the San Diego Padres baseball team, John also was a member of The Carter Center board. We heard that as many as 250,000 eyelid surgeries for people who suffered multiple scarring infections would be needed. To accomplish this goal, health workers would need to be trained and health centers built.

I asked, "How much would that many surgeries cost?"

Answer: "Well, we could really make an impact with a million dollars; we could do even more if we had two million."

John Moores and I looked at each other. It didn't take us long to figure out how to raise the $2 million.

I said, "Are you good for half?"

He said, "Yep. Are you good for half?"

I said, "Yep."

And that was it.

Many others contributed over the years to fund these simple, fifteen-minute surgeries in Ethiopia, Mali, Niger, Nigeria, Sudan, South Sudan, and Uganda. In 2013 alone, The Carter Center supported fifty-eight thousand corrective eye surgeries— a quarter of the surgeries performed worldwide—conducted by local health workers who were trained and equipped for the procedures. In the same year, the center supported construction of more than 150,000 household latrines, upping the total since 2002 to approximately 3.1 million.

It turns out the number of surgeries actually required in Ethiopia was underestimated: In 2015, The Carter Center discovered that 791,000 surgeries were still needed. Undaunted, the center has set a goal to end blindness caused by trachoma by 2019 in Ethiopia, Mali, Niger, Nigeria, and Sudan.[15] More than forty million people, mostly women and children, had active cases and needed treatment in 2015.[16] Estimates among global health professionals suggest cases are so numerous that advanced trachoma blinds one person every fifteen minutes. Yet the disease has already been wiped out in Ghana. With that proof of success, and strong progress in other countries, hope is high.

"We Have Not Yet Made the Commitment to Share"

When Jimmy marked his ninetieth birthday in October 2014, he was still in good shape, optimistic as ever, and continuing to work hard. Every minute of his day was scheduled. Shortly before one meeting would end, a staff member would open the door to his office—the signal for him to wrap up, walk back to his desk, and prepare for the next one.

Less than a year later, Jimmy's doctors discovered four small cancerous tumors in his brain, a few weeks after removing a malignant tumor from his liver. As he approached his ninety-first birthday, my family and I joined with hundreds of his friends in offering our greatest hopes and encouragement as he began advanced treatments for four small melanomas. "I'm at ease with whatever comes," he said at an August news conference.[17] Before the year was out, Jimmy told his Bible study class the hopeful news that his cancer was in remission, explaining that his latest brain scan "did not reveal any signs of the original cancer spots nor any new ones." Cancer experts greeted the results as another sign that cancers can be defeated by combining changes in the body's immune system with radiation therapy.[18]

Even after the cancer diagnosis and his ongoing treatments, Jimmy organized each day in his Atlanta office or traveling on Carter Center activities with the precision you might expect from a onetime senior officer of the precommissioning crew of the *Seawolf*, the US Navy's second nuclear submarine.

By comparison, I long ago learned to count on other people to help me stay organized. I can be easily distracted. A

Mali–Ghana–Togo trip with Jimmy after I joined the center's board offers proof. When we walked into our hotel in Accra, the capital of Ghana, I was fascinated with the architecture. The main building featured a cathedral-style ceiling supported by large beams rising over a central fountain. As I strolled into the main lobby carrying my briefcase, looking at the ceiling, I walked straight off a ledge into the fountain pool. The drop was at least three feet. Luckily, I stayed on my feet and kept my balance, but my briefcase, pants, socks, and shoes were drenched. When we got to my room and dumped out my briefcase, things I hadn't seen for years poured out with the hotel fountain water: documents, notebooks, photos, and so forth. John Hardman later remembered the incident as hilarious, saying, "I had towels out, trying to save pictures and keep ink from ruining documents, but Dick would stop and reminisce about some photo or document and say, 'Oh, look at this!' It was a childlike excitement over finding things he thought he had lost forever."

Well, maybe so. Jimmy and I are very much alike in the conviction about our personal responsibility to help others less fortunate. Dianne and I were honored to be part of a small group invited to attend the ceremony in 2002 where Jimmy accepted his Nobel Peace Prize. The prize is awarded every December 10, the anniversary of Alfred Nobel's birth, at historic Oslo City Hall in Norway. "Obviously they were two of our closest possible friends," Jimmy later explained. Some have said that he should have been awarded the Peace Prize in 1978, alongside Egyptian President Anwar Sadat and Israeli Prime Minister Menachem Begin, for his role in the Camp David Accords—thirteen days of secret negotiations that led to a peace agreement between their countries. But Jimmy told me he was glad his prize came decades later for The Carter Center achievements, which he considered even greater than his pursuit of peace between Egypt and Israel. "I felt the Nobel Prize was given to me because of the work of

The Carter Center," he said, "and in many ways Dick was a partner with me in that work."

In his Nobel Lecture in 2002, Jimmy said the greatest challenge the world faces is the growing chasm between the wealthy and the destitute:

> Citizens of the ten wealthiest countries are now seventy-five times richer than those who live in the ten poorest ones. . . . The results of this disparity are root causes of most of the world's unresolved problems, including starvation, illiteracy, environmental degradation, violent conflict, and unnecessary illnesses that range from Guinea worm to HIV/AIDS. . . .
>
> Tragically, in the industrialized world there is a terrible absence of understanding or concern about those who are enduring lives of despair and hopelessness. We have not yet made the commitment to share with others an appreciable part of our excessive wealth. This is a necessary and potentially rewarding burden that we should all be willing to assume.

I could not agree more.

Part 2

What Smart Investing Teaches Us about Development

Chapter 5

Risks and Rewards

"It is hard to fail, but it is worse never to have tried to succeed. In this life we get nothing save by effort."

—Theodore Roosevelt

If we had a caste system in the United States, I would have ended up in the clothing business like my great-grandfather, grandfather, father, mother, and even stepfather. My maternal great-grandfather, Louis B. Heil, immigrated from Dieburg, Germany, made his way west, and opened a store to outfit silver miners in Montrose, Colorado. When the mines began to dry up, he moved his family, including my Grandmother Cleve, to El Paso, Texas, and opened the Union Shoe and Clothing Company. When my grandmother married Charles Hirsch, he joined my great-grandfather in the business. And as I described in chapter 2, my father and mother kept the tradition going by becoming State-O-Maine western region sales representatives.

Maybe it isn't surprising, then, that when I was well into the MBA program at the University of California, Berkeley, and looking for work, a family friend offered me a job as a sales representative for Van Heusen shirts. The job came with a guaranteed income of at least $1,100 a month, a sizable amount in that day. It would have been easy enough to accept. But I had been around the garment business enough to know that it was not for me.

By the time I was a teenager in the early 1950s, I had seen enough of life to know that one day I would have to make money for myself and probably support a family. Although there never was any question in my mind that I wanted to major in business, I studied as widely as possible in other fields. Your college experience should open you up to the world and challenge your thinking, beliefs, and assumptions. Your classes and activities should suggest an array of possibilities in the contemporary world for a life well lived—a life by which you make important contributions to society. My years at Berkeley did all this for me.

My time at Berkeley and the rising arc of my business career—into the world of investment and finance—helped me develop a strong capacity for analyzing facts, assessing risk, and identifying emerging trends or opportunities. These skills have certainly benefited me personally, but they also have shaped how I approach any global development work I play a role in, whether it's philanthropy, public policy, education, or something else. The American Himalayan Foundation would not have had the impact it has without these disciplines baked into our core processes. When I've seen initiatives from other nonprofit groups fail or end in disappointment, it's often because one or more of these management competencies—fact-based analysis, risk assessment, or knowledge of local and global trends—was missing from the start.

Of course, all this focus on gathering knowledge, developing insight, and taking action has to be framed by both a passion to make a positive impact in the world and an inspiration that flows naturally from the values of empathy and altruism. Life is simply a series of decisions that lead to action. The risks and the rewards are sometimes obvious—and oftentimes not.

Six Months in Europe and North Africa

One day when I was a sophomore, I happened to pick up *The Daily Cal*, the campus newspaper, and noticed an article about a foreign study program at the University of Vienna, organized by the Institute of European Studies.[1]

The only time I had traveled abroad was during a weekend assignment with the Navy Reserve in San Diego, when a few of us from the reserve unit drove down to Tijuana. Unlike today, in the 1950s study abroad programs were few and far between, even at major universities. The Vienna program sounded ideal and certainly appealed to my instinct for adventure. I applied for the program while studying for what was the equivalent of junior-year credits and was accepted for the spring semester of 1957. I would study in Vienna after a few weeks of touring with a group of college students across Western Europe. In the summer, I would be able to travel wherever I wanted.

I learned somewhat late in the process, though, about academic requirements I had to meet before leaving campus for Europe—a mistake. The registrar's office informed me that I would have to take six classes for the next two semesters in order to fulfill my degree requirements and graduate on time following my return from Vienna. These classes also happened to be some of the most difficult ones I would need to take.

I hadn't been a great student in my first few semesters at Berkeley—procrastination and cramming for a class like I did in high school didn't work so well anymore—and I might not have made it through those two semesters if I hadn't met an attractive young woman named Andrea Schwartz. She was studying to be a physician and had never, ever gotten a grade worse than an A.

It didn't take me long to realize that the only way I could see her during the week was to study with her. We were taking the same art history course, and when I came in second to her top marks, a light bulb finally went on. I became a much better student. A few years later, Andrea would become my first wife and the mother of my three wonderful daughters—Annette, Heidi, and Eileen.

During those two rough semesters before my planned travels abroad, it seemed that I was nearly killing myself trying to get it all done—the endless reading, the papers, the tests. But I certainly learned a lot. Once I had run that gauntlet and my grades were in good shape, I was tremendously relieved.

Well, not so fast. Two weeks before I was scheduled to leave for Vienna, an official in the registrar's office told me, "We made a mistake. You can't spend your last year off campus and get credit for any courses you take. That would violate a residency requirement. Your senior year has to be at Berkeley."

I was not happy. "I'm going anyway," I told them. I figured I would have any backing I needed from my professors in the business school if I had to arm wrestle with these bureaucrats when I got back. It never came to that.

It was a risk, but sticking to my plan was absolutely the right decision. I would learn more in the next several months in Europe about life and what the world was like than I did growing up in San Francisco and those first years at Berkeley. Most important, I came to understand for the first time how much poverty there was in the world.

One of my first impressions drove home for me a glimmer of what it must be like to live your life on the edge of poverty. I had traveled from New York to Liverpool, England, on a passenger ship with about twenty-five other college students. We'd had five days of high seas, late nights, and good times before coming into port and boarding a bus. Now, we were riding through a tunnel that was dark and filthy with coal soot that had been accumulating from chimneys and smokestacks across Liverpool for a hundred years. Our bus suddenly passed very close to a guy who was working in the tunnel, trying to scrub the soot off the inner walls with just a rag. I was appalled. The air must have been full of deadly contaminants, unbreathable and stinging his eyes. I couldn't imagine how anyone could work under those conditions, and I never forgot it.

As we traveled by bus through England, Belgium, France, Germany, and Austria, we saw people still trying, more than ten years later, to recover from World War II. Housing was old and cramped, because so much of what had once stood in these towns and cities had collapsed to rubble. There wasn't enough food because the food and agricultural industries had been so hard hit. When we arrived in Vienna, it was less than three months after the Soviets had brutally ended the Hungarian Uprising of 1956. The city was full of refugees who had escaped Hungary. People were queued up in lines that went on for blocks, hoping to get visas at the US embassy to go to America.

I rented a room from a family who lived on the sixth floor of an apartment building with no stair lights. The elevator didn't work because the Nazis had stolen the elevator cables during the war. Many steps were broken. Just getting up to my room was dangerous—good training for years later when I was climbing mountains in Nepal.

I wasn't going to get academic credits for any classes I registered for at the University of Vienna, so although I was taking some interesting courses, I stopped attending lectures by early spring and for most of my remaining four months hitchhiked through more of Europe and a little of North Africa. Many towns and cities I saw there were impoverished too, especially in Yugoslavia, Greece, and Spain. Spain was dreadfully poor.

In Morocco, both France and Spain had been imperialist colonizers off and on for more than a century. You could see in the eyes of people on the streets in Casablanca a distrust, even hatred, for Europeans, especially the French and Spanish. Unfortunately, Moroccans I encountered in shops and on the streets appeared to assume I was French, not American.[2] They were not very friendly. One day I got into a scuffle with a guy in Casablanca who was trying to pick my pocket and wouldn't take his hand out. I was much bigger physically, and I grabbed him by the throat and slammed him against a wall. He yelled out. Suddenly I was being chased by guys in turbans who seemed to be coming from everywhere. It was like a scene in a movie: I dashed away down a narrow alley, ducked behind a wall, and hid there as they all ran past, my heart pounding. I'm thankful they never found me. I decided to get out of Casablanca fast and took the next train to Marrakech.

After quickly crossing northward from Morocco back into Europe, I soon had several more interesting trips, including hitchhiking into Soviet-occupied East Germany and sleeping on a wooden bench for three nights in Berlin's expansive Tiergarten Park, and eventually returned to Vienna and then Berkeley. Back on my home campus, I felt a new sense of purpose.

Paying Attention to Trends

After completing my undergraduate degree, about six months after I returned, I enrolled right away in the Berkeley MBA program, finished in a year, and continued on with PhD studies in economics. I wanted to travel and see more of the world while making a living, but I needed a job in the meantime to pay the bills while in graduate school.

In these first years after World War II, large American firms sold their goods abroad through international trading groups. These groups provided a better understanding of local marketing conventions and practices, and they oversaw each step of in-country sales transactions. A family acquaintance got me in the door at a trading company on California Street in downtown San Francisco, and I met with the managing partner. I'll never forget the scene. Only two people were within sight—the managing partner and another partner—and in front of them were forty desks, all of them empty. It looked like these two guys might be the only ones left.

The managing partner promised me a position, but after he returned from a business trip two weeks later, he called and said, "I'm going to do you the biggest favor of your life. I'm not going to give you a job," he said. "Don't go into this business. If I were a young man, I wouldn't." These trading companies, it turned out, were fossilizing, in their dying days. Improvements in shipping and communications had made it possible for major companies to work directly with foreign buyers.

I abandoned my idea of working with a trading company. Not long after, a few friends from an investment club I had belonged to while an undergrad at Berkeley introduced me to people in some of San Francisco's top investment firms. The club, with the grandiose name of The Midas Investors, turned out to be a valuable learning and networking experience; I went in not knowing the first thing about how to choose stocks. I quickly realized the atmosphere in these investment firms was completely different from the trading company. Instead of pessimism, I saw optimism. I heard of one broker in his twenties who was making $30,000 a year, a *phenomenal* sum then. *That could be me*, I thought.

I signed on as a junior analyst and trainee at Sutro & Co., a traditional brokerage firm that made most of its money on commissions from its clients' stock trades, not on profits from investments or trading in its own accounts. This was 1958—seventeen years before the old system of fixed commission rates would be abolished by the Securities and Exchange Commission (SEC), and the year Sutro marked its one hundredth anniversary.

For decades, Sutro & Co. was the largest investment house west of the Mississippi. It was a conservative enterprise in every way. Over the course of a century, the firm had been led by only three senior partners. Each was so innately risk averse that the firm *rented*—and never bought—the property where it maintained offices—in the 400 block of Montgomery Street, near the heart of what is today's thriving financial district—for more than 110 years.

I was assigned on my first day to the research department. There were five of us, all crowded into a single room with a long row of filing cabinets crammed with company reports. My first assignment was to throw out enough outdated documents to empty two filing cabinets, thereby creating space for my desk.

For weeks, I sat and read annual reports on hundreds of companies, most of which I knew nothing about. I took a lot of notes, though, and by the time I earned my little desk, I had absorbed information about scores of industries and their major players. Though I wouldn't suggest this as a training program today, at the time I saw it as a great opportunity. I *wanted* to be in the research department.

I was comfortable with the intrinsic nature of the work because it flowed seamlessly from my MBA studies. A lot of research back then wasn't all that hot, frankly. If you could do your own research and have your own company contacts, you would have more confidence in what a company was saying and how to assess the value of its shares for clients. I felt sure I could learn more that way, and I have believed ever since in getting as close as possible to the best source of relevant information in everything I do.

My breakthrough at Sutro came about a year later, after market research firm AC Nielsen went public. I wrote what probably was the first research report by any brokerage on AC Nielsen. I had studied the business in one of my MBA classes; I understood it and liked it. I gave Nielsen a strong "buy" recommendation, and in the following months, the stock did extremely well.

It wasn't long before many of Sutro's two hundred brokers discovered me. "What other companies can you recommend?" they would ask. Varian Associates was one I could suggest with confidence, again thanks to my MBA studies. I had finished the core course requirements for my MBA by the time I started at Sutro and had decided to take further advantage of Berkeley's cornucopia of offerings to add some courses on finance. I had written about Varian Associates—one of the few providers of the klystron microwave tubes the National Aeronautics and Space Administration relied on for its satellite communications and radio astronomy programs—for one of those classes, and had interviewed Varian's treasurer, Jim Donovan. He couldn't have been nicer. We stayed in touch after I joined Sutro, and I occasionally would go see him to understand better what the company was doing. We recommended, and bought, Varian shares in the twenties. The price soon climbed into the seventies before falling back.

In addition to writing reports, I also analyzed investor portfolios and began working with my own clients. It was pretty basic stockbroker activity. I would call clients with a new idea I liked for a promising investment or just to check in with updates on their portfolios and the market. Ewald Grether, the dean of Berkeley's business school for many years, who had taught a few of my courses, asked me to manage his investments. He didn't have a large portfolio with us, but his was a huge vote of confidence for a young kid like me just getting started. He was a renowned expert in marketing and pricing, and I had often sought him out for academic and career guidance.

I continued to do my own company research and enjoyed it. The reports were benefiting clients, our firm, and me, and I knew that continuing to unearth good investment opportunities ahead of competitors was going to be *my* best opportunity for a rapid rise in the firm.

Hard Work's Rewards

At first my goal at Sutro was to earn at least $1,000 a month as a broker. I knew that if I could push that to $2,500 a month, I would be on track to actually earn that $30,000 a year. I topped $1,000 in the first month, at $1,100—more than triple my initial salary in commissions alone—and was now making as much as if I had taken that job selling Van Heusen shirts. It was exciting.

I was earning money on my own terms, and that was important to me. I had watched my mother and grandmother struggle financially at various times. My grandmother had a penchant for falling for financial and investment schemers later in her life. And my mother had been forced to use up much of the money left to her by my late father, who was reasonably successful. She had quit her job with State-O-Maine after remarrying when I was twelve. My new stepfather, Morrie, was a men's clothing manufacturer's sales representative, but he gambled excessively. Bob and I were back home from the military boarding school we hated so much, and my mother had to pay all the household expenses whenever Morrie's income was squandered to cover his gambling debts. As a young man, it had stuck in my mind that I needed to move beyond the prospect of diminishing resources and learn how to make money for myself. Now I felt I was making quantum leaps in that direction.

I gained the equivalent of ten years' experience in my first five years at Sutro because I worked twice as hard as anybody else. I often was the first guy in the door in the morning and the last guy out at night and always wanted to be at my desk at least an hour before the opening bell rang on the New York Stock Exchange at seven a.m. Pacific time.[3] After the market closed at twelve thirty p.m., I worked on either research or client calls. At home in the evenings, there were company reports and *The Wall Street Journal* to read to get ready for the next day.

One day, after three or four years at Sutro, one of the brokers said to me, "Well, you almost got there."

I had no idea what he was talking about. "What do you mean, I almost got there?" I asked.

"You were almost our largest producer," he replied, glancing back to a tally sheet for a period that had just ended.

I was stunned. Looking back, I shouldn't have been so surprised. I always say, my inspiration comes from perspiration. That's how you succeed. But many of my colleagues operated without detailed information about industries and companies. The longer-tenured Sutro brokers would fill their days simply charting price movements of their favorite stocks, never looking at research or developing fresh ideas. They thought every client should own some shares in General Motors, Bank of America, and Pacific Gas & Electric.

I was much more interested in finding and studying companies with promising business models and exciting growth prospects— similar to the philanthropic and global development opportunities I would later seek. Clearly, this was working well. I narrowed my sights even further: toward making my first $1 million.

Embracing Risk

One trait I've retained from my youth is a perpetual curiosity about virtually any subject. This has always driven some of my associates and family members a little crazy, but I am sure insatiable curiosity has helped set me apart from the crowd. It allows me to see opportunities where others see threats or obstacles. Curiosity inevitably tests your appetite for risk, because you are attracted to situations or circumstances most others avoid.

Risk is a great teacher. Sometimes you win and sometimes you lose, but the more frequently you take risks and are able to step back and learn the right lessons from those experiences, the better you are able to calculate the dangers and the rewards when each new opportunity arrives. Now that I'm older and presumably wiser, I am asked occasionally how our firm, Blum Capital, has been able to invest so successfully over the years. The answer is that my partners and I knew how to assess risk. We have been willing to make big investments despite keen competition and great uncertainties. Even at times when a situation might have looked bleak, we would hold fast to our plans and analyses. In order to do well, you need to have the courage of your convictions.

To reach that level of confidence, insight, and conviction about potential opportunities, you need to start taking risks in your career and in your investments when you are young, the stakes are relatively low, and there is plenty of time for you to change course if necessary and recover. Better to make mistakes while you are young and the numbers you are working with have fewer zeroes at the end. It's far easier to recover, if you have to.

I had tested this theory twice by the time I was twenty-five. Mark Twain once wrote that a cat only sits on a hot stove once.[4] If that's true, I guess I wasn't as smart as the average cat.

Not long before I joined Sutro, I had gone into business with a friend's father. We opened San Francisco's first—and last of its era—trampoline center. It was 1957. Trampoline centers were all the rage in Los Angeles, where 150 of them had sprung up and young people were queuing up by the hundreds at each location to experience the latest fad.

Soon after we opened up with new trampolines neatly spaced on a vacant lot that we had rented, however, a customer was seriously injured in a fall at one of the Los Angeles centers. Those centers all shut down as quickly as they had opened, and it wasn't long before we cratered too. In business for about four months, we lost all the money we invested. For me, that was $3,000, or about half my net worth. I was pretty shaken up. I hadn't realized you could lose so much money so quickly.

After I started at Sutro, I began putting money I saved into stocks. When I inherited $10,000 from my grandmother after she passed away in 1960, I invested all that money in high-tech electronics companies down the Peninsula. This was early days in the nascent Silicon Valley, before it was even called Silicon Valley. I figured I'd be really smart and buy even more on margin—that is, borrowing another $10,000 to double down on these stocks and use the shares as collateral.

It wasn't long before my $10,000 in inherited cash had turned into $100,000—on paper. I was riding high. But then the market plunged. I came to work at eight o'clock one morning and was greeted with the shocking news that my losses had triggered a margin call: I had to deliver $11,000 in cash by eleven a.m. or all those tech stocks would be sold at prices drastically lower than what I had paid.

Asking me to come up with $11,000 in cash in a few hours then was like asking me to come up with tens of millions in cash in a few hours today. *Oh, my God*, I thought. *Where am I going to get eleven thousand dollars?*

One of our branch office managers had a brother who was a loan officer at the Mechanics Bank of Richmond, California. I knew him only slightly but called anyway and told him my predicament. Reluctantly, he agreed to see me. I drove as fast as I could over the Bay Bridge to Richmond and showed him my portfolio.

"You shouldn't have bought these speculative stocks," he said.

"Yes, I know," I replied. "But I did, and it's too late. Can you lend me the eleven thousand dollars?" I promised to repay the money as soon as I could.

With no security other than my pledge to pay him back, he handed me a cashier's check for $11,000. I was relieved, but only for a moment. I raced back across the Bay Bridge to San Francisco. Ten minutes before the deadline, I ran up to the cashier's window, delivered the check, and narrowly averted having all that stock dumped in a forced sale. That would have been a disaster: Those tech stocks rallied a week later, and I quickly sold enough of them to repay the bank.

I'll never, ever put myself in that position again, I told myself. I was never going to leverage any stock holding to the point that it could be subject to a margin call. I was never going to risk money I didn't have, in one form or another. And I never have. For more than fifty years, the only money I have borrowed from banks is through term loans backed by hard assets on real estate projects.

EAST OF TIMBUKTU

Taking risks is fundamental for investing in or supporting projects in underdeveloped countries and communities. You do your best to research and analyze the situation, but instability and change are rampant, and your best efforts to make wise decisions will never guarantee the best outcomes.

Jimmy Carter, John Hardman, and I took a trip through West Africa a few years after I joined The Carter Center's board in 2000, stopping in Mali, Ghana, and Togo. During a meeting at the American embassy in Bamako, the capital of Mali, the head of US Agency for International Development (USAID) programs told us he wanted to start a health care training program a little east of Timbuktu, in a town called Gao. He needed a financial partner. His plans and enthusiasm appealed to me, and I made a commitment to get started.

Within a year, though, that director had moved on, and his successor didn't seem interested in that training program. I couldn't get any status reports. Jimmy and I planned to visit the project in Gao for ourselves a few years later, but by 2012 the area was too dangerous.

The Tuareg rebellion in the north had displaced more than four hundred thousand people and driven government forces out of Timbuktu and Gao. Human Rights Watch reported horrible attacks centered in Gao that included "sexual abuse, looting and pillage, summary executions, child soldier recruitment, amputations, and other inhuman treatment."[5] I never heard from USAID what happened to the people in our nurses' training program, or even if the program still existed in 2012.

None of what came later made me believe that supporting the program wasn't the right decision at the time.

Who Assumes the Risk? Who Reaps the Reward?

While it's true that I'm comfortable taking measured risks, I never expect others to take undue risks only for my benefit. This principle applies in my personal life just as it does in business matters, and is why I find so inexcusable the grave dangers confronting Sherpas with expedition companies operating on Mount Everest. The situation has become, in a word, obscene.

It was late February 2014, and Norbu Tenzing was chatting with visitors in his American Himalayan Foundation office. "It's just a matter of time until there is another big disaster on Everest," he predicted. Within two months, as Everest's spring climbing season was gathering momentum, Norbu was proven horribly correct. Tumbling, splintering blocks of ice high on Everest's South Face crashed onto twenty-five Nepali men, each ferrying more than sixty pounds of food, oxygen tanks, cooking equipment, and other supplies on their backs for guided expeditions. Sixteen mountaineering workers were killed—thirteen

Sherpas and three other Nepalis. It was the worst disaster in Everest history, adding to the carnage of three other Sherpa deaths earlier in the year, four in 2013, and three in 2012. The shock and anger that reverberated across Sherpa communities shut down the 2014 spring climbing season.

The avalanche struck in the most feared expanse along the route to the summit: the Khumbu Icefall, which Jon Krakauer in his 2014 *New Yorker* article described so well as "a jumbled maze of unstable ice towers."[6] The Icefall's greatest risks by far fall upon the Sherpas. They must cross this danger zone as many as thirty to thirty-five times for each expedition, carrying heavy loads for people who often will cross it only twice or possibly four times.

The core issue here is this: Who is assuming the greatest risk, at what potential cost, and who is reaping the greatest rewards, with what potential benefits?

What Sir Ed and Tenzing Norgay accomplished together to the world's amazement some sixty years ago was summiting the highest mountain on earth and returning safely to tell the story—something no men before them had ever done. "Even using oxygen, as we were, if we did get to the top, we weren't sure whether we would drop dead or something of that nature," Sir Ed said in a 2000 interview with *NZEdge*.[7] It was the mid-century equivalent of the following generation's quest to put a man on the moon. Seven major expeditions over the prior three decades had failed, including one mounted by Swiss climbers a year before in 1952.

The journey hundreds of people now complete each year—to the top of Everest and back to Base Camp—bears little comparison to the arduous challenges overcome by Sir Ed and Tenzing. Everest expeditions follow essentially the same route these pioneers climbed, but the comparison ends there. The majority of climbers on guided expeditions are tourists, really, who pay $60,000 or more with the full expectation they will reach the summit and return safely. Many have never before worn crampons before.

"There are fewer hard-core mountaineers," Susmita Maskey, a Nepali who has climbed Everest and other major peaks, told *The Wall Street Journal*. "It's a circus."[8] Almost every step is choreographed along miles of fixed ropes secured by Sherpas who routinely must work precariously within a few feet, or less, of what they know could be a fatal plunge. Most carry haunting personal memories of someone, perhaps even a family member, who died while laboring on Everest. Various sources cite different figures for fatalities on Everest, but all are ghastly. According to government statistics, around three hundred people perished there from 1953 through 2015.[9]

The idea that people expect others to continually risk their lives so that they can amuse themselves in a high-altitude adventure just seems wrong.

A Sherpa working above Base Camp is nearly ten times more likely to die than a US commercial fisherman (the job rated most dangerous by the US Centers for Disease Control and Prevention) and more than three and a half times as likely to die as a US Army infantryman was during the first four years of the Iraq War, according to the Himalayan Database.

"As a workplace safety statistic, 1.2 percent mortality is outrageous," said *Outside* magazine's Grayson Schaffer in his cover story "The Disposable Man: A Western History of the Sherpas on Everest," published *nine months before* the April 2014 catastrophe. "There is no other service industry in the world that so frequently kills and maims its workers for the benefit of paying clients."[10]

In a country as poor as Nepal, Everest Inc. puts a lot of money into many pockets. It is the wellspring of Nepal's $370 million trekking-and-tourism industry. Norbu's home village, Thame, is one of the few where Sherpa tradition and culture remain strong. Some people still work the land and raise yaks. A three-hour trek from Namche Bazaar and twenty miles west of Mount Everest, Thame (pronounced Tha-mey) is home to several famous climbers—including Apa Sherpa, who has summited Everest a record 21 times. Dozens of young Thame men risk their lives to work as he did on Everest expeditions: their best potential source of income.

In the spring of 2014, we saw more than a thousand potential climbers at Base Camp. In 2013, more than 450 people made it to Everest's peak, about double the number in 1990. The government issues too many permits for Everest because expedition companies, most based in the United States and Europe, keep the money flowing.

But how much of that money do the Sherpas see? The biggest issue for me, Norbu, editors at *Outside* and *National Geographic*, and others who despise the spectacle on Everest is that an abysmally low share of Everest Inc. money ever reaches the Sherpas and other local guides and porters who bear the heavy loads and biggest risks. Guides on the staff of Western expedition companies often make $50,000 in a climbing season, but top pay for Sherpas, who must make many more trips, is only $5,000 (roughly ten times the average per capita income in Nepal).[11]

Before the 2014 disaster, surviving families of Sherpas killed on Everest expeditions above Base Camp received only $4,600 in death payments from expedition operators. The Nepal government raised the death benefit to $11,000 after the catastrophe, but that amount still is far too meager. If the amount of life insurance paid by the government in 1971 had kept pace across more than four decades of inflation, payments to Sherpa families in 2014 would have been equal to $45,000 in today's dollars. Making matters even more unconscionable, expedition companies rarely step in with contributions to cover much of that shortfall. "When a Sherpa dies, the family pays all that money for last rites and other religious activities, and then is just left to fend for itself," Norbu has said. "Foreigners make promises. Most don't keep them."

Our American Himalayan Foundation and others raised a decent sum of money after the 2014 disaster for the sixteen families left behind. Working through Sir Ed's Himalayan Trust, we committed to help educate the thirty-one children of those families from kindergarten through high school. The government provided some help to families directly for living expenses, but the Sherpas had hoped for more.

Apart from death benefits, actual incomes for Sherpas and others who work on the mountain don't reflect the dangers they face. More Indians and Asians, riding the wave of expanding middle-class economies, want to climb Everest. They are looking for cheaper ways to get there, a demand some Sherpas have met by setting up their own operations. Sherpas today have more education and, with a clearer awareness of the exploitation, rightly believe they deserve a bigger share of the Everest money. Yet Norbu has witnessed how these new companies, often operating from Kathmandu, have aggravated price cutting that has lowered community income and increased risks by putting more young, poorly trained Sherpas on the mountain. "We're going to see more deaths," said Norbu. "It's inevitable."

As Norbu has written, anyone planning an Everest expedition through Western companies or local operations in the Khumbu should get the facts in advance on how Sherpas and other local support staff for the expedition companies are trained, paid, and insured. They should ask themselves: *Is my conscience clear about how a climbing Sherpa's family would be compensated and protected if a father, husband, uncle, or brother is killed during the expedition? Do I and the expedition leaders understand the ethics of our choices?*[12] And we believe Sherpas working on the mountains need to get more organized among themselves to push for better training, safety precautions, insurance, and pay from all expedition operators.

Everest Inc. is not going away. Nearly 300 Westerners converged for summiting expeditions in the 2016 climbing season. This was down by half from the average total before the deadly avalanche and earthquakes, but clearly the mountain will remain a primary source of income in eastern Nepal. There will always be some segment of the Sherpa community living along the Khumbu trails that makes a living off trekkers and climbers.

"By Their Deeds, Laddie"

About a year after I joined Sutro & Co., the partners elected a new senior partner, a Scotsman named Alastair Hall. He was just the fourth senior partner in the firm's century-long history and the first one who was not a member of the Sutro family. Alastair Hall stood six foot four. Everyone called him Shorty.

There are two things you need to know about Shorty. First, he was the epitome of integrity. Second, in many ways, he was the father of my business career, with more influence in my formative years than anyone else. He taught me the importance of being consistent and forming opinions that are firmly rooted in an abiding philosophy of life. We had very different personalities—he was reserved, methodical, and wise, and I was hard-charging, unpredictable, and passionate—but we developed a close relationship.

I was especially impressed by the many ways Shorty showed empathy for the problems of others yet never expressed any self-pity. He endured more than his share of personal tragedy before and after joining Sutro. He was imprisoned for most of World War II by the Japanese in the largest civilian prison camp in the Philippines, Santo Tomas. Before the war he had had his own commodities trading firm in the Philippines, with a seat on the Manila Stock Exchange. Most of the four thousand prisoners in the camp were American or British, and conditions were harsh. The average man lost fifty-three pounds, the life-threatening equivalent of one-third of his body weight.[13] Shorty's wife was among many Western women living outside the prison in Manila who were rounded up by Japanese soldiers to serve as hostages in the days before Americans liberated the prison in 1945. Tragically, many of the women were executed before the Americans could rescue them. Shorty's wife was one of the victims.

Years later, after Shorty moved to San Francisco with his four children and a new wife, one of his sons caught meningitis only a few weeks after graduating from Stanford and died. I couldn't imagine the grief he was suffering, but this memory often calls to mind something Shorty once told me: "When you walk down the street and look into people's faces, you never know what kind of sadness they may be enduring."

Shorty regularly shared his wisdom in refined Scottish sayings. When I would tell him how some deal promoters were positioning an investment that looked promising, he would turn, look me in the eye, and say, "By their deeds, laddie. By their deeds." His message was a crucial one: *If you go ahead with the deal, be sure to watch what they do, not what they say.* In those days, your word was your bond, particularly in trading. For me, it still is. About the worst thing someone can do in any kind of relationship, in my opinion, is lie.

Shorty's guidance helped me develop an expectation of honesty and integrity in all my dealings—business and philanthropic. In well-managed organizations—including nonprofits, where there can be pressure from both inside and outside to bend the rules to court, mollify, and retain benefactors—hard-nosed accountability is essential. Our commitment over the decades at the American Himalayan Foundation to local, accountable partners has proven remarkably effective in avoiding or, when necessary, shutting down programs that weren't legitimate. You won't be surprised to learn, then, that although we were an early supporter of Greg Mortenson, the now infamous founder of the Central Asian Institute and author of *Three Cups of Tea*, we pulled our funding after a few years when we couldn't get him to provide reports or even photographs on the schools supposedly built or the students supposedly attending. It wasn't an easy decision for the board. He still had many supporters at the time, and we all put such a high value on education. A Jon Krakauer exposé years later confirmed that our halting fundraising in the mid-1990s was the right decision.[14]

Hunting for Value

The business world was less specialized in my first years at Sutro than it is now, so I was able to be a merger-and-acquisitions guy one day and an investment banker the next. I learned a lot about the different parts of the business and gravitated toward making deals.

My approach was to look for undervalued companies, work to persuade our partners to buy a stake and maybe get a seat on the board of directors, and then work with management to improve the business over a period of years. This style of investing is favored today by many fund managers and institutional investors, but it was virtually unheard of in the 1960s and '70s. It was so effective for us that in 1964, when I was twenty-nine, I became the youngest partner in Sutro's history.

I have embraced this approach—investing with big stakes, then nudging top executives toward success with advice both strategic and operational—for forty years now. We called it the Art of Friendly Persuasion. It allows me to take certain risks because I know I'll be involved in such a way that I can help mitigate them. I get to do more of what I love, which is to add real value to an organization and create a positive impact on the people who work for or with that organization. Really, it's much the same approach we take at AHF.

Possibly the most fascinating example of doing this at Sutro was the deal I developed to buy "The Greatest Show on Earth"— the Ringling Bros. and Barnum & Bailey Circus. An attorney in Washington, DC, with whom I had become close friends through a couple of investment deals, Lewis Jacobs, brought the idea to me. Sure, buying the country's biggest circus was a proposal about as radical as you could invent for Sutro's low-risk, by-the-book culture. I had to campaign hard. I persuaded, cajoled, and scrambled at every turn initially to raise the money. But in the end, it was how I made my first million dollars and achieved a spectacular return on a modest investment. Smart risks based on good opportunities to add value that others overlook can deliver the best rewards.

Over the years, the Ringling Bros. and Barnum & Bailey Circus had become rundown. Performers wore old costumes, train cars and other equipment needed to keep the circus acts rolling from city to city were poorly maintained, and morale was low. John Ringling North, nephew of the late impresario John Ringling and residing primarily on an Irish manor, led the family enterprise but had little interest in the operations. He never crossed the Atlantic to see his uncle's circus and what was becoming of it.

Irvin Feld, a concert and theatrical promoter along the East Coast, wanted to buy the circus. A onetime record-shop owner, Feld was early in staging rock 'n' roll concert tours, and his clients included big names such as Fats Domino, Bill Haley and the Comets, Paul Anka, Elvis Presley, and The Beatles. Feld knew Ringling Bros. was profitable (a virtual monopoly) and had healthy cash flow (due to advance ticket sales) because he had booked it into local arenas around the country for several years. But, as he explained in our first call, he didn't have enough money to buy the circus outright. He needed partners and wanted to know if I would be interested in putting together a group to make the purchase.

I was ready to put up some of my own money and thought Sutro should invest, too, so I went to see Shorty Hall.

"Shorty," I said, "you are going to think I am out of my mind, but let me tell you what we need to buy. By the way, the biggest assets have four legs, and they walk around and poop."

I can still picture Shorty peering at me over spectacles for a long moment and wondered if he was going to throw me out of his office. Instead he said, "Maybe it's interesting, laddie."

Some older partners were more skeptical. This came as no surprise. The idea of buying into a circus was foreign to anything they had ever done. To address their doubts, I invited our correspondent firm in New York, the prominent, buttoned-down Loeb, Rhoades & Company, to have a look. This led to another round of nit-picking scrutiny that Feld detested. He found the Loeb, Rhoades accountants humorless, rigid, and overly cautious. At one point, Feld took his revenge. During a restroom break, he stood side by side at the urinal with one of the Loeb, Rhoades bean counters. He came out smiling and whispered to me, "I pissed on his shoe." Feld was a character.

Eventually, we formed our investor group, including the bigger-than-life Texas entrepreneur Judge Roy Hofheinz, former mayor of Houston and builder of the Houston Astrodome. I was the primary investor from Sutro. With the money in play, the real deal-making began within a diverse ownership group: John Ringling North and the Ringling Family Trust, composed of his six siblings. After many months of negotiations and work to convince the family it was a good idea, we bought the circus in 1967 for $8 million.

As planned, we moved quickly after the closing to get the

circus in better shape and build revenues and profits. All the performers got new costumes. We upgraded the rail and highway transportation equipment and facilities. With only a few clowns still working, and all of them over the age of fifty, Feld had to find a new pipeline for clown talent, so he opened the Ringling Bros. and Barnum & Bailey Clown College in Florida to train young recruits. We even doubled the circus capacity, adding another full touring company so we could bring the production to twice as many cities each year.

How about licensing circus toys? We did that, too. I introduced Feld and Hofheinz to Ruth Handler, creator of the Barbie doll and cofounder and mastermind of Mattel's business, and her husband, Elliot. I had only licensing opportunities in mind, but it wasn't long before the Handlers became determined to buy the whole circus. It was 1971. They were offering $50 million—*more than six times* what we had paid just four years before.

Feld was all for it, but I was against. After calling around to toy distributors, I was convinced the Handlers were overstating their financial strength. Feld didn't want to hear it. So although I wasn't happy about it, we sold the Ringling Bros. and Barnum & Bailey Circus for $50 million, netting a return of 600 percent in just four years. I had made my first million dollars, but even so, that sale was bittersweet for me.

The SEC determined a few years later that Mattel indeed had doctored its books, and it forced all directors, including the Handlers, to resign. Irvin Feld and his son, Kenneth, got an incredible bargain in 1982: reacquiring Ringling Bros. plus a few live touring shows the Handlers had added, all for $22.8 million. Feld Entertainment later diversified further into live concerts and touring shows, and expanded internationally,[15] staging events attracting an estimated thirty million people annually in more than sixty countries.[16] In 2014, *Forbes* magazine estimated Kenneth Feld's net worth at more than $1 billion. It is just a hunch, but by my reckoning the Ringling Bros. and Barnum & Bailey Circus alone must be worth hundreds of millions of dollars. *The greatest show*, indeed.

In my days at Sutro, and in the early days at Blum Capital, I would look at anything where we thought we could do well. Exercising my expansive curiosity means I am never quite sure what I'm going to be interested in next. When I find something fascinating, I like to dig into it and figure out how we might want to capitalize on the opportunity. As some have said, I'm a deal junkie. I don't exactly disagree. I have always enjoyed the adrenaline rush of putting a deal together. But it may be more accurate to say that I'm a value seeker who loves to find opportunities where other people can't see past the downside.

The Right Time to Exit

On May 1, 1975, the SEC's mandate ending fixed-price commissions went into effect, as I had long anticipated. It was a loud signal that the time had come for me to move on. I was approaching my fortieth birthday, bored with the situation at Sutro, and extremely restless.

Just a few years before, I had told the partners, "You have a model that's served this firm well for a hundred years, but it's not going to work anymore. We have a good name. We've been around a long time. But the core of our business will probably become unprofitable. The commission business will almost assuredly be a tool to sell other products." I had then made the case for the firm to begin focusing on three themes for future growth: wealth management, real estate, and Asia. Most of the older partners weren't paying attention, but the business world—and I do mean business *world*—was changing drastically. You could see first light in the dawning of globalization.

For three years I had pushed these strategies. And for three years my partners had either resisted or taken half measures that had no chance of succeeding. No matter what opportunities I pursued, it all seemed too risky for them.

It was time for me to leave, and in retrospect, it certainly was the right choice. Seven years after I left and put up my shingle as Richard C. Blum and Associates (RCBA), Sutro & Co. was acquired by John Hancock Financial. In 2001 the last vestiges of Sutro & Co. disappeared when the few remaining assets were bought by another investment firm.

When I left, I did so without rancor. The dividend was that I remained friends through the years with many of the firm's partners. But before I left, I told them, "Deep down, you guys don't really want to do what I want to do." I said I respected their position, but I reiterated my concern that Sutro's future would be in doubt if the business model did not change.

"You don't really believe the world is going to change," I added. "I do."

Chapter 6

Innovation and Value:
A Long-Term Commitment

*"Only those who risk going too far can possibly
find out how far one can go."*

—T. S. Eliot

Our approach to investing and global development projects has always been similar. Deal junkie, value seeker—call it what you will. I have always seen myself as a value investor. We're fascinated by situations with potential to turn possibility into reality, preferring to focus on a few companies that I like and to work with management on strategies to help grow the business. We are perfectly willing to stay in these companies for years if they do well for their shareholders, their markets are growing, and they are on the ball. We've stayed in some companies more than twenty years, believe it or not. That's rare for an equity investment group (most private-equity funds have a time limit for returning funds to investors), but it's my idea on how to make a good return—or a good impact.

To stay involved that long requires a focus on relationships.

If people like doing business with you, and you are committed to long-term relationships, more often than not you will be much more successful. So we at Blum Capital have tended to be friendly investors. We have never believed in squeezing the last dollar out of a deal. Being greedy is bad business because it's bad for relationships. We have never bought into a business with the idea of dismantling it and selling off the components for a profit. And we have never been interested in a buyout predicated on laying off large numbers of workers and shipping jobs overseas. My principle has always been *Don't go in looking for a fight. Make love, not war.*

When we invest, we work with companies to make their operations better, and I think we have developed a reputation at Blum Capital for helping build companies in ways that have benefited all the key constituents: employees, customers, owners, and the community. *BusinessWeek* summed up our investing style well in a 1996 article by Linda Himelstein, "Reaping the Rewards of Friendly Persuasion":

> After doing exhaustive due diligence, [RCBA] takes stakes—on average 5 percent—in midsize companies that tend to be rather obscure, often troubled, and undervalued. The firm has a knack for identifying weaknesses. Then, over a period of months or years it will coax management to adopt its usually elaborate recipe for change.[1]

From the start we were collaborators, often working with other investment groups who wanted to help companies be great by solving some of their more complex problems. We knew the global development community would benefit from a similar mind-set focused on results, not simply on concocting grand ideas and competing for attention or recognition.

Shankar Sastry, director of the Blum Center for Developing Economies at Berkeley, summed up typical frustrations well: "Development is lots of pilots—and no planes!" Foundations, think tanks, and NGOs are rife with ego-driven empire builders. The results, no matter how well intentioned, too often are needless, overlapping efforts and expenses—and a lack of accountability, efficiency, and results. All this generates organizations and initiatives that just come and go, like fireflies that flicker alluringly before vanishing into the night. Big, real-world problems today in global poverty are moving targets; they never stop evolving. There is no point at which you are "finished" and can walk away. Early exits sometimes can be more disastrous than not doing anything at all.

My philosophy of long-term investing and value-building is very similar to what we have done at the American Himalayan Foundation in identifying and backing local champions, often for twenty years or more, and at the Blum Center for Developing Economies. As we will see in chapters 12 and 13, the Blum Center is turning out thousands of innovative students collectively on all ten campuses of the University of California—the largest public institution of higher education in the United States—plus Hebrew University in Jerusalem and Central European University in Budapest. Many of these students are making important contributions to development projects in different parts of the world. In any scenario, I try never to abandon the long-term strategy for building a business or organization that can effectively serve its customers or clients. That is the big opportunity.

Solve Problems, Create Value

About the time I set up my firm in 1975, the CEO of a small engineering services company known as URS called me with a problem. I owned some stock and had some clients in it, too.

He was very concerned that two blocks of his company's stock might soon be bought by an investor planning a hostile takeover. URS stock had been issued as payment for some small-company acquisitions he had recently completed. "Why don't you buy that stock?" he said. "You'll be the largest shareholder in the company. You can come in as vice chairman."

I was intrigued but would need to raise between $3 million and $5 million to buy the stock. I had not yet raised any money from investors for my first fund at Richard C. Blum and Associates. Over the years our firm's investor base would grow to where about 90 percent of our capital came from large state pension funds; insurance companies; sovereign wealth funds; and institutions in Europe, the Middle East, and Asia. Two of our bigger investors over the years were California's large pension funds, CalPERS and CalSTRS. But back then my clients were all individuals.

I knew whom to call to raise the money for URS.

Gene Friend was the first person I pitched. He was the father of one of my buddies, Bob Friend, when I was growing up in the Ingleside neighborhood of San Francisco. I had worked in Gene's clothing store on Market Street during the Christmas holidays, and he still remembered the time I sold more blue suede shoes than anybody else. (Remember, this was the 1950s.) Gene was a good guy but a tough, tough sale. He had me sit on a stool in his kitchen while he walked around asking the toughest questions. I felt as though I were on the witness stand in some courtroom. But in the end I raised the first $50,000 for my firm.

Through more conversations with other people in my network over a couple of months, I raised the funds to buy the URS shares. It was the first official transaction for Richard C. Blum and Associates, and it had to go right; otherwise, going back to raise more funds would have been hard. It was a bumpy ride, as

URS went through a couple of up and down cycles, but when we sold our position in 2005, it was worth $300 million.

Over the years, companies came to us because they needed a partner. Maybe they didn't have a major shareholder, were concerned about a takeover, or needed to get financing to grow a product line or make an acquisition. What drove our decisions? I listened to the thesis, met the people involved, and read all the summary memos. I looked at the numbers enough to know whether we were crazy or not in our valuations, but I was never a number cruncher. I was much more into the people and culture within each business.

We were drawn especially to businesses we thought had a really solid core but might have lost their way. Maybe they had branched into related businesses where they didn't have the capacity to compete and had refused to retreat. If there was a problem that management wasn't addressing properly, however, throwing more money at it wasn't going to fix it. We would seek out the opportunity to fix the problem, encouraging management to refocus on what we saw as the company's core strengths.

The considerable returns on this work have been the source of most of the funds I've dedicated to help support people committed to fighting poverty and income inequality in myriad ways.

When you take aim at solving complex problems, you need to be clear in your own mind that your long-term commitment will be imperative for making an impact. When you actually realize the impact, you will be rewarded beyond what you might have imagined at the beginning. We saw this in the stories in Part 1, showing how thousands of people have benefited from the planning, persistence, and values of our foundation and our many partners, and of course from their own long-term commitment and hard work to make the most of new resources we helped gather and provide. For me, the parallel in value here—between investing for the long term in businesses with great potential and investing for the long term in people with great potential—is just obvious.

PEPPER'S PRAGMATISM

When I was at Berkeley, many undergrad students took a philosophy class with a professor named Stephen Pepper because it was supposed to be an easy A. It was held in a big lecture hall, and if people went, they often spent the class dozing. But I was intrigued.

Professor Pepper was an expert in the tradition of pragmatism. In his most influential book, *World Hypothesis*, published in 1942, Pepper argued that you need to apply both common sense and rigorous analysis when considering any problem, because there is no such thing as pure, objective fact. Anytime you accept something as pure, objective fact, he believed, you inevitably open yourself up to false conclusions.[2]

I wanted to understand Pepper's lectures better, so I started dropping by to talk with him during office hours. I never had to wait; nobody ever went to see him. But to me it was a real privilege to spend half an hour with this man. He talked about how to frame your perspective about the world—basically, how to think. He wanted you to step outside the world you knew and question it from all angles, to dig into the details.

His ideas struck a chord. They certainly served me well when I was coming up as an analyst at Sutro—and far beyond that time. I imagine this was at least partly because my faculty advisor at Berkeley, a truly brilliant man named Choh-Ming Li, had driven home a related idea in his lectures on international economics: "When you say something, understand the implicit assumptions of what you are saying." I've quoted Professor Li on this point at one time or another to most every partner and colleague I've worked with.

> If you want to be a problem solver and add real value, you always need to address and test your assumptions. The better you understand those assumptions, the better your decisions and solutions will be.

Innovation and the Long View

In 1989, Blum Capital made the biggest investment we had ever made: $100 million as part of a $3.65 billion leveraged buyout (LBO) of Northwest Airlines. Gary Wilson, onetime chief financial officer of Marriott Corporation and the Walt Disney Company and a close friend with whom I have invested and served on boards for thirty years, proposed the deal, and we took the company private.

Airlines had been struggling, since Jimmy Carter deregulated the industry in 1978, with high legacy costs; new, low-fare competitors; and frequent fare wars. Northwest was reeling from poor labor relations and bad customer service in the wake of the largest merger in airlines history, with Republic Airlines. Yet Northwest had the best position of any US airline on routes to Japan and elsewhere in Asia, plus several hometown corporations based in Minneapolis–St. Paul. With the LBO, Northwest management would buy a controlling share of the company using outside capital—from us. We saw a route to success through leveraging the company's strengths, making the cost structure more competitive with low-cost rivals, and adding routes and passengers through acquisitions. Over time, we would get expenses under control, achieve more pricing power, rise as one of a few industry consolidators, and become respectably profitable. That was the plan, anyway.

"We both were fascinated by the airlines business. We had this connecting-the-world philosophy," Gary later recalled. More than that, though, we saw opportunities for major innovations in the industry to capitalize on trends we could see just over the horizon.

To begin with, Dutch airline KLM signed up for nearly 20 percent of the private ownership. The Northwest–KLM equity partnership led to the first international airline strategic alliance, approved by international transportation authorities in 1993. "It was a great leap forward," KLM executives said later, noting that most major airlines adopted the strategy to form international route connections through alliances with other airlines over the following decade.[3] Northwest and KLM also were the first airlines to create a single brand to reflect this alliance; we provided benefits for frequent flyers along the international routes involving any combination of airlines that were members of our alliance. Another innovation: We called it SkyTeam, and it still exists today.

We took Northwest public with an IPO in 1994, only our second year of profitability after the 1989 buyout. The US economy was recovering from the 1991 recession, and passenger volume for Northwest was rising after two bad years following the Gulf War. We had weathered some hard times and narrowly escaped bankruptcy in 1992. But the IPO was profitable for the LBO investors. I kept a large share of my firm's holdings as well as my seat on Northwest's board of directors. A year later, the value of our investor group's stake in Northwest had tripled to $300 million, capping three years of outsized performance that helped our firm attract more funds from large institutions, mainly public and private pension funds. Those prosperous years helped fund more innovation at Northwest. For instance, we were the first large US airline to offer passengers Internet check-in.

Good times never last forever, though. A ten-day Northwest pilots' strike in 1999 cost us $1 billion from operations before the Clinton administration ordered the pilots back to work. A collapse in air travel after the 9/11 attacks in 2001 sent

Northwest further into a downdraft. We were forced to lay off thousands of employees and to accelerate plans to take aging aircraft out of service.

We didn't like the way the airline was being run and concluded the pay issues with the pilots' union were intractable. If your airline is not the lowest-cost producer and you lose customers to lower-fare competitors, you eventually go bankrupt. We could see the writing on the wall and, by 2004, had sold much of our firm's holdings. Northwest filed for a Chapter 11 bankruptcy reorganization in 2005 and, in 2008, agreed to merge with Delta. The last plane flying the bright red tail that had marked Northwest aircraft since World War II was repainted with Delta colors in 2009.

We could have sold our firm's shares in the years after the IPO for a huge gain. We did make a return in the end, netting out in the high single digits, but the fact is, we would have done better if we had simply bought US treasuries with that $100 million back in 1989, when they were yielding more than 9 percent.

At a farewell dinner when I was leaving the board in 2004, I surveyed our ups and downs in my parting remarks and concluded wryly that my fifteen years with Northwest had been "long on theater and short on returns." In the end, the Northwest investment didn't cause our firm any damage, but it did require a lot of my time and effort. John Dasburg, Northwest's CEO from 1990 to 2001, summed up the lesson from Blum Capital's prolonged connection with the company: "No matter how difficult it became, Dick stayed with it." I believed then, and believe still, that to build a great company or organization, you have to keep the long view, even in bad times.

Reducing Global Poverty through Innovation

In all that I do—with the American Himalayan Foundation, the Blum Center for Developing Economies, the Brookings Blum Roundtable, and our private-equity work—I believe emphatically in the power of innovation. As I had told Sutro's more traditionalist partners when I left, our world of course would continue to change. To keep pace and improve lives, we as a society as well as global citizens have to innovate in everything we do, whether it's how we partner, how we develop strategies, how we teach, how we give, or how we invest.

Technological innovation in particular is a huge area of interest for me. It's why we formed the Blum Center on two pillars: innovation (in partnership with the College of Engineering) and the Global Poverty and Practice minor. Later, we added Big Ideas, a campuswide competition that provides seed funding for undergraduates with world-changing ideas.

I am confident we will see quantum leaps within the next fifteen years in the ways advancing technologies help millions of people who otherwise would continue to struggle in poverty. Renewable energy may provide some of the most far-reaching benefits. First, global climate change affects poor, underdeveloped communities (through drought and severe weather) dramatically more than developed communities. Second, improved access to energy at affordable rates leads to better living standards, attracts more investment, generates growth in local economies, and more.

For former US Energy Secretary Steven Chu—a Nobel laureate, former UC Berkeley professor of physics and of molecular and cellular biology, and distinguished member of the Blum Center's board of trustees—climate change is the biggest long-term obstacle to a sharp reduction in extreme poverty.[4] "We're heading into an era where, if we don't change what we're doing, we're going to be fundamentally in really deep trouble," he has said. "We have to transition to better solutions."[5]

Many national security and migration challenges are tied to climate change. Severe drought, crop losses, and high food prices resulting from rising temperatures contributed to political upheaval sparking the rise of terrorists in northeast Nigeria and civil war in Syria. Rising oceans linked to melting ice caps are submerging low-lying coastal communities. These may be only the beginnings of our global predicament.[6]

Steven favors many steps to accelerate renewable energy supplies, including policies to put utilities or other third parties in the forefront of owning, installing, and maintaining rooftop solar systems. "If distribution companies and regulators got behind this, then all of a sudden they're making money by deploying solar-energy systems, instead of fighting it or dragging their feet. It's now in the profit/win column. You have to allow people to make money; that's what motivates them."[7]

We know that the costs of producing solar energy and wind power are declining faster than most anyone anticipated. This is hopeful news for the entire world, especially for developing economies across Africa and in India, where vast swathes of the population have no access to reliable sources of electricity. And more than 80 percent of the world's one billion people struggling with extreme poverty live either in sub-Saharan Africa or India.[8]

Over time, I and others believe, hydropower will be a larger source of global renewable energy than solar and wind systems. Several governments in Africa and Latin America have approved massive hydropower projects over the past several decades that require construction of colossal dams on major rivers. The projects created vast new supplies of reliable energy. However, these benefits often were accompanied by cost overruns, corruption, significant ecological damage, and the dislocation of millions of people.

Run-of-the-river projects have become a preferred alternative since the turn of the century, a compelling engineering breakthrough often with financial backing by the World Bank. These smaller systems harness the force of a river as it flows downhill, capturing the water to turn turbines inside a small power generation plant. They are vastly cheaper and much faster to construct than large hydroelectric dams. This innovation has enormous potential to make reliable, low-impact energy available to hundreds of millions of people.

Since my first treks with P. K. in Nepal in the late 1960s, I had often thought of the vast potential all across the Himalaya for generating hydroelectric power. Here was an abundant natural resource, concentrated among eight of the world's fourteen tallest mountain peaks. If rivers originating from snow packs on these peaks could be tapped, the hydropower could bolster the wealth of Nepal and several neighboring countries.

So in 2015, we invited Dr. Rajiv Shah, USAID's administrator for the prior six years, and a team of proven professionals to join us in forming a private-equity firm, Latitude Capital Partners, with the purpose of raising funds for several clean energy projects, either hydro or solar. This is our newest effort to combat global poverty, extending the work of the American Himalayan Foundation and the Blum Center in important ways. More than $2.5 trillion in investment will be required to build new power-generating capacity in Africa and India by 2035. That's for 700 gigawatts of generating capacity—the equivalent of 350 Hoover Dams! And although our work at Latitude Capital is just beginning, we expect our results to provide sorely needed resources for poor people in both southern Asia and Africa—resources they can use to improve their lives.

Life-changing innovation requires long-term commitment. Big advances do not happen overnight as if delivered by lightning bolts from the sky. They take years of research and planning. They require huge capital investments. But when the result is environmental, political, and social stability and an improved standard of living for millions of people, it obviously is worth the effort.

Strategy and Values

I was more confident than ever in the early 1990s about our firm's investing fundamentals. The big trends of economic growth in Asia and expansion of international businesses were creating opportunities with tremendous potential. You only had to know where to look, stay focused, and take action.

There weren't many in private-equity firms who thought CB Commercial, a forerunner and the foundation for what is now CBRE Group, was one of those opportunities. "The real estate industry before then was scattered to the four winds," according to Mickey Kantor, US Trade Representative and Commerce Secretary during the Clinton administration, a CBRE board member for many years, and a colleague of mine in Democratic Party politics since the early 1970s. "But Dick saw a time coming in commercial real estate when globalization would hit and there would be opportunities if you could find the right kind of acquisitions."

Over my twenty-plus years on the board—I joined in 1993 and served as chairman from 2003 to 2015—I can count at least a dozen acquisitions that were essential in creating the global CBRE Group platform. Two UK transactions in 1998 positioned us as the first vendor able to professionally manage real estate services for companies in major cities around the world. Those acquisitions put CBRE on a trajectory toward becoming a global organization. Acquiring and integrating companies has become a core competency: In 2013 alone, CBRE made eleven acquisitions, all funded from cash flow with no added debt. This is a formula for rapid, profitable growth.

The CBRE Group is now the world's largest commercial real estate services and investment firm, entering 2016 with more than seventy thousand employees, annual revenues approaching $13 billion, and approximately 450 offices worldwide. It was the only corporate real estate services firm in the Fortune 500—ranked number 363 in 2014. It also was Blum Capital's largest single holding, with a market value exceeding $500 million.

CBRE is a case study in how strategic focus and corporate values are mutually reinforcing. Commitment to values is why the company has topped its industry sector on the *Fortune* magazine World's Most Admired Companies list for four consecutive years. We continually emphasized ethical standards and behavior—doing the right thing. All too often, acquisitions create bad blood and poor outcomes, especially when executed internationally. It's essential to establish a high bar for all employees, including the management team, no matter where they're based.

From the start, the culture we wanted and supported was to do good while doing well. We wanted senior management and the board to always keep in mind that in effect we were taking care of the families of tens of thousands of people who worked for us. When the economy softened in early 2009 and our revenues declined, we put salaried employees ahead of managers and executives as we cut expenses.

According to Brett White, a close colleague at CBRE for more than twenty years, "We didn't provide salary or bonus increases for senior management in a tough market, but we always did for lower employees regardless of the market."

When revenues were falling and no one knew where the bottom would be, Brett, then the CEO, told me he was going to eliminate all executive bonuses across the company—after having just committed $11 million to give employees making less than $150,000 a year a 3 percent merit increase. My answer was, "Of course."

You can't succeed in mergers and acquisitions without dealing with personal issues. They are inevitable. After one big merger when I was chairman, I had to work out a peace treaty between the leader of the company we acquired and the head of a CBRE business unit. They disagreed over multiple issues: titles, the formula for splitting commissions, and so on. Both leaders stayed, however, and made important contributions to CBRE's success. That wouldn't have happened if we hadn't been listening to our people and treating them with respect.

I have learned over the years that strategy and finance are secondary to people and values. You can do well personally with the former, and obviously many do, but creating an organization with lasting value also requires listening closely and doing the right thing for people.

BEING TOUGH ON DOING WHAT'S RIGHT

The CEO who originally brought me in to URS in 1975 made a few acquisitions that some of us on the board weren't all that thrilled about, and for good reason. They failed, and URS nearly went bankrupt in the late 1980s. We brought in new management, the new CEO was successful, and URS grew impressively.

But this CEO miscalculated in 2005 when he agreed to partner with Lockheed Martin and the University of Texas to compete against the University of California for the contract to manage Los Alamos National Laboratory in New Mexico, the famed research institution for national security sciences.

The University of California (UC) had managed Los Alamos since its inception in the 1940s. I thought it was highly inappropriate for a major San Francisco engineering firm to join another state's university system in competing against the University of California. I had been on the URS board for nearly thirty years by then, and a member of the governing Regents of the University of California for three. In my view and that of professionals who knew the nuclear science field well, the advanced science capabilities of UC were far superior to what URS, Lockheed Martin, and the University of Texas could offer. And indeed, UC would go on to easily win the contract.

But the competition created the perception of a conflict for me, and a nasty public controversy ensued. I requested a letter from URS confirming that in fact I had no conflict related to the URS–Lockheed Martin bid. Three days after I received that letter, I sold all my URS stock and resigned from the board. I had been a URS vice chairman all those years, but I refused to go against the University of California.

If I invest in a company and don't think management is doing the right thing for shareholders, I'll let them know. I can get tough then. I don't go looking for fights, but I am not afraid of them.

Chapter 7

Capital and Finance in Developing Communities

"If you confront your problems rather than avoid them,
you will be in a better position to deal with them."[1]
—His Holiness the Fourteenth Dalai Lama

Doing the right thing can enrich your life beyond whatever numbers end up in the financial ledgers. In 1964, the year Congress passed the historic Civil Rights Act, I heard about a group of investors who were having trouble raising money to start a bank in Harlem. Just north of Central Park in Manhattan, Harlem was a wellspring of African-American culture but often neglected by big banks in lending to residents, churches, and local businesses.

The new bank's chairman was Jackie Robinson. During his celebrated baseball career as the first African-American player to break the color barrier in the major leagues, and after his retirement from the game in 1957, Robinson was a tireless, courageous advocate for equal rights. The bank was going to be called Freedom National Bank of New York, with headquarters on Harlem's main east–west thoroughfare, 125th Street.

Many small businesses and churches in Harlem were putting up money in the hope that people in the community would have a better chance to get loans. The bank's directors didn't need to raise more than a few hundred thousand dollars, but they just couldn't find investors.

I was glad to see what I could do. After meeting with a few of the directors, I went to a bunch of my Sutro clients and said, "Look, I think you ought to buy some stock in this bank. It's a good thing for the country, and it's a good thing for New York." We succeeded, and Freedom National Bank of New York soon had enough capital to open its doors.

Not long after we delivered those funds in 1964, one of the bank officers asked what our fee would be. "Nothing," I replied. "Harlem needs a bank, and you guys seem like the right guys to do it." We didn't ask for a penny, but I did have one request: a personal lunch with Jackie Robinson.

It was a thrill for me to meet him. He was a warm, decent guy. I could see why, when I was a teenager, he had been voted the second most popular person in the entire country after Bing Crosby.

The bank did become a vital part of Harlem's business community—the first commercial bank owned by African-Americans. For years it was the largest financial institution in New York State owned by African-Americans and among the largest in the country.[2] A spate of bad loans forced Freedom National to close in 1990, as New York City stumbled through a three-year economic downturn and home values in Manhattan dropped by an average of 25 percent. Freedom National had twenty-two thousand depositors at the time, and its failure was a blow for Harlem's economy.[3]

This project helped me appreciate why a strong financial sector is vital for communities in need of development. For the world's poorest communities—in underdeveloped countries with poorly functioning governments and fragile banking systems—financing often has to come from foreign investment. The traditions of a closed economy and a closed society hold countries back. We've certainly seen the effects in Nepal, a country closed to foreigners until the mid-twentieth century. And we've seen how the opening of closed economies to foreign investment—including funds committed by me and my partners—has helped improve the lives of hundreds of millions of people across Asia.

Abundant Value in Asia

If you looked at opportunities to invest outside the United States in the 1970s, Asia was hands down the bet you wanted to make. Hard work is just part of the culture in Asia; France has a thirty-five-hour workweek, which is just three working days—*half* of a workweek—to people in China. From Japan to China to Singapore, the people are creative. And Malaysia and Indonesia are seeing growing economies and rising employment.

The most obvious economic trend in the world by the mid-1990s was the growth of the middle class in Asia. The standard of living was going up. I could see this every time I visited, beginning in the early 1960s. There was an emerging middle class in China, India, Indonesia, and so on.

Considering all this, you can understand how mystified I was to learn that my partners in Blum Capital were not excited about Asia's growth potential or investing there. They may have held the same opinion communicated in a 2003 *BusinessWeek* article: "Doing business in China is not for the fainthearted."[4] The statement was perhaps even more true a decade earlier.

But David Bonderman, a founding partner of TPG Capital, was as enthusiastic about Asia as I was, so we teamed up to start Newbridge Capital. When we opened the doors of the Newbridge Hong Kong office in 1994, we were the first foreign private-equity firm to put down stakes in China—"pioneers in globalization," as David has said, pointing out that "most every major private-equity firm today is global, but that wasn't the case twenty years ago."

We set our sights on identifying opportunities to restructure banks, and then direct their products and services toward the expanding economy of middle-class consumers and away from the industrial sector. It took a few years to get our first big win, but when Newbridge was folded into TPG a decade after opening, we had posted 28.7 percent annual net returns in Asia. If we had not encountered a fair amount of leakage due to corruption, our returns would have been much higher. Of course, we expected to encounter some corruption along the way—as you do anywhere, including in the world's most industrialized economies.

One of our guiding beliefs about investing in emerging markets is to use local people. Most employees of the companies you believe in and back should be from the local culture. They understand things on the ground far better than you or I ever will. We knew that having a good grasp of local politics in any emerging market in Asia would be imperative. And every market has its own unique politics. Most of our Asian teams comprised young Chinese, Korean, Indian, or Japanese professionals, many of whom had studied for their MBAs in the United States. For us it was the best of both worlds: They knew *their* countries, and they knew *our* style of investing. To be successful in emerging markets, you need to have that kind of cross-fertilization.

The local expert that David and I hired to open and manage our Hong Kong office initially was an ethnic Chinese private-equity banker working with Bankers Trust in Hong Kong, Peter Kwok. Peter knew the territory. So did the American we paired him with, Dan Carroll. A talented Harvard MBA, Dan already had nine years' experience in Hong Kong deal-making. For the next ten years with Newbridge, Dan and Peter traveled to Asia and Australia every few weeks, meeting prospective partners, bearing down on deals in the works, and staying in close touch with executives running our businesses.

We made a commitment to open a local office so we could meet people, get educated, and build the Newbridge name. Dan developed a good relationship with the leaders of one of Hong Kong's most prominent real estate companies, Kerry Properties. When the Asian financial crisis rocked the equity markets in 1997 and 1998, Kerry Properties' stock price plunged from the midteens to below four dollars. The company's principal owner, Robert Kuok, was blocked from buying more shares because Kerry Properties' public float had to be at least 25 percent or the company might be delisted. Kuok's family holding company, the Kerry Group, already owned 75 percent. Dan and Peter had often explored ways we might work with Kerry Properties. Here at last was the opportunity.

We bought a 10 percent stake of the public float because we thought it was a good value, as did another US firm we brought in, Colony Capital. Less than two years later, we sold our Kerry Properties holding for $70 million—more than twice our original investment. I hated to sell, which won't surprise you, but the Kerry executives had found a buyer and asked us cordially if we would sell our block.

Robert Kuok has since become a good friend, and a great partner and advisor.

BALANCING INVESTMENT AND ETHICS

Human rights issues in China, particularly the harsh treatment of Tibetans and the People's Liberation Army's destruction of Tibetan Buddhist culture, were already well known in the 1990s. It is fair to say that hardly any other American individual or company doing business in China at the time was more outspoken or willing to discuss Tibet with the Chinese government than me.

Although Dianne and I often spoke candidly in private meetings with Chinese officials about Chinese human rights abuses in Tibet (including several situations I recount in chapter 11), my strong views on Tibet never were challenged or even mentioned by our Chinese counterparts on Newbridge business across Asia.

It never occurred to me that our strategy at Newbridge in exploring opportunities in China was the wrong thing to do. China's critics can say what they want—maybe they don't like the government or they've suffered through bad business deals—but when you talk about all the people who came out of poverty during that decade, most were in China. *Several hundred million* Chinese people joined the middle class. That happened because the country opened itself to foreign investment and trade, promoted rapid growth and urbanization, and dedicated more resources to improving access to safe water and to basic health, education, and transportation services. Without foreign capital, in what conditions would these hundreds of millions of people be living today?

Common Challenges in Developing Economies

Some of our other early investments in China probably would not make anyone's list of good deals. The disputes were hair-raising at times, but we learned a lot.

One of Newbridge's first deals was the partial buyout of a company called North Dragon Iron & Steel Group, which gave us management control of an iron mine and a pipe fabricating plant in northeast China. I remember driving there from the major industrial city of Shenyang for the first time, a two-hour journey toward the North Korean border. Our car passed several old, grimy steel mills, including a classic giant that was perhaps a half mile long. I was thinking, *This must have been what the early days of the Industrial Revolution looked like.* People working there were dressed in rags. It was one of the most depressing areas of the world I've ever seen.

The Chinese government had purchase orders on the books for as much drain pipe as North Dragon could deliver—no limits. That seemed like a good situation. The only problem was, we were never paid during the first three years. One of our top Chinese colleagues on the North Dragon project, W. K. Zhang, was determined to get our money back, though. It took W. K. more than ten years, but he succeeded.

It can be difficult for foreign investors to hold governments accountable, but it's worth the effort. This was neither the first nor the last time we would have to deal with that sort of challenge. Foreign private-equity firms contribute sorely needed capital to developing economies. They take these risks based at least partly on expectations that the nation's legal system will adequately protect their ownership rights. You have obligations to investors, of course, to take legal action when you believe your rights have been abused. It's important, too, for local government officials to know that when foreign investors pursue and receive justice in the courts, the courts demonstrate to other investors and prospective investors that the legal rights of private ownership and capital are respected. Going forward, this benefits the entire nation.

Another deal was acquiring the candy-making part of a food conglomerate controlled by the Shanghai government, Guan Sheng Yan. The business—whose name in English was "Big White Rabbit"—was the biggest maker of hard candy anywhere in China. Big White Rabbit candy was sold everywhere, but we thought the candy was mediocre and could be improved.

Not long after we took over, revenues fell sharply. Our lead Chinese colleague for Newbridge on this project discovered that our candy was now being sold at big discounts as a kind of loss leader for Guan Sheng Yan—that is, to reap higher margins on other products. And pirate crews—not our employees—were running some of our machinery at night, making more product and presumably pocketing whatever money they got for selling that candy. We experienced other types of skullduggery, but you get the idea.

We didn't give in. One of our Chinese partners went up to Shanghai to protest to the company's senior managers in person, and we continued to press our case. Over time the managers arranged for the government to buy the company back. We did get our money back, plus 10 percent.

Another challenge in Asia was creating strong financial institutions. We looked for troubled financial institutions with good franchises and good prospects for a profitable recovery. In nearly every case in which our offers were successful, our approach was similar: to convert these institutions from commercial lending to consumer lending. We did this with banks in South Korea, China, Indonesia, and Taiwan, and with financial services companies in India and other places.

Two particular opportunities we came across in South Korea and China fit our criteria. Both were complicated, which appealed to us because complexity in deals often discourages a lot of potential competing bidders. Moreover, national and local politics were unstable and unpredictable. Legal and regulatory rulings likely would be extremely uncertain in both countries, because authorities were only starting to experiment with opening their economy to foreign owners. Still, we believed hostile takeover attempts from potential rivals would not go far. We figured that regardless of any resistance we encountered after making a successful offer—and we were well aware there would be resistance—we would stick with our strategies because the rewards could be substantial.

We were persistent and patient in taking on numerous challenges. And as events played out in our push into consumer lending with Korea First Bank and Shenzhen Development Bank, we were right.

MAKING A CASE FOR A STOCK EXCHANGE

Years before we first formed Newbridge, I had already gained some experience in the financial sector in China. Shanghai had become a sister city to San Francisco, and I traveled there with Dianne often after she became mayor in 1978.

During my first trip to Shanghai in 1978, I gave a talk at an international business school about reviving the Shanghai Stock Exchange. It had been shuttered since Mao Zedong's Communist Revolution in 1949. Workers at the time had been allowed to buy stock only in their companies, but I counseled that to fund growth, the companies would need outside capital. This was only three years after Mao's death, and I was speaking in the world's largest communist country.

I chose my words carefully.

Instead of saying *stock exchange*, I explained that if Chinese companies were going to attract outside capital, they would need a mechanism to "transfer those funds" into businesses. Dianne, sitting in the front row with Shanghai Mayor Wang Daohan, shot me that look of disbelief that seemed to say, *Oh my God! What are you doing?* I managed to keep an air of decorum.

After the event, Wang came over. "You were talking about a stock exchange, weren't you?" he said. He was old enough to remember the Shanghai Stock Exchange before the Communist Revolution. He knew.

"Well, if you want to bring in outside capital, you need a way to create liquidity," I replied delicately.

"Can you come to my office tomorrow morning?" he said eagerly. "I want to bring my staff and start talking about doing this."

We had some meetings, and a few years later, in 1990, they got the Shanghai Stock Exchange going again. It was so quiet on some afternoons after the exchange opened, you could have taken a nap on the trade floor. But a new generation now rises: In 2014, the Shanghai and Hong Kong stock exchanges together listed more new issues than the New York Stock Exchange.

A Shift toward Consumer Lending, Efficiency

Standing in an elevator as it rose to a top floor in a Seoul office tower, Frank Newman, onetime deputy secretary of the US Treasury Department, could hear beating drums in the distance, getting louder and louder. When the elevator stopped and its doors opened, Frank stepped out. He was surrounded immediately by scores of chanting, shouting demonstrators—all wearing black ninja outfits. As he walked ahead, a path slowly opened toward a boardroom. Several masked men lined each side. Some were beating on *taiko* drums, totems Asian warriors over the centuries had pounded to intimidate their enemies.

This was early 2000, in the aftermath of the Asian financial crisis. Many emerging economies were only beginning to stabilize, including South Korea's. State-controlled financial institutions there were foundering in a sea of delinquent debts. Government officials had moved haltingly to reduce state ownership and bring international investors into the South Korean economy—part of their deal with the International Monetary Fund for a $58 billion package of loans to prop up the economy.

The sale of the government's stake in the country's eighth-largest bank, Korea First Bank, was big news. Nationalized two years earlier to prevent its collapse, Korea First was a lender to many of Korea's biggest *chaebol*, or flagship, family-controlled global conglomerates. Allowing such a valued lender to fall under foreign control was, for some Koreans, a national embarrassment and cause for alarm.

Korea First was in serious trouble because, like nearly all major banks in South Korea, it had been drawn into what was sometimes labeled a corrupt government–chaebol strategic alliance: Politicians needed money for political campaigns; chaebol groups needed funding to expand further in global markets. Banks lent too much money to the chaebol that didn't work out, and bank officers had often been leaned on by friends in the government who needed money.

To investors like us, though, Korea First had appeal, believing as we did in a recovery from the financial crisis and the inevitable rise of middle-class consumers across Asia. Gross domestic product in South Korea had increased an average of 8.2 percent for three decades in a row. Average annual incomes had risen to $10,000 from $80 in 1960.[5] When details of the IMF bailout for South Korea were announced, news of Korea First's pending sale caught our eye. "We had a clear view that the bank could be fixed, and that life would get better in South Korea," David Bonderman later said. "So we injected ourselves into the bidding process."

WEIJIAN SHAN

Weijian Shan was my best partner based in Asia, and remains a great friend. He was instrumental in the success of Korea First Bank, Shenzhen Development Bank, and many other Newbridge investments.

Shan has led an amazing life and enjoyed a remarkable investing career. Today, as group chairman and chief executive of Hong Kong–based PAG since 2010, he is on all the short lists of Asia's private-equity geniuses.

When Shan was only twelve, his formal education in Beijing was abruptly halted by the turbulent Cultural Revolution of the 1960s. Less than three years later, he was making bricks, tending pumpkins, and living in a shack in a poor farming village in the Gobi Desert. He was stuck there for six years. But he learned to read English at night by kerosene lamp and while listening to the Voice of America. He also learned not to give up on life. "Once you have experienced hardship—starvation is the worst—you don't think anything is hard anymore," he told *The Economist* decades later. "You learn patience."[6]

As Chairman Mao's extreme doctrinaire socialism faded, Shan's work unit got him a chance in 1975 to study English. He finished his degree in 1979 as Deng Xiaoping was opening China's economy, and the US-based Asian Foundation tapped him for a scholarship in undergraduate studies at the University of San Francisco. He then completed at Berkeley a master's in economics (1984) and a doctorate in business administration (1987). One of his Berkeley professors then was a young economist, Janet Yellen, who today as Federal Reserve Board chair still remembers Shan as one of her brightest students.

We recruited Weijian Shan in 1998 to be Newbridge Capital's managing partner in Hong Kong. Our major investments in Korea First Bank, a 50–50 partnership with the South Korean government, and Shenzhen Development Bank, a classic strategic-block investment, delivered combined returns for our investor groups amounting to $4 billion within six years. These two investments certainly were highlights of Shan's initial work with us, but he was well-regarded in China as an expert in Asian banking and private-equity investing long before our huge gains in those deals.[7] In my book, for this singular epoch of Asian private equity, Weijian Shan is *the* guru.

Korea First was the first bank Newbridge acquired. It took us about a year to get the deal done. We had to work with government negotiators to agree on, among other things, the real value of the bank's assets, how nonperforming loans should be classified, and our right to sell unrecoverable loans to the government. It was a long and drawn-out process, but we never let go because we could envision the potential results. We had seen an American version, a decade before, of how Korea First might play out: David had been chief strategist for investor Robert M. Bass of Texas in the group's takeover of a failed savings and loan in Los Angeles. The experience was a good win for the Bass Group and, according to David, "the blueprint" for our Korea First investment.

Late in 1999, we agreed to invest $500 million of our investors' funds for a controlling stake of 51 percent (and 100 percent of voting rights); agencies of the South Korean government owned the rest. The government agreed to gradually cover all the nonperforming corporate loans on the books in exchange for government-obligation notes. The South Korean government had never done this before and never did so again. Throughout our negotiations, we held to our view that at least $1.5 billion of bad loans had to be written off—and absorbed by the government—which is how things turned out. The deal closed as agreed early in January 2000.

This was the backdrop when Frank Newman, who had a long career in the banking industry and had most recently been chief executive of Bankers Trust Company in New York, arrived for that first official session of Korea First's new board of directors, including me. That rowdy reception, drums and all, was political theater of a uniquely Korean style, staged by the bank's employees union.

"We could hardly hear each other in the board meeting, the drums were so loud," Frank remembered later. "But we were told that this was the way things worked. The union wanted to give a message to the new board: *We're here! Don't forget about us!*" In South Korea, a company is not permitted to keep union protestors out of its building. We never knew when they were coming.

The perennial joke on the Korea First board was that, as the house liberal, I always would take the lead in dealing with the union guys. Once, toward the end of our time there, a new union leader came in with his group in all their regalia—jackets, headbands, ninja outfits. He launched into a rant that was so emotional, he was tearing up. I did the only thing I could think to do: walk over and give him a hug. The Koreans in the room—the board members, the staff, and the union guys—all stood up and applauded.

At our meeting the next day, the union guy showed up again with his entourage.

What now? I thought.

It was a peace offering this time, a show of respect: They gave me a jacket and a headband and made me an honorary union member. The union's tactics did get our attention, but we never found the union to be a problem. What they really wanted, just like unions everywhere, was to keep their jobs and make more money.

Almost the entire staff of the bank during the four years we owned it was composed of local Koreans, except for the CEO. He was a seasoned French banker named Robert Cohen, and a very smart man. Robert (pronounced *Ro-BEHR*) had taught finance and economic for sixteen years at leading business schools in Paris. A twenty-five-year veteran of the Paris-based

Credit Lyonnais organization, he had led Credit Lyonnais USA for eight years when we recruited him to Korea First. He did an excellent job, tripling the value of loans on Korea First's books while paring the bank's ratio of nonperforming loans—a standard measure for well-managed banks—to the lowest among South Korean banks.

The leadership team had a three-pronged approach: build consumer assets, improve multiple processes such as credit collection, and win the hearts and minds of employees. Total employment rose, despite the fact that the team closed some branches. Efficiency improved. Loan approvals accelerated sharply, with processing time falling by 75 percent.

We like to think that by helping build a culture of credit in South Korea, with strong standards, ethics, and practices, we helped set an example of how modern banking should be done there. That may indeed be one part of the story. Another is that most South Korean banks learned a painful lesson from the financial crisis and, over time, better managed themselves by adopting Western standards.

We never worried about losing money by writing mortgages. South Korean law limited mortgage loans to 50 percent of either the appraised value or the purchase price of a home, whichever was lower. This is very conservative, especially in contrast to the free-lending times for housing in the United States that were just gathering steam. I think a 50 percent limit is too tough—coming up with half the value of a house isn't easy, especially in developing economies. But if we had some rules like that and more discipline in our own nation's markets, the United States never would have experienced the housing and financial crisis. In South Korea, you were never going to lose money on a portfolio of mortgage loans, and Newbridge never did.

Our strategy to convert to a consumer bank had worked: Over time, mortgages had amounted to the majority of Korea

First's assets. Our timing was right: The South Korean economy became much stronger after the millennium, loan demand kept pace, and we had good momentum from all the restructuring work within the business. And with the Asian financial crisis well in the past, global banking organizations were eager to expand in South Korea. In early 2005, we agreed to sell Korea First to Standard Chartered, one of the world's biggest international banking institutions. The price was $3.3 billion in cash. Our Newbridge share was around $1.6 billion—a gain of more than $1 billion in five years and more than triple our initial $500 million investment. We made an excellent return on our investment—and we handed Standard Chartered a profitable, well-managed institution.

SUPPORT FROM THE PRESIDENT

A lot of people in South Korea didn't really understand what we were doing during the five years we worked to revive and rebuild Korea First Bank. As we anticipated, there was resistance from many directions: the government, the media, and the business community. One exception was the president of the country, Kim Dae-jung. For decades he was the country's foremost dissident against military rule. Never given the credit he deserved, Kim was one of the great heroes in Asia after World War II. This was a fiercely resilient, tough guy. He survived at least five assassination attempts and a death sentence while in prison. Eventually, Kim brought democracy to South Korea. He was the first opposition political leader to be elected president, serving from 1998 to 2003.

President Kim initially opposed terms of the IMF bailout during the 1998 political campaign, but he soon changed his mind. His priority was reviving the South Korean economy, and he wanted to meet with us before Newbridge bought the bank.

I thought this was a bad idea. We didn't want to be in a position where anyone could complain that the reason we won the Korea First bidding was because the process was influenced by the Blue House—the executive offices and main residence of South Korea's head of state.

Mickey Kantor and I had agreed to meet with President Kim only if we were successful and after the deal was closed. We were well aware by then that executives in South Korea could be thrown into jail simply for mismanaging a company.

When the day arrived, the president met us with a stern gaze. Through an interpreter, he said, "Reforming this bank is at the center of my reform plans."

His expectations were clear. Any misstep by our group would bear grave consequences. We took his admonition seriously. Around that time, one of President Kim's political associates termed our investment a "showcase" for Kim's push to open up the South Korean economy to the global marketplace.[8]

President Kim came to understand that our strategy at the bank was working not only for us but for his country, too. We never saw him again while he was president, but after we sold the bank to Standard Chartered and Kim had left office, we requested a meeting to talk about our results.

This time he was smiling.

Through an interpreter, he said, "You helped my reform plan. You fixed the bank. And you made money." Then, in English, Kim added, "Win . . . win . . . win."

We laughed and shook hands. That meeting symbolized what we had hoped to accomplish: We had made a very good return, we had earned the president's trust, and our investment had helped revive the South Korean economy.

Fighting Perception—and the Government

One of several terms China accepted in joining the World Trade Organization in 2001 was opening its domestic banking system for the first time to foreign investors. China's banking sector needed capital. Here was an opportunity for Newbridge to get in early and acquire a failing bank, just as we were doing in South Korea.

We took aim at the Shenzhen Development Bank. Founded by several local credit cooperatives, Shenzhen Development potentially was a solid franchise. It had a nationwide banking license and was well established as a commercial and retail banking institution. All of China's largest banks were state-owned, which greatly complicated prospects for foreign investment. But Shenzhen was publicly traded with about a thousand individual shareholders. The city's stake was the largest block.

In the twenty years leading up to 2000, GDP growth in the Guangdong area was phenomenal, averaging approximately 18 percent. GDP per capita was nearly four times the national average. The area accounted for one-third of China's total trading activity and nearly 7 percent of investment in fixed assets.[9] Guangdong was the epicenter of China's unprecedented economic modernization. This is largely because of its proximity to the free-market haven in what was then British-ruled Hong Kong, just a few miles to the south. (Today you can take a subway train from Hong Kong to Shenzhen in less than an hour.) Deng Xiaoping initiated reforms opening China to foreign investment and the gradual, limited market liberalization that ensued after succeeding Mao Zedong as head of China's Communist Party.

Like many Chinese banks we analyzed, Shenzhen Development was virtually bankrupt by Western standards. Nonperforming loans were reported at around 11 percent but in fact were above 20 percent. Loss reserves were depleted, meaning the bank would require a major infusion of capital to recover. The potential for a collapse was real—but so was the potential for a turnaround. We were convinced implementing good management and a strategy focused on consumer lending, just as we were doing with Korea First, could put Shenzhen Development on solid footing.

A key question was, could we negotiate the right terms? We needed a proposal the Chinese would consider more favorable than competing bids. We also needed terms that would protect us financially and legally. We were making the first foreign private-equity investment in China's highly regulated banking sector. There would be setbacks and obstacles—both anticipated and unknown. We needed to control our fate as best we could. In this situation, would "as best we could" be good enough? We thought so.

In October 2002, the city government of Shenzhen agreed in principle to sell us its 18 percent stake in the bank. Several details remained to be worked out, but the outlines were clear: We would have management control as the biggest shareholder, with the next largest shareholder owning only 3 percent or less. Weijian Shan had persuaded Shenzhen city officials and Chinese banking regulators over several meetings that Newbridge could deliver better than any foreign commercial banks with competing bids. Moreover, we were the only strategic buyer backed by private investors, not a global banking group. An acquiring banking group would be more likely to keep existing operations and leverage its global strengths to compete against China's domestic banking giants from a base in the country's most vibrant regional economy. JP Morgan and HSBC were known to be interested.

Newbridge, on the other hand, would have an incentive to sell the bank ("cash out," as investment bankers say) in the future. Chinese financial institutions—banks, insurance companies, brokerages—might be interested buyers at that point. This appealed to Chinese regulators.

In May of the following year, though, or about six months later, Shenzhen Development's board unexpectedly aborted the deal. Within the closely wired international private-equity community, Newbridge now was seen as a victim of its own misjudgment: underestimation of China's political resistance to foreign ownership. In fact, there was some truth to this perception at the time. The bank's existing management, deeply wary, was against us. Many executives had come from Shenzhen's city government or local state-owned companies. They were political operatives, not bankers. Job security, not operating efficiency, was their priority. Many wondered if we would replace them.

Within days we filed a lawsuit, accusing Taiwan's Chinatrust Commercial Bank of unlawfully mounting a competing bid for Shenzhen Development. Our swift move to the courts surprised people, but this is the kind of determination you must make clear at times to prevail in emerging markets. People said, "You can't sue the Chinese government." But it was the right thing to do. We had a signed agreement, and as I told the Chinese bank regulators in Beijing, "If we don't fight for our rights, we might as well pack up and never return."

The regulators in Beijing actually were happy we filed the lawsuit. They had already approved our deal and did not want to see it fail. They believed it would benefit the Chinese economy. But they had surprisingly little leverage to sort out and resolve the situation with Chinatrust. In the United States, bank regulation is centralized under various government agencies, but in China at the time, bank regulation was somewhat decentralized.

After filing the lawsuit, we initiated international arbitration hearings against Shenzhen Development's executives, seeking compensation for their scuttling the 2002 deal after it was approved by Chinese banking and securities officials. "It's rare for even the most frustrated foreign investors in China to turn to the courts, for fear of jeopardizing future relationships," *Business Week* wrote. "But Newbridge isn't a normal investor."[10]

A year later, Shan, Dan Carroll, and the rest of our team had reassembled the essential pieces of the deal. We paid $160 million to the city of Shenzhen for the 18 percent stake. Chinese banking law limited foreign ownership to less than 20 percent. We were the largest owners, but were limited to four seats on the bank's fifteen-seat board. All other board members were Chinese representing other ownership groups. Their view was mostly the same as the Beijing regulators we worked with: "Keep us informed. As you long as you are heading in the right direction, we are not going to shut the bank down."

After a year, as we were completing the sale of Korea First thirteen hundred miles northeast of Shenzhen early in 2005, we were able to bring Frank Newman in as chairman and chief executive with full board approval. Our regulators were progressive and knowledgeable, but they initially resisted giving Frank both titles. Chinese banks had never had a designated chief executive—a chairman and a president, yes, and also a party secretary, but never a chief executive. In our view, Frank needed the chief executive title to make clear to employees, partners, government officials, customers, and others that he was vested with the bank's most senior authority on strategy and management.

We had a lot of smart financial guys at Newbridge who knew how the Chinese financial system worked, but Frank was in a class by himself. He was fully aware of Shenzhen Development's challenges. The city's vice mayor for finance once told Frank the city's ownership of the bank was "more a liability than asset." Rising expenses, plus the widening shortfall in loan payments, had starved profits for years. The city of Shenzhen had poured in millions of dollars to shore up capital.

There were two major priorities for fixing the Shenzhen bank:

Edmund Hillary and Tenzing Norgay, after their historic ascent of the earth's highest point, the peak of Mt. Everest, on May 29, 1953. *Photograph by AP.*

Pasang Kami, my Sherpa guide on many treks and countless acts of kindness.

Younger brother Robert, me, mother Louise, and father Herbert Blum circa 1942, three years before cancer took my father's life.

With my seven grandchildren, on the same slide of my own childhood. Left to right: Mitchell, Spencer, Tristan, me, Julien, Eileen, Léa, and baby Benjamin.

Reclining along the Khumbu Glacier with briefcase
(a gag for my Sutro partners). Mt. Everest in background, 1972.

Boyhood dream: standing with Tenzing Norgay and Sir Ed
at the Potala Palace in Lhasa, 1981.

We pledged to help educate P. K.'s six children and his grandchildren. Years later, his oldest daughter, Nawang (here, in 2009), established the Khumbu's first dental practice.

A little girl in traditional Tibetan dress at Dakmar day-care center in Nepal's Upper Mustang, 2014.

Guided by Italian artist Luigi Fieni, three dozen Newaris and Lobas have been restoring exquisite wall paintings in LoMontang temples for more than a decade. *Photo by Luigi Fieni.*

The ancient walled city of LoMontang, 2010.

Raja Jigme Bista, king of Mustang, the 26th in an unbroken line dating back to the fifteenth century, with me on the preferred method of transit, LoMontang, 2010.

With Erica
Stone, president
of American
Himalayan
Foundation,
and ladies of the
Jampaling Tibetan
Settlement in
Nepal, in 2010.

Dr. Aruna Uprety and
Stop Girl Trafficking
students. SGT has
protected more than
17,000 Nepali girls from
being trafficked into
slavery by keeping them
informed and in school.

An iconic temple
at UNESCO
World Heritage
Site in Bhaktapur,
reduced to rubble
by the magnitude
7.8 earthquake
on April 25,
2015. *Photo by
Luigi Fieni.*

Bruce Moore (left), American Himalayan Foundation's regional director, in Sindhupalchok, bringing emergency relief bags filled with clothes and supplies to SGT girls in the aftermath of the 2015 earthquake. *Photo by Luigi Fieni.*

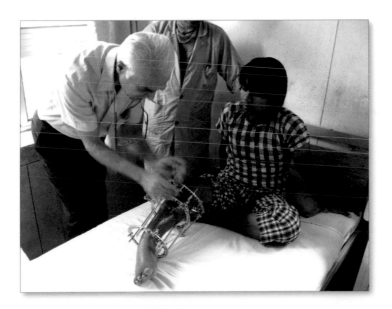

Dr. Ashok Banskota, with a young clubfoot patient. 70,000 poor, disabled Nepali children have received life-changing surgery and care at the Hospital and Rehabilitation Center for Disabled Children over the past 25 years.

President Jimmy Carter and Nawang Tenzing, Incarnate Lama of Tengboche, with a crowd of young monks at Tengboche Monastery, 1985.

President Carter speaking to villagers in Ghana about Guinea worm in 2007. Carter Center efforts reduced the cases of the dreaded disease from 10,000 in 2005 to 22 by the end of 2015. *Photo courtesy of The Carter Center.*

Celebrating the purchase of Ringling Bros. and Barnum & Bailey Circus, in 1967. Judge Roy Hofheinz and Irvin Feld made it on time to Rome's Colosseum. I arrived too late, coming from South Vietnam. *Photo courtesy of Feld Entertainment.*

With His Holiness in Dharamsala a few days before Dianne's first (and only) Khumbu trek, November 1978.

A city hall wedding, 1980.

Greeting Queen Elizabeth II in San Francisco, 1983.

With Pope John Paul II at the Vatican, 1982. Dianne and I presented him with a cross sculpted from 15 melted-down handguns, including one she once owned.

With Dianne and Fritz Mondale in San Francisco during his 1984 campaign for President. American government, he said, has a duty to "protect the disadvantaged." *Photo by Vici MacDonald / San Francisco Chronicle / Polaris.*

At his Inauguration in 2009, President Obama carried a Tibetan khata (ceremonial scarf) in his pocket that I had handed to him earlier that day—a gift from His Holiness.

Jiang Zemin, China's leader in the 1990s and a friend since the 1980s. The tension in the photo reflects our discussion about his army's oppression of Tibetans.

What's better than a hug from His Holiness the Dalai Lama?

With George Shultz and Dianne, inaugurating a new home for the Blum Center for Developing Economies, at the University of California, Berkeley, in 2010.

The first crew in Sudan to assemble Darfur Stoves, a Blum Center innovation that improves fuel efficiency for cooking in the refugee camps there.

Walking toward LoMontang in some of the world's most breathtaking landscapes, and among some of its most hospitable people. The range behind us is the Annapurnas.

An aerial view of Namche Bazaar, with 22,349-foot Ama Dablam in the distance, 2015. *Photo by Norbu Tenzing.*

With brothers Jamling and Norbu Tenzing at the unveiling ceremony of their father Tenzing Norgay's statue in the Khumbu, 2014.

Traveling with yaks was a way of life for most people in the Khumbu in 1972, the year I took this photo. Sherpa living standards have improved markedly since then.

Tsedo, AHF field director, visits the prayer room in a home for Tibetan elders in Nepal, 2015. Tsedo's parents escaped Tibet in 1959, shortly after His Holiness had fled the Chinese. *Photo by Luigi Fieni.*

Kangshung Face aerial view. *Photo by Bill Thompson.*

Ama Dablam with Tengboche Monastery in foreground.
Photo by Gil Roberts, 1999.

With President Bill Clinton on stage at UC Berkeley, where we welcomed 6,000 people to "Courage to Create," the opening session of Clinton Global Initiative University's annual meeting in 2016. *Photo by Max Orenstein / Clinton Global Initiative.*

First, strengthen basic lending operations with tighter standards and more efficient processes, including more advanced information technology. And second, transform the culture from a sleepy, top-down bureaucracy into a vibrant, bottom-up meritocracy while remaining true to local Chinese culture and traditions.

At the first executive session with his twelve-member executive team, Frank purposefully took a seat near the center of the long conference table, not at the head. He was surrounded by team members who came with notepads—and no questions—expecting Frank to deliver instructions as prior authority figures had done. Instead, Frank said to them, "It's not going to work that way. I have a lot of experience in banking, but not in China. You know your bank. You know your markets. We're going to have to do this together." This was a big change for the leaders, but the meetings became far more productive. "I clearly was the leader," Frank explained later, "but I also saw myself as a teacher and a coach."

Frank knew how to build a team. Over the next four years, he promoted several people to different positions at headquarters and in the branches. He recruited talent, such as a new credit officer and a new chief financial officer, from outside the bank. He created an incentive system with bonuses throughout the organization, not just for senior executives. "Handing out bonuses based on accomplishing objectives rather than on how much your boss liked you was energizing for them," Frank said. He also took on the prevailing culture of cronyism and nepotism by promoting a new person—previously the bank's deputy secretary of the Communist Party in charge of discipline—to lead human resources and be responsible for benefits *and* a new code of ethical and professional conduct.

"The woman we promoted was very smart, very upstanding, and it worked out well. This was the first code of conduct the bank ever had," Frank said. "We decided at the board level we were not going to investigate everything that happened before. People had never been told what the rules were. They operated in a different environment then."

Once the transformation was well under way in mid-2009, we agreed to sell the Newbridge stake in Shenzhen Development Bank to the giant Chinese company Ping An Insurance Group. The price was about $2.4 billion—*fourteen times* our initial investment on behalf of Newbridge investors.

Capital Allocation, Wealth Creation, Rising Living Standards

The banking organization we handed to Ping An was one of China's strongest in terms of operations, profits, and all key ratios for sound banking. Ping An Bank Company, as it has been known since 2012, was a success story. Net profits and earnings per share under our stewardship had increased by an average of 69 percent a year. Market capitalization rose nearly five times, at an annual pace of 33 percent. Deposits, loans, and total assets each tripled, rising by more than 20 percent a year. The percentage of nonperforming loans, one of the highest among significant Chinese banks early in the decade, now was near the lowest, at less than 1 percent. And employment had doubled to fifteen thousand.

It's vital to respect and understand as best you can local cultural traditions and practices when conducting business as an outsider in a developing economy. The basic fundamentals for financial success, however, are more or less the same everywhere.

Improving management in the banking and financial sector is essential in developing economies (just as in developed economies, of course) because financial institutions can channel capital inflows, typically from foreign direct investment and local savings. More efficient allocation of capital, when combined with abundant (or even just sufficient) labor resources, is the wellspring for economic growth. As labor becomes more skilled—and capital allocation, more efficient—a virtuous cycle develops that can attract more foreign direct investment and further accelerate growth.

To be sure, when banking and financial services are not well managed, the consequences can be disastrous. While we tend to think about these problems being confined mainly to developing economies, the problem can be even more pronounced in developed markets. We need look no further than the mortgage-led meltdown of the US financial system that created the Great Recession in 2008 and 2009.

It was exciting to be among the early foreign participants contributing to the growing financial sector in Asia. This was a time of unprecedented quantum leaps in creating new wealth, wealth that was essential in helping people raise living standards, and in reducing extreme poverty, and we remained eager to pursue more intriguing situations there.

Part 3

Policy and Practice to Bridge Divides

Chapter 8

Poise and the Middle Path in Local Matters

*"There are two kinds of people in the world:
problem makers and problem solvers.
At some point there is a choice."*

—Senator Dianne Feinstein

Local government is often the best place to make or see progress happen. Leaders are more directly connected to the issues they're charged with solving, and getting things done means marshaling smaller numbers of resources and people.

That said, my biggest problem with government has always been that government doesn't serve the people as efficiently as it should. The obligation that leaders have to take responsibility often is too diffused. Bureaucracies in general make me crazy. You wind up with people in three different departments, who know nothing about each other, doing the same thing. Among many concerns about the University of California's Office of the President when I joined the UC Board of Regents in 2002, this was one of the biggest.

Bias comes into it—people's preferences, political affiliations, even place of birth. Don't misunderstand me. Many people in government are bright and motivated. But rigid rules and procedures can grind them down and cause them to fall back on the way they've always thought about certain issues, or to adopt the perspective of the old-timers in their departments. I've seen many talented people with new ideas get stymied or slapped down. Others fall into routines, lose their creativity, and get comfortable with the safety net. The status quo, by definition, always has constituencies that work to oppose change.[1]

I have been very fortunate when it comes to local governance. I've been able to contribute to initiatives in San Francisco and California, and I've had a ringside seat to much broader governance issues through my wife, US Senator Dianne Feinstein. When I first met her, she was president of the San Francisco Board of Supervisors—and was soon to be pushed by tragic events onto the national stage.

Why does my involvement—and Dianne's—in local and state government matter in the context of global development or the battle against poverty around the world? Because authentic progress on a large scale must be strongly connected to people at the grass roots. Very little happens in any community without the involvement of local leaders, agencies, administrators, or councils.

And while I may be biased, I believe that Dianne is one of the best kind of leaders: someone who is truly committed to solving the problems and is willing to work with whoever has the best answers to those problems. I think her story offers powerful lessons about what we should look for in our leaders and in the leaders we partner with in any development initiative.

JFK's Resonating Idea: The Peace Corps

It was a speech by John F. Kennedy, laying out his inspiring case for the Peace Corps, that first sparked my interest in government initiatives. I was in the crowd at the Cow Palace in San Francisco, six days before the 1960 election, and I loved the idea. I could visualize how teams of American volunteers committed to two years of humanitarian work would have made life better for many people I had seen in my travels a few years earlier in Europe and North Africa. When we started the Blum Center for Developing Economies at UC Berkeley some forty-five years later, part of our inspiration was drawn from the Peace Corps model JFK put into action in the first months of his presidency.

But my first connections with city officials and public policy in San Francisco came a few years later, after Joseph L. Alioto, a centrist Democrat and high-profile corporate antitrust lawyer, was elected mayor in 1968. One of his priorities was stabilizing the city's finances.[2] I was recruited through a friend and former White House Fellow, Howard Nemerovski (or "Nemo," as we called him), to help them target good people to serve on a new mayoral finance committee.

"Joe was very business-oriented, and that is how he looked at running the city. He needed people with talent who knew budgets, business, and corporations," said John De Luca, then Alioto's deputy mayor and now an old friend of mine. Before I got involved, Alioto's team already had approved construction of many high-rise buildings, including the Transamerica Pyramid (until recently the city's tallest building), the Embarcadero Center on ten acres near the wharf, and the fifty-two-story Bank of America Center— "all controversial at the time," according to John.

When Nemo first introduced me to John, I didn't have any specific role in mind for myself at city hall, so I just said, "I'd like to be involved in helping out the city."

John, perhaps assuming I had an agenda to push, like most volunteers he encountered, asked reflexively, "Well, what do you wish?"

"Nothing. I just want to be helpful if I can be."

Around this same time, in the early 1970s, I was doing well at Sutro and meeting more people involved in national politics: Martin Agronsky, a political TV analyst based in Washington and first host of the *Face The Nation* program; Walter "Fritz" Mondale, then a Hubert Humphrey protégé in the US Senate and future vice president under Jimmy Carter; John Burton, a state senator and later US congressman from my district north of the Golden Gate Bridge in Marin County; and Barbara Boxer, an aide to Burton who later was elected to the same congressional seat and then to the US Senate along with Dianne in 1992.[3] This network widened just naturally, informally, and as it did I developed an itch to get involved, but with nothing specific in mind.

Taking the Port

"I'm having a bunch of people over to meet George Moscone, and I'd like you to meet him," said the voice on the phone— Nemo. It was 1975, and Joe Alioto was heading into the final year of his second term as mayor. Moscone, a populist state senator and a *bête noire* of Governor Ronald Reagan, was going to run that fall to succeed Alioto. I was moderately interested in what Moscone might have to say, but it was a particularly busy time for me. I was just leaving Sutro to start my own firm. Plus I was going back and forth to Washington once a month to help Fritz Mondale on some projects. I didn't want to add anything else to my schedule. But Howard was a friend, so I agreed to join the gathering at his house.

Moscone was a classic San Francisco liberal of that era—a charismatic champion of the underdog; a former all-city high school basketball player with strong support in lower middle-class, poor, hippie, and gay communities; and a man with few fans among the mainstream business interests that thrived under Alioto.[4] I wasn't sure what to expect. Moscone explained that he wanted to take a fresh look at all the city government activities, and then talked through what he thought about each department.

I purposefully sat in a chair behind a big potted plant, trying not to be noticed by Nemo or Moscone. I thought I was in the clear as Moscone got to the last point on his list: the Port Authority of San Francisco. After more than a hundred years of oversight, dating to the 1849 gold rush, the state government was handing over jurisdiction of harbor activities to the city and county.

Fisherman's Wharf in the mid-1970s was a tableau of older piers occupied mostly by boats of Sicilian fishermen plus one or two good restaurants, including Alioto's own establishment. In other words, it was nothing like today's tourist mecca. The boom in Pacific container ships, mostly from Japan at that time, was happening over in Oakland, not in San Francisco, and many longshoremen jobs were moving across the Bay.

"What should we do with the port?" Moscone asked, speaking to no one in particular.

"Hey, Dick, why don't you take the port?" Nemo shouted my way.

I wasn't enthusiastic. "Why?" I replied. "I don't know anything about it. Because I like to go swimming?"

"That's a good enough reason to go have a look," Nemo said, grinning.

How could I say no? We put together a somewhat extensive analysis, talking to people who made their living along the harbor or who might consider investing in one thing or another. We evaluated the entire San Francisco side of the port for its potential as both a modern transportation center and a tourism hub. Then we gave Moscone several recommendations. I talked to him about it a little, and as we finished up he said simply, "Thank you very much."

I figured he would just toss the report into a wastebasket without bothering to read it. But when he announced a ten-point platform during his mayoral campaign, I was shocked to see that most of my ideas for the port were there. *Oh my God*, I thought. *This is a politician who actually listens.*

Moscone was running for mayor against two members of the San Francisco Board of Supervisors, an elected eleven-member body comparable to many city councils across the nation: John Barbagelata, a conservative realtor, was old school and deeply resistant to the social changes happening in the city. Dianne Feinstein was the other candidate.

I knew who Dianne was, of course, but had never met her. Most people figured Barbagelata would lose in the first round and the runoff would be between George and Dianne, the moderate candidate. She had run for mayor four years earlier, finishing a distant third. Barbagelata and Moscone were first-timers in a mayoral campaign. But Barbagelata rode a conservative wave across the city to finish second, knocking out Dianne, who finished third again, and he nearly overtook Moscone in the runoff. The official victory margin was fewer than five thousand (a result Barbagelata contested unsuccessfully for another two years).

It was clear to me that mounting public opposition to rising taxes, and not reactionary social issues, was the main force behind Barbagelata's surge. This was just three years before California voters would signal to the country that a 1980s tax revolt was brewing, by overwhelmingly approving tax-slashing Proposition 13.

The night after the runoff, during a dinner celebrating Moscone's victory, I made a suggestion. "George," I said, "there was a message from the Barbagelata vote: The taxpayers have had it." I suggested he establish an advisory committee to recommend ways to cut spending and improve the efficiency of the city's operations.

"Dick," he responded, "that's the best idea I've heard since I started this campaign. Will you chair it?"

I agreed.

Along with Rudy Nothenberg, Moscone's highly capable deputy mayor, I signed up financial and business experts from around the city and established a pipeline for reports and recommendations on how to finance the city's debt, how the municipal railroad could operate more efficiently, and so on. I'm sure we made a positive impact. Four decades later, our little committee—now called the Municipal Fiscal Advisory Committee—is still active. I believed strongly then as I do now that government works best when responsible public officials regularly involve people with substantial financial and business experience. (I wish President Barack Obama had done more of this; if he had, his administration would have made more progress.)

Moscone took our work seriously. So did Dianne Feinstein, who had become the first woman to serve as president of the San Francisco Board of Supervisors after winning more votes than her peers in the prior election. She called me one day in 1977 to ask for our committee's latest report to the mayor. It was an analysis of financial trends comparing San Francisco with other big cities. The analysis was complicated, so I said, "Would you like to have lunch? I'll explain this thing to you."

The eldest of three daughters of Dr. Leon Goldman, a prominent surgeon at the prestigious University of California, San Francisco, Dianne had been passionate about politics even before her days as a campus government leader at Stanford University. Her uncle Morrie Goldman was fascinated by local politics, and on Monday afternoons he often took young

Dianne with him to follow the action at meetings of the county's board of supervisors—or, in Uncle Morrie's words, "board of stupidvisors."

"He would always say to me, 'Dianne, you get an education, and you do the job right,'" she would later remember. "It was my uncle who really gave me my desire to participate in society."[5]

She majored in history, earning her degree in 1955. In her successful application that spring for a fellowship with the Coro Foundation, which trains young people for careers in public affairs, she wrote, "I plan to run for political office on a local and possibly a national level."[6]

Now she was forty-five years old and in her third term as a San Francisco supervisor. We met at Jack's Restaurant in the Financial District and talked mostly about the numbers in the report. We both agreed later that it was a fairly boring lunch—maybe because of the presence of a police officer at our table. He was part of a detail the city police department had assigned for Dianne's personal security. A radical group called the New World Liberation Front was in the midst of a nerve-racking multiyear bombing spree across California. Power stations, office buildings, and banks had been hit, although no one had been killed.

Dianne had been targeted too. One night, the group placed a bomb in a flower box below her daughter Katherine's window. The detonator went off, but subzero temperatures that night, during an unexpected and rare cold snap, prevented an explosion. "I was very lucky," Dianne has said. Sometime later, members of the group shot out windows at Dianne's vacation home near Monterey. She was twice lucky: No one was at the house.

In the summer of 1978, I had been divorced for two years, and Dianne's husband of seventeen years, Dr. Bertram Feinstein, had passed away only a few months earlier after a long fight with cancer. He was a renowned neurosurgeon and a colleague of her father. They had a wonderful marriage, and Dianne and

Katherine both adored him (he had adopted Katherine, whose father was Dianne's first husband).

"It was such a painful period. I hate to go back to it," she has said. Indeed, she fell into a deep grief until Katherine told her, "You've got to stop this, mother. Life is for the living." Only then did Dianne begin thinking about seeing anyone socially again.

Our fiscal committee a year later had updated our report to the mayor, and one day I called Dianne and asked her if she would like to see the revised report. She suggested that we have dinner the next Monday night. The board of supervisors would be meeting, she said, but we could go out during the dinner break.

We drove across the Golden Gate Bridge to Scoma's, a romantic restaurant along the waterfront in Sausalito. There was no police bodyguard this time, and we didn't talk much about the numbers. She never made it back to the supervisors' meeting, which was totally out of character for her. Neither of us went out with anyone else after that. It was June 14, 1978.

Dianne and I went to dinner one evening in July when we were in Lake Tahoe, surrounded by the Sierra Nevada mountain range, and she asked what it was like in the Himalayas. I was planning a fall trip for another trek in Nepal and to Dharamsala in northern India to call on His Holiness the Dalai Lama, whom I hadn't seen in six years. So I described the rugged, spectacular peaks . . . the wonderful Sherpa people . . . the invigorating challenge of trekking in the cold at high altitudes and sleeping on the ground in a tent.

I was certain Dianne would not want anything to do with a Khumbu expedition like this, but as a courtesy, I invited her to come along. She picked up her glass of wine, took a big swallow, and said, "OK, I'm coming." When Dianne told Katherine she was going trekking with me in Nepal, Katherine told her mother she had lost her mind.

Our trip began splendidly. His Holiness happily accepted the invitation we carried in a letter from Mayor Moscone to visit San Francisco the next year. Then fortune's bright smile soon became an awful glare after we left Namche Bazaar, heading toward Everest Base Camp in the Khumbu with my friend Gary Wilson and his son, Derek. Dianne had contracted dysentery before leaving India. In retrospect, she was too weak to have even attempted the trek.

"We had been campout walking with no facilities in thin air for ten days," Gary later remembered. "Dick is very good at high altitude and would go off on a hike, while we would just sit there in the woods, cold and tired, without having had a shower for a week. The scenery was spectacular, but at fifteen thousand feet, we all got pretty sick."

Dianne and I had been together only six months, and here she was suffering acute nausea and fever, far from any modern comforts or medical care. It was a real test of our relationship. "Just get me out of here," she told me, "and we never have to see each other again." Compounding her misery, we were not able to call in a helicopter or small airplane for a lift back to the airport. Aircraft service was so spotty in those years you could wait three days or more and still have no idea when you would depart. Dianne had to ride a yak, with me walking alongside, much of the way down the mountain to Namche.

Aside from contending with her physical distress, Dianne was using this time away from city hall as best she could to decide her future. She had been elected three times to the board of supervisors but lost twice in her campaigns for mayor—a moderate squeezed from contention by rivals on the left and right in 1971 and again in 1975. "I was convinced that I was unelectable as mayor, that the city would not elect a woman," she has said often.[7]

Of course, she was wrong. But her path to that position would be one of epic tragedy.

A City's Horrific Fortnight

Luckily for me, Dianne did not follow through on her promise in Namche to ditch me. From Nepal, Dianne and I flew to Rome for a few days before heading home. That is where Dianne learned that Supervisor Dan White had abruptly resigned from the board and then, regretting his decision a week later, was pushing Mayor Moscone to reappoint him. (White had called Dianne earlier during our trip before we arrived in Rome to tell her he planned to resign his low-paying supervisor seat because he needed to earn more money to support his family.) But Moscone had other ideas. The board was split, and Moscone was planning to appoint a liberal to the open seat to further bolster prospects for the board to approve more of his political agenda.

A onetime fireman and police officer with a blue-collar Catholic upbringing, and at age thirty-two the youngest supervisor on the board, White was under pressure from his supporters among uniformed city employees and the Chamber of Commerce to return to the fray and oppose policy shifts pursued by the gays, minorities, and labor groups who had elected Moscone.

Meanwhile, as we headed back to San Francisco, Dianne had decided to abandon her dream of becoming mayor and get out of politics. She would announce the decision after she was back at work.

Less than an hour after arriving in San Francisco, we heard the disturbing news on our car radio that a local congressman, Leo Ryan, was reported missing on a trip to Jonestown, Guyana. A few days later, news reports confirmed Ryan had been gunned down at a Guyana airstrip. He had been attempting to depart with a handful of defectors from a remote encampment where the Reverend Jim Jones had lured hundreds of his followers in the San Francisco–based People's Temple congregation.

Two days after Ryan's death, Jones had led his followers in

a stunning mass suicide and murder; most victims swallowed grape-flavored punch laced with cyanide. More than nine hundred people died in the jungle, one-third of whom were children fed poison by their parents or others.

San Francisco went into mourning. The horrific event dominated the national news for several days, but it was only the beginning of what became San Francisco's darkest fortnight since the aftermath of the 1906 earthquake.

Still regaining her strength after Nepal, Dianne didn't go back to her office for another week. When I dropped her off at city hall on Monday morning, November 27, 1978, she planned to announce that afternoon she would not run again for the board of supervisors. She had already told several friends her political career soon would be over.

We didn't know what Moscone was going to do about Dan White—whether or not he would reappoint the young supervisor—but on the preceding Friday I had encouraged the mayor to call Dianne before making any announcement. "She *is* president of the board of supervisors," I said, simply noting protocol. "Whatever you decide, don't let Dianne read about it in the newspapers first."

At nine a.m. that Monday, Moscone called to say that he was going to replace White with a community activist named Don Horanzy. The mayor assured Dianne she would like Horanzy, adding that he would be sworn in at eleven o'clock that morning.

White had told friends that if he was not reappointed, he would come to the board meeting that afternoon and take his seat anyway. Knowing this, and after getting the news from Moscone, Dianne went to the office hoping to persuade White to not make a scene at the board meeting. She was depending on the mentoring relationship she had built with him as she tried privately to help him learn the ropes after he was elected to the board of supervisors a year before. But she couldn't locate him.

What she didn't know was that White was already heading to the mayor's office. Wearing a three-piece suit and packing the same .38-caliber revolver he had carried as a police officer, along with extra bullets in his pockets, White avoided the metal detectors at the doors of city hall by crawling in through an unlocked basement window. He first went to the mayor's second-floor office, where he confronted Moscone. When the mayor told White he would not reappoint him, White pulled out his gun and shot Moscone four times, twice in the head.

Before anyone could react, White escaped through the door of Moscone's smaller back office and hurried to the warren of tiny offices on the opposite side of city hall, where members of the board of supervisors worked. Spotting him rushing through the main door, Dianne called out, "Dan? Can I talk to you?" but he didn't break stride. "In a minute!" he shouted. He was looking for Harvey Milk, a masterful politician and the first openly gay member of the supervisors.

White and Milk had met weekly, and talked often, but over the weekend White grew livid after learning that Milk and two other politicians close to Moscone, State Assemblyman Willie Brown and Supervisor Carol Ruth Silver, had pressed Moscone to reject White's reinstatement. White later confessed (after being released from prison) that his intent that morning was to slay all four.

Dianne heard the door to Milk's office slam. Moments later, five shots rang out. For a moment, she thought White had committed suicide. Then she realized there had been too many shots. She could smell the cordite. "After I heard the shots, Dan walked right by my office and out the door," she remembered later. No one else was in the hallway, and she heard only the sound of silence. "Everyone disappears. No one is around. All the doors are closed."

She quickly walked down the hall and opened the door to Milk's office. "I found Harvey on his stomach," she remembers.

"I tried to get a pulse and put my finger through a bullet hole. He was clearly dead." Dianne said it was "one of the hardest moments, if not the hardest moment, of my life."[8] She repeatedly tried calling Police Chief Charles Gain and couldn't understand why she was unable to reach him. Then the chief walked into the suite of supervisors' offices and told her Moscone was dead.

As president of the board of supervisors, she was automatically acting mayor.

Lucid in Crisis

Political commentators have observed over the years, beginning with the assassinations, how calm and purposeful Dianne is during times of public crisis. "I needed that ability when I became mayor," she said, "because the city was falling apart."[9]

Dianne credits her late father, Dr. Goldman, for his constant counsel. He had always urged her to research exhaustively and then look for the essential truth amid complex or conflicting ideas. Whatever the source, Dianne's inner steel, her toughness, and her conviction were essential—and evident—as she carried on that day and in the weeks following.

Her first official comments as mayor were broadcast the night of the assassinations by the three commercial TV networks and reported with photographs the next day in national newspapers: "As president of the board of supervisors, it is my duty to inform you that both Mayor Moscone and Supervisor Harvey Milk have been shot . . . and killed," she said, gazing into the TV spotlights and photographers' flashbulbs. She then paused for a few moments amid city hall staff and journalists' shouts of "Quiet! Quiet!" before she added, to even greater shock and disbelief, "The suspect is Supervisor Dan White."

White turned himself in to police and confessed to the killings that afternoon. Incredibly, a sympathetic jury returned a manslaughter verdict, not murder, at the conclusion of White's trial six months later.

The city was stunned. "I thought he would get the death penalty," Dianne has said. "He killed two people—no question about intent." The verdict touched off major rioting in San Francisco's gay community, in what became known as the White Night riots. Within a few years of his release from prison, White committed suicide.

A week after the assassinations, following a contested election among its members, the board officially named Dianne mayor by a one-vote margin. Under the most abhorrent circumstances, she now held the office she had dreamed of since high school. She had become the first woman to serve as mayor of any major city in the United States.

The following year would be the toughest of her career.

Nonpartisan Stability

Dianne quickly decided one way to preserve Moscone's legacy was to retain his staff. Some of her advisors encouraged her to bring in her own people, and in fact, Moscone's people expected to be let go. But she quickly decided that the political operations of the city should not change as a result of the killings. She kept his team, which was very smart. Many ended up becoming her most loyal supporters and, in some cases, good friends.

Dianne was tough-minded and nonpartisan. As mayor, she led the public in mourning and helped pull the city back together. "This was a real crisis. There was deep hate," she has said, looking back. "I had to do a lot of things to put the bricks back together. And we did that." This is the talent of the very best leaders—pulling people together, not driving them further apart.

In Dianne's first six months as mayor, I spent nearly all my time working on city matters, trying to help her however I could.

We were together twenty-four hours a day, seven days a week. In the midst of all this, Dianne and I became engaged (she had forgiven me for the Nepal trip), and by the summer of 1979 she was campaigning to win the mayoralty in her own right in the fall election.

It is easy to forget after all the years how people then viewed the role of women in politics. Many questioned whether a woman could be tough enough to lead a major city. Dianne found herself in a bitterly contested race against Quentin Kopp, an old-style conservative member of the board of supervisors who certainly thought that way. Nonetheless, Dianne won the election with 54 percent of the vote and, on January 8, 1980, was sworn in for the first of her two full four-year terms.

Twelve days later, we were married in a private ceremony in the mayor's office with about twenty family members and close friends attending, including Willie Brown and city protocol chief Charlotte Swig (who later married our good friend, former secretary of state George Shultz). I had returned to my investment business months earlier, resigned as chairman of the fiscal advisory committee, and even stopped attending public events with Dianne. The point in part was to make it clear I was keeping my business and personal affairs separate from Dianne's. But to celebrate our wedding, we invited the entire city to a reception downstairs in the city hall rotunda. More than eight thousand people came. Our hope was for everyone to feel they were part of the celebration as San Francisco continued to recover from the tragedies of 1978.

Nearly four years later, Dianne easily won her second term as mayor, running without serious opposition in the general election after soundly defeating a recall effort six months earlier, mounted by a short-lived right-wing group, the White Panther Party, that opposed her push to ban handguns in the city. (Dianne carried her own registered handgun in the years immediately after the threats on her life when she was on the Board of Supervisors, then turned it in as part of her successful 1982 campaign to ban handguns in San Francisco. Her pistol and fourteen others were melted down and sculpted into a cross, which Dianne presented to Pope John Paul II later that year at the Vatican.) She captured more than three-fourths of the official vote in both the primary and the general elections in 1983. In 1987, *City and State* magazine named her the nation's most effective mayor.

In his best-selling account of San Francisco's two turbulent decades from the late 1960s to the late '80s, *Season of the Witch: Enchantment, Terror, and Deliverance in the City of Love*, journalist David Talbot assessed Dianne's impact as mayor:

> It has become fashionable in recent decades to disparage public service. The political profession is widely scorned and reviled. But there are times when political leadership seems like a blessing. San Francisco in November 1978 was a broken vessel on a dark sea. The city had endured so many blows and afflictions that it seemed cursed. When deliverance finally came, San Francisco owed it in large part to an unlikely leader . . .
>
> Feinstein was well grounded, resolute, firm, managerial . . . She turned out to be precisely the right leader for the time. While she shifted the city back toward the center, she stabilized it enough to allow many of the revolutionary changes that preceded her to become fully absorbed by the body politics. Though she herself was not in harmony with all of these "San Francisco values," they became enshrined under her leadership.[10]

Term limits prevented Dianne from running again when she stepped down as San Francisco's mayor in January 1988. Fortunately, that constraint has never applied to her as a US

Senator. Dianne has represented all of California since winning her first statewide election in 1992 by a sixteen-point margin. Four women were elected that year to the Senate—a record at that time. In her last reelection campaign in 2012, Californians embraced Dianne with the most votes tallied in the history of US Senate elections, nearly 7.3 million. And for the second campaign in a row, her margin of victory over her opponent topped twenty-four points.

The Difference a Great Leader Can Make

I'm proud of all Dianne has accomplished. Her entire political career has been about solving problems and helping people. Among her most significant lawmaking achievements in the Senate are a ten-year assault weapons ban (which Congress foolishly let expire in 2004); restrictions on manufacturing, and criminal penalties for possession and distribution, of methamphetamine; security and visa reforms aimed at targeting terrorists attempting to enter the United States; an increase in fleetwide fuel economy standards for cars and trucks by ten miles per gallon by model year 2020 (the largest increase in more than two decades); and the largest federal park land to be set aside in the lower forty-eight states, creating Death Valley National Park, Joshua Tree National Park, and Mojave National Preserve.

I was never more proud of Dianne, however, than the day in December 2014 when she took to the Senate floor—in the wake of intense objections, especially from the Central Intelligence Agency—to explain the release of a summary of more than five hundred pages of the Senate Intelligence Committee's 6,700-page report on the CIA's unlawful interrogation practices in Iraq. Dianne later said:

I've been on that committee for fourteen years. There are two ways of looking at what we do. One is that we are comrades-in-arms with the intelligence agencies, and the other is that we're an oversight committee and that when you see things are wrong or should be changed or done differently, you say so. The CIA and the sixteen different intelligence agencies that this government has *need* oversight. They are brotherhoods, and their tradecraft is deception. Simply put, that's a unique combination.

Dianne is one of the most nonpartisan members of the Senate, a good-government pragmatist respected by Democrats and many Republicans in Congress. She is not ideological. She tries to reach across the aisle, even at times when it is almost impossible. Her core belief about effectively representing constituents in any elected position is to be a problem solver and to use compromise as a way to find workable solutions. "If you think you're going to get everything you want, that you'll stop the place until they come and do your bidding . . . It's not going to happen," she has said. "You're going to create a lot of animus, and you aren't going to accomplish it. On the other hand, if you are a centrist, you can reach out to all sides and help create compromise."

Chapter 9

Higher Education and the Case for Efficiency in Public Institutions

"The search for efficiency is the administrative equivalent of painting the Golden Gate Bridge. The work never ends."

—Janet Napolitano

We were asking a basic question: How many full-time employees were being paid in the president's office of the University of California system? To answer it, Katie Lapp, the newly recruited head of business operations, had to do something astonishing, almost embarrassing. She went through all the payroll slips, counting them one by one, for nearly *two thousand* employees. Short of that, there was no way to answer the question.

What Katie found was that departments had been understating their head counts by hiring "temporary" workers who wouldn't count against the approved levels, but the temporary workers had actually been working there for years. The same practice was happening at the ten campuses, making it all but impossible to know how many people actually worked for the university system. This was just one among several dismaying administrative problems that I learned about in my first few years as a regent for the UC system.

It was a big deal for me personally when Governor Gray Davis appointed me in 2002. With all the time I spent in Washington, I could have raised my hand for a number of high-level appointments. But the only assignment I ever wanted—with real authority in the public sector—was to be a member of the UC Board of Regents.

I'd spent much of my career trying to analyze organizations, identify future trends, and help them solve problems. I figured I had developed a good sense of knowing when an organization was well run and doing what it was supposed to be doing, and tried to apply this to my role as regent. It turned out I knew less about the UC system than I thought. A lot less.

My first impression as a new regent was jarring: The university administration wasn't properly focused on its mission. The bureaucracy was unwieldy. Financial planning and operations management were lagging. It was difficult to get information or identify key actors on an issue. I was astonished—angered, actually—by how the ineptitude in basic management harmed students and faculty and how it prevented teaching and research across UC from continuing to excel.

The Office of the President's senior finance team, although well-meaning, for years embraced a policy of keeping individual campus administrations and the regents in the dark about systemwide budgets and funding. The board of regents wasn't briefed on many important issues, sometimes by design and sometimes through neglect.

We couldn't even review a budget for the president's office, because we couldn't find one. There was a systemwide budget (mostly for funds that needed to be raised), and there was an expense budget that was so opaque, you couldn't tell whether it was good or not. *What's going on here?* I thought, *This is not some rural community college educating a hundred students in the 1950s.* We were talking about the University of California, with nearly 190,000 students and 165,000 faculty and staff in 2002.[1] It was the biggest university system in the country! The absence of budgets and other financial planning tools was distressing, to put it mildly. I would never consider investing or working with any business that was run like this.

During my first six to nine months as a regent, I wondered at times if I wanted to serve out my term, which was *twelve years.* One of my colleagues on the board, a highly accomplished entrepreneur and CEO, did resign after a few years, saying, "This place just wears me down."

What appeared to be willful disarray in the headquarters for the UC Office of the President in Oakland was dismaying. The prevailing culture at the time reflected a belief that because UC was the largest and best public university system in the world, surely it must *be* the best at everything, including administrative processes, with nothing to learn from others. Resistance to change was high, and excuse-making widespread. Occasionally we would hear that administrators offered this excuse: "Oh, the regents don't want to do it." It was nonsense.

We discovered many missed opportunities and looming threats that, in our view, were due mainly to ineptitude, indifference, or inaction within the administration. These failures were avoidable. The regents' mission was to work with the administration to face awkward facts about how the university was being run, and to push for better results and generally do whatever possible to maintain and strengthen the UC system's outstanding academics and research.

I survived my first and second years and then headed the finance committee for two years beginning in 2004. In 2006, I was elected to chair the full board. I had the flexibility to put long hours into confronting these long-simmering internal administrative challenges *and* the reductions in state funding, before an even greater challenge flared between 2009 and 2012: a crisis created when the state legislature slashed $900 million, or 30 percent, from the state's contribution to the UC annual operating budget.

Our country is full of public institutions that are the envy of the world. Their roles are to help keep us safe, improve the quality of life, and support people in need. But the United States needs more of our institutions to be equally focused on how they can deliver greater impact with the fewest funds. My time as a regent has made me wonder what is happening at some of these other institutions. If the best public university system in the country (according to *US News & World Report*, which in 2016 put six of the ten UC campuses in the top ten of all public universities in the United States) was being managed so inefficiently—wasting resources, money, and big opportunities to further its mission— what is happening elsewhere?

The US Agency for International Development (USAID) used to be a manifest example, until Dr. Rajiv Shah, a former executive with the Bill & Melinda Gates Foundation, got his hands on it. (Chapter 12 describes some of Raj Shah's important USAID initiatives.) For years USAID was burdened by a deserved reputation as slow-moving and arrogant in its choice of aid and how it delivered that aid to poor countries. I can't count the times USAID's unimaginative responses left Erica Stone and me shaking our heads. In most cases, we just decided to find other partners for the American Himalayan Foundation in Nepal—or just go it alone.

Of course, that's just in the United States, where government transparency is higher than in most developing and many developed countries. The ineptitude, even corruption, of public institutions in developing countries is much worse and much more dangerous. People die as a result of such inefficiency, and hundreds of millions more continue to live in severe poverty. No, better-run public programs and services won't solve all the world's problems.

But it's a sad situation when those same programs, services, or institutions create or exacerbate those problems.

To many people, an organization like the UC system seems so complex, it's almost impossible to change in meaningful ways. The American public certainly holds that opinion of our government system right now. But it's simply not true. As a group, the regents proved change was possible. Our efforts highlight some important lessons about pushing for change in these types of organizations—lessons that I believe are valuable for anybody working in development.

Rescuing Our Greatest Comparative Advantage

If you count all students, faculty, and research and administrative staff, the University of California has more people engaged in advancing knowledge and innovation than even global industrial giants like IBM and GE. Truly a national treasure, the UC system embraces an astonishing array of people whose collective activity is breathtaking in sophistication, breadth, and impact on the world. UC has ten campuses, five medical centers, three national laboratories, and dozens of professional schools, with 250,000 students and 199,000 faculty and staff. Their work deserves to be supported with the best management practices available to any modern organization, especially one *dedicated to improving the quality of life on earth*.

Year after year, the Berkeley campus is ranked number one in teaching and research among all public national universities in the country, and is the only public university among the top five global universities in academic research.[2] Other UC campuses—Los Angeles, Santa Barbara, Irvine, San Diego—are regularly included in the top ten list of public universities. The value that all the campuses together bring to California, the nation, and the world is immense.

My biggest desire in becoming a regent was to give back to the UC system that gave so much to me. More broadly, I wanted to support public higher education. Reestablishing strong support for public higher education is essential, but older generations today are not doing enough. If we do not invest more in our young citizens and provide greater opportunities for an outstanding education, our nation's economic future will suffer.

"Most people don't realize that America's greatest comparative advantage is our system of higher education," former president Bill Clinton said in a handwritten note to me shortly after I was named chair. "We need to keep it that way." In his first address to a joint session of Congress a few years later, President Obama said, "The countries who out-educate us today will out-compete us tomorrow."

Slowly we gained a reputation as the most activist group of regents in recent memory. To begin, we sought an independent assessment of the facts, with recommendations to build our case for better management. We brought in two management consulting firms—McKinsey and Company, followed by the Monitor Group—to perform organizational diagnostics, identify big issues, and then dig into those details and make change happen alongside sharp-eyed expert Betsy Horan, whom we brought on to help lead and coordinate the projects when I became chairman.

Betsy knew the players and surfaced several key issues. She supported and trusted excellent, reform-minded midlevel managers and was as impatient as any of us on the board with whatever stonewalling, lack of focus, or outright incompetence she encountered in these analyses. Teaming with the consultants, working day and night, Betsy made major contributions to reforms and restructurings.[3]

The Office of the President had more than two thousand employees, and staff groups were Balkanized much as all the different campuses were, doing mostly what they wanted. Different blocks of people within the same headquarters buildings in Oakland wouldn't even talk to each other. Problems just festered.

Worse, we had no centralized purchasing practice across the system. We might have been the only major organization in the country with employees paying retail prices for Microsoft software instead of buying at big negotiated discounts. The same was true for pens, paper, copiers—all the basics. It was clear that we could be saving millions of dollars a year. There was so much waste. At times I said some rather harsh things because it was the only way I could get enough people to listen. My statements were all rooted in one central criticism: *Your inefficiencies are forcing students to pay more to go to school here. If you're not efficient, you're driving up tuitions.*

Pension finances were another worry. For fifteen years, the university had not contributed *anything* from its yearly revenues to pension pools for faculty and staff; nor had any employees done so. The people in charge, evidently blinded by a long bull market in equities, were leaving it to appreciation alone to keep retirement funding on track. When the markets collapsed in 2008 and 2009, the pension plans for more than fifty thousand retirees of the UC system suddenly were only 70 percent funded.

I began to focus on two main objectives: first, improving salaries so we could retain outstanding faculty, and second, helping these faculty stars get new buildings approved and constructed to improve their prospects of attracting funds from the federal government and other sources. These scientists had big dreams of their own; they were working on projects that would be vital to the future of the state, the nation, and the world: all good. I wanted UC to support and keep them.

On the issue of salaries, it's my belief that you're only going to get the most skilled professionals if you pay them well. Yet the chancellors of the ten UC campuses, who typically were paid 40 percent less than their peers around the country, were an inspiring exception. I told this group several times before the legislature slashed UC's funding that I would walk the plank for them. "You guys deserve more money. You want it, I'll propose it." Each year, unanimously, they said no.

We pressed to simplify the university's bloated bureaucracy, raise noncompetitive salaries for faculty, restart contributions to pension plans, and recruit a new team of outstanding leaders and managers. We also tossed out ridiculously low, self-imposed limits on debt financing and streamlined approval processes to unlock and accelerate funding for several state-of-the-art research centers and other much-needed new campus buildings.

Yet it can take a great deal of time, persistence, and persuasion to make progress with organizations large and small. This is certainly true in the world's developing economies and poor communities—and also here in the world's largest economy and our nation's most populous state.

Spending Where It Matters

The first time I learned about low spending limits for capital projects on each campus was when a vice chancellor at Berkeley said he couldn't spend more than $50 million.

I said, "A month?"

He said, "No, a year."

Well, you can hardly keep toilets fixed for $50 million a year on a campus the size of Berkeley. How could this be? So I asked him to give me a course on Berkeley Finance 101.

Each of the UC campuses had debt caps assigned arbitrarily by the finance team in the Office of the President. Their belief was that the university's systemwide debt capacity was less than $1 billion. The effect was every department was cowed by these limits. New residence dorms weren't built. Hundreds of buildings needing seismic retrofits were untouched, an enormous liability for the regents and the administration because we all were aware of the risks. New buildings intended for important research ready to be funded weren't built.

Some of us looked at the balance sheet and the income statement, and thought, *This makes no sense. We have to have much more debt capacity.*

We were able to get a group of debt-financing experts at Lehman Brothers to study the situation, and they agreed. "Your debt capacity is not $1 billion," they told us. "It's between $9 billion and $11 billion over the next five years."

Meanwhile, campus and university-system administrators had been working with the regents and the Monitor team to simplify the process for reviewing and approving capital projects, which were often delayed by months because of little tweaks— like the color of tile—being made late in the approval process. The new methods greatly accelerated construction timelines and saved millions of dollars in administrative costs alone.

As chairman, I thought I should try to use the position as a bully pulpit—to dig deeper into details and understand issues better, and then make recommendations to my colleagues. I was often mulling the question, *How can I best help this place?*

Advances in Renewable Energy

One answer from the beginning was to try to help UC's faculty superstars, who had become entangled and frustrated by the bureaucracy. Steven Chu was one of them. With colleagues at the Lawrence Berkeley National Laboratory, he mapped out scientific research needed to discover and create technologies for harnessing solar power (and other renewables) and converting it to power transportation. President Obama would later appoint Steven as energy secretary, a post Steven held from 2009 to 2013, often using it to champion nuclear power and renewable energy as the best global response to easing climate change.

But back on campus in the mid-2000s, he wasn't going to get far in his renewable power research without a building designed and built specifically to conduct that research. And he wasn't getting *anywhere* with the finance and planning staff in the UC Office of the President. They had placed a debt cap of zero on UC's national laboratories.

Our idea was to demolish some old California Department of Health buildings on the Berkeley campus and construct a new building with advanced laboratories that would research how to efficiently produce renewable, carbon-neutral biofuels. Known as the Helios Energy Research Facility, it would be the new home for the Energy Biosciences Institute and would include space for future use by the university's Department of Bioengineering. The US Department of Energy had committed millions for the research, funds that would partially be used to repay loans needed for construction.

UC president Robert Dynes was on board, but his staff stonewalled the project. They were ignoring his mandate to plan and develop the building in partnership with the federal government, arguing that the Energy Department funds technically were not a permanent source of income because Congress had to approve the appropriation each year. They concluded, therefore, that budgeting plans for the building were "against policy."

It was unusual for a regent to get involved in individual campus projects, but I became quite agitated about this. I had kind of gotten out my metaphorical AK-47 by then, and Steven Chu and Betsy Horan were no shrinking violets. We pushed back: "Whose policy?" we asked. "The state's or the university system's?"

"Well, no," came the response. "It's just a practice by the staff." One that nobody bothered to question, of course. "We've always done things this way." It was a phrase I heard many times.

"That's not a reason to keep doing things the same way now," I would reply. "If that's the thinking, I guess I shouldn't be surprised to find an employee whose job it is to make sure students don't ride horses too fast across the campus!" It was Management 101: If we have some practice tied to our policy, and we want to change the practice, we should just change the policy.

To break the logjam on Helios, I met with Bob Dynes and we found a simple solution: The Energy Department would send a letter assuring the university that there would be a steady stream of revenue to repay the loan required for the building.

Not long after we announced plans and timeline for Steven's building, the global energy company BP pledged $500 million over ten years to fund the new research on cleaner fuels in partnership with the Lawrence Berkeley National Laboratory, the University of Illinois, and UC San Diego. Three of the world's great private universities had been competing for that funding and were on BP's short list: the Massachusetts Institute of Technology, Cambridge University, and the Imperial College of London. If we hadn't gotten the Helios building approved and moving forward, UC Berkeley wouldn't have gotten that BP commitment to fund the research.

"Addressing the major problems that face our society is our public mission," UC Berkeley's chancellor Robert Birgeneau said at the time of BP's announcement, adding that the project would deepen UC's legacy of research, teaching, and innovation "in service to our state, our nation, and the world. This is our generation's moon shot."[4]

Early in 2015, against the backdrop of collapsing oil prices and a steep new financial burden after settling lawsuits from the Deepwater Horizon oil spill, BP decided to halt its development of a cellulosic biofuels business. The company asked the Energy Biosciences Institute to wind down research in that field while exercising its option to pare its original funding commitment proportionately. BP generously agreed to honor its pledge to support graduate and postdoctoral students for up to thirty months longer. BP also extended its partnership with the institute through 2020 (at the reduced funding rate) and supported the university's efforts to raise funds from other corporate sources.

Researching Cures for Diseases of the Brain

Dr. Stanley Prusiner, a 1997 Nobel laureate, and Dr. Stephen Hauser, leaders of the best neuroscience faculty in the world, had been asking for a new building at the new UCSF campus in Mission Bay so they could expand their research teams, upgrade equipment, and make faster progress in their research.

When we started investigating, the UCSF development staff advised us that the building would cost several million dollars more than the actual proposal from private donors (who would fund development and construction, and lease the building back to UCSF). Yet a UCSF executive who looked over the initial budgets explained that people in the planning office must have padded the initial estimate. "They have made this thing look ridiculously expensive," he said. In one example, estimated monthly lease costs for UCSF were put at $21,000, 50 percent above actual plans for a donor-built project. Why would they do this? In the proposed model, which required fewer university administrative resources, some of them might lose their jobs.

Financially, the case for constructing the building was beyond dispute. Dr. Prusiner had proven the existence of a type of protein known as the prion that can cause normal proteins in the brain to fold abnormally, triggering rare neurodegenerative disorders. He held dozens of patents (fifty as of this writing), all of which were assigned to the University of California and represented hundreds of millions of dollars of potential future revenue. His research center receives $7 million a year in funding from the

National Institutes of Health and he leads the world's most talented team of researchers in neuroscience at UC San Francisco's Institute for Neurodegenerative Disease, exploring for cures for dementia, Alzheimer's disease, Parkinson's disease, and other debilitating disorders of the brain. Dr. Hauser researches genetic factors for developing multiple sclerosis and leads the UCSF neurology department. It would have been a terrible loss for UCSF if Stan and Steve had decided to leave due to lack of support from the university. More important, *their research really matters.* Countless people all around the world will benefit from it.

The financing for what became the Sandler Neurosciences Center was a masterstroke as a public–private partnership. Once again, after construction was under way, a major pharmaceutical company agreed to fund a significant portion of Stan and Steve's research program over many years. With any sort of research facility especially, you first must build it, and then they may or may not come. In this case they did.

Seeing this project take shape and the research move ahead in Mission Bay has been a thrill. When Stan and Steve explained their work and plans at the groundbreaking in 2010, I was so proud of them and what they would accomplish. Who knows what potential advances in medicine might have been missed because of low-level politics in a slow-footed bureaucracy.

Averting Catastrophe

When Dianne was mayor of San Francisco, the head of the city's Department of Public Works came up to her one day and said, "We've done some studies, and we're concerned that the concrete rim around at Candlestick Park will come down in an earthquake."

The City and County budget had no extra money and the odds of an earthquake occurring during a sporting event were long. But Dianne said, "Now that I know about this, we've got to fix it. We have a moral and legal responsibility. How much is it going to cost to fix the problem?"

The head of public works said, "We'll need $6 million, but we don't have any money in the budget."

"We need to find it," Dianne replied. And they did.

The engineering team updated a study, and crews completed the three-year repair project shortly before the 1989 World Series between the San Francisco Giants and the Oakland A's. On October 17, less than an hour before the third game of the series—and the first game at Candlestick—a 6.9-magnitude earthquake struck the San Francisco and Monterey Bay region. The death toll across the Bay Area from what became known as the Loma Prieta earthquake was limited to sixty-three people. If Dianne hadn't insisted on those repairs a year earlier, thousands of people under the rim might have been killed.

Fast-forward nineteen years. University of California officials had known for years that a major earthquake fault line, the Hayward Fault, ran beneath California Memorial Stadium, the bowl-shaped coliseum where Berkeley's Golden Bears football team played. Nearly a thousand athletes and hundreds of staff used the stadium facilities on a regular basis, and more than seventy thousand fans often filled the stadium for home games.

The regents had been unaware of an administration report concluding that an earthquake could take down the entire west side of the stadium, which had been built on a landfill. When we learned of the report, with the close call at Candlestick Park in the back of my mind, I raised concerns about what could happen if an earthquake struck during a home game. Some people in the administration responded, "Yeah, but it's a million-to-one chance."

And I said, "Well, let me tell you a story."

The UC Office of the President and the Berkeley Office of the

Chancellor were not interested in a serious seismic retrofit that would cost hundreds of millions of dollars. Some opposed me publicly, initially. They had in mind a cheaper solution: build a small athletic center adjacent to the stadium to relocate the few dozen students and staff who used stadium facilities regularly, and then eventually complete a simple retrofit to address major safety concerns in the stadium structure.

But I was convinced we had to take stronger action. Over the decades, the steady seismic creep had shifted the interior of the structure of Berkeley's Memorial Stadium so much that some doors no longer shut properly. Worse yet, several concrete columns designed to support hundreds of seats above were visibly leaning, with cracks showing at the top.

If an earthquake caused any deaths or injuries around the stadium, in my view the regents could be civilly and possibly criminally liable by allowing Berkeley's athletic department to schedule Bears games at Memorial Stadium without a seismic retrofit. In 2008 a few of us regents made a stand: No games would be scheduled in the stadium after the 2010 season until the comprehensive retrofit project was completed.

It took nearly two years and $321 million financed by loans and an athletic department fund-raising campaign to get the work done. Although the athletic department is taking longer than expected to find buyers for three thousand reserved seats (each bearing a fifty-year contract) and to provide a cushion of capital, financing for the project was secured through bond sales without requiring one dime of public funds.

For me, when the question is whether or not to spend money that could—and very likely will—save hundreds or even thousands of lives, the answer is obvious.

Improvising to Do What Is Right

This past year, my daughter Heidi gave my wife and me a pillow with the words *Yes, dear* embroidered on it. It's a long-standing joke in the family: Dianne expresses her opinion about whatever new idea or project I've come up with. I say, "Yes, dear." Then (more often than not) I go do whatever I had planned to do in the first place.

I call it "persistence" and "focus." Other people have less positive words for it. But I think persistence and focus explain how we can get things done.

Yes, I am known as a bit of a maverick, and as I've said, my tolerance for arbitrary displays of authority or unnecessary policies and procedures is extremely limited. I realize this is a slippery slope. I recognize that it's the argument many have made when accused of fraud or corruption. Here are the lines I hold firm: I don't believe that the end always justifies the means. I don't carry a blatant disregard for *all* rules and policies, even the ones I sometimes ignore. I don't bypass rules for personal gain. And I don't work around regulations when it would place other people at risk or potentially cause harm.

None of these ethical guardrails was breached during the months I spent with a few other regents identifying, vetting, and courting a new president for the UC system. We had to be efficient and effective, and as matters turned out, we were.

Recruiting and hiring a new president is the most important decision any board of regents can make. When Bob Dynes agreed in 2007 to step down and return to his physics lab at UC San Diego, it was my responsibility as board chair to lead the search committee. I told Governor Arnold Schwarzenegger and his chief of staff, Susan Kennedy, we would need to sharply increase compensation and do a few other expensive things to attract the best possible candidate. The governor was in full agreement. "We need to be competitive," he said. "Do what you think is right."

The University of California is a huge, $25 billion enterprise. We were looking for someone with proven management skills, strong academic credentials, and experience leading a multicampus university system—a rare combination. The first decision we made was to hire somebody from outside the system. In more than one hundred years, the regents had never done this, but we needed someone with broad experience, an outsider's perspective, and no allegiances among ongoing administrative power struggles.

A leading candidate from day one was Mark Yudof. He was president of the University of Texas (fifteen campuses and 215,000 students today), former chancellor of the University of Minnesota (five campuses and sixty-five thousand students today), and a constitutional law expert who became dean of UT's law school. But he wouldn't even take my calls.

My friend John Moores, a Texan, had just left the UC Board of Regents and arranged for Mark and me to connect. When we did, Mark made it clear he had no appetite to be part of a beauty contest at UC. "I was perfectly happy where I was at Texas," he later explained. If word got out that he was talking to the University of California, his rock-solid support among most UT regents, alumni, faculty, and students could be shaken. "It was too risky."

But we soon were convinced that Mark would be an excellent fit. He was smart, a savvy advocate and negotiator, and as a former visiting professor at Berkeley, he knew a lot about UC. I reviewed the UC system's unmatched qualities with him, adding, "UT is half the size. This is the biggest job in the land. You'd be surrounded by brilliance."

Mark was intrigued, but he had two imperatives before he would even consider being a candidate: the recruiting process must be private, and we must not interview other candidates. I agreed. My one condition for him was that UC not be forced into a bidding war with UT if we made him an offer. I knew we would have to pay more than Mark was getting at UT—and double what Bob Dynes earned at UC—and I didn't want to ask our board or the governor even one time to raise the ante. Mark agreed, and we secretly went to work.

There are times when following procedures could block progress toward an important goal, and you have to weigh the trade-offs. This was one of those times. While alumni, faculty, and student representatives should have been part of the screening process, I knew that if word leaked out Mark was talking with us, he immediately would take himself out of the running.

As the regents' chair, I controlled the recruiting process, so I invited only the regents I had put on the search committee to join me in private dinners with Mark. These were people whose judgment I respected and who I knew would move quickly once we found the right candidate. We did two meetings with three regents at each. They were all enthusiastic about Mark. After the second meeting they said, "Just hire him."

The formal process for naming a new president called for the faculty group known as the Academic Senate to provide an initial list of candidates for the regents to consider. When the list arrived, it was a relief: It included Mark Yudof. We asked if the group would have objections if the regents went ahead and chose a president from the names on their list. They said no.

Mark was confirmed unanimously, by the full twenty-six-member board. It took only eight days after the board's green light for Mark and me to negotiate his contract, get sign-offs from the regents and the governor's office, and work out compensation details with finance and personnel staff in the Office of the President. This was handled at warp speed.

"Dick is a tenacious fellow," Mark said later. "Once he gets a bullet between his teeth, he gnaws at it with grave energy. He took a lot of body blows later, but he got it done. Recruiting me may have been one of the most difficult, uphill things he did as the regents' chair."

Mark and his team made great progress. He put in place an outstanding senior team to help manage the entire UC system. One of his biggest achievements was changing the conversation with the public about UC's dual problem of declining state funding and rising tuition. By the time Mark stepped down in 2013 to teach in Berkeley's law school, the Office of the President was managed much more efficiently and professionally. Regents were much better informed. During Mark's five years as president, the administration head count was reduced by one-third. Priorities were addressed. Things got done. We had more resources to pay better faculty salaries. And we kept a lid as best we could on rising student tuition.

"Mark Yudof is one of the best presidents we've ever had at UC," said Sherry Lansing, former chairman and CEO of Paramount Pictures Motion Picture Group for more than twelve years, the first woman to head a major film studio, and member of the UC Board of Regents since 1999 (including two years as chair). She continued:

> But we would never have gotten Mark if Dick hadn't been the maverick. Dick's view was, "Mark is everyone's first choice. I'm not going to follow the process (involving all recruiting committee members), because if I do, we'll end up with someone less than Mark." He took a tremendous amount of heat. A lot of people were angry with him—the faculty regent was angry with him—for not involving everyone.
>
> Dick has the ability to take criticism and not get upset by it. In fact, he doesn't care if he is criticized,

as long as he feels he did the right thing. This is a very unique and wonderful quality.

Janet Napolitano, a former Arizona governor and former head of Homeland Security, the third-largest agency of the US federal government, has continued the same discipline about budgets, management, and efficiency in the UC Office of the President.

Rising Costs, Lower Funding, and the Potential of Public–Private Partnerships

One day, when he was president of one of the nation's outstanding private universities, former treasury secretary Larry Summers said he was troubled by the ebbing support by legislatures across the country for state universities, including the UC system.

"Why," I asked, "would the president of Harvard University—with the largest endowment fund of any private university—be concerned about the funding of public higher education?"[5]

"Public higher education is part of what makes America great," Larry replied. He expanded on why these gateways must be preserved for young dreamers today:

> Without great public universities, we will not be Thomas Jefferson's aristocracy of talent. Our elite will increasingly be a closed club. And without the pluralism great public universities represent, the academic enterprise will be increasingly cloistered and isolated from public purpose.

It remains a mystery why state governments, not just in California, continue to underfund public and higher education. After all, every dollar the state invests in the university adds nearly ten dollars to the gross state product.[6] Yet in the UC system, we were educating sixty-eight thousand *more* students in 2015 with the same amount of funds we had received from the state twenty years before, in 1995. The only way we did this was by increasing class size and raising tuition, strategies we would have liked to avoid.

Our biggest challenge, a loss of $900 million from the state's annual contribution to the university system's budget, began during my last year as chairman. The ongoing and pressing problem of insufficient long-term funding became urgent. How could we cut costs and replace revenue? What could we do about huge funding shortfalls in pension plans? Would we have to implement tuition hikes or reduce course offerings? How would we maintain world-class academic programs and continue to enroll thousands more students each year?

The federal government contributes $3 billion a year toward research and other sponsored programs at UC, plus $1 billion to the Lawrence Berkeley National Laboratory and $1.6 billion in student aid. But the truth is, our nation has been putting fewer and fewer resources into public higher education for many years. Long before the Great Recession, state legislators were cutting spending for public colleges and universities. The financial crisis just deepened the cuts and amplified the rhetoric.

It has been apparent for many years that the State of California no longer can, or has the will to, fund the University of California in such a way that UC can remain competitive with the best universities in the country. Pure and simple. One day during one of the debates in Sacramento with politicians, I complained to one high-ranking official about the short-sighted policy of slashing state funding for the UC system.

"Look, I'm not getting paid anything for this," I said, referring to my work as a regent. "In fact, I have committed tens of millions of dollars to this university. So I'm going to do what I think is right."

"You know, a guy like you can be dangerous," he said. It was a welcome compliment, offered with a knowing smile.

We all caught a lot of heat for nearly doubling tuition, to $12,192 for the 2014–2015 academic year, compared to the start of Mark Yudof's tenure in 2008. But it is important to emphasize that Mark's administration increased enrollment and financial aid for low- and middle-income students.[7] He had the board's support at every step.

One of our most important achievements, thanks to Mark, has been changing the public's perception of reasons driving the rising tuition. We won a big political victory in 2012 when voters blocked Governor Jerry Brown's plan to trim $250 million in state funding for each of the state's three systems for higher education, and the state agreed to provide another $125 million so tuition would not be increased that year.

"Dick would get into the numbers with compassion," Sherry Lansing observed later. "He would spot duplication and spending that wasn't necessary. He would challenge the governor. He would challenge the legislature. He would challenge the chancellors or the students. And he would do this from his heart, not just from pure numbers."

There were many campus demonstrations against rising tuitions. "You always blame the authority figure who's closest," Mark has said. "No one wanted to raise tuition, but when one-third of your state budget is cut . . . " Most demonstrations were organized by the American Federation of State, County, and Municipal Employees Union, which of course was arguing with the regents for contracts with higher pay and benefits. Some union members raided my office one day in 2009. I told them they didn't understand the budget issues restricting what the regents could pay. "Why are you yelling at people like Mark Yudof and me?" I asked. "Why aren't you talking to the legislators in Sacramento? What is it about the legislators' decision to cut $900 million from UC's budget that you don't understand?"

You always want to lobby for as much state money as you can, but I think we spend too much time whining in Sacramento for what we get out of it. It seems better to understand and accept that the state is going to do whatever the state is going to do. We simply have to pursue other options, including running the university more efficiently (which we continue to work on); raising tuitions (which we have had to do); increasing federal funding for faculty research, student aid, and national laboratory research; and raising whatever money we can in the private sector through philanthropy and research grants.

Giving back to UC Berkeley is a privilege, a chance to show appreciation for everything I've learned and for a better understanding of the world. The UC system provided a foundation for my success in life; having achieved that success, taking the opportunity to give back for all I have been given seems the right thing to do. My financial commitments over the years to the UC system amount to more than $40 million.

Many of my friends feel the same as I do: The University of California was the best education for the money you could get anywhere in the world. Is that still true? Without question. But not everyone can afford it.

I am certain there is a deep well of untapped financial support out there among California business leaders. They profit either directly or indirectly from a strong public university. With state funding at a low point and the urgency to keep tuition affordable, we need more campaigns to go after that untapped support.

When you ask anybody in the business community if they want the University of California to be as good in ten years as it is now, the answer, of course, is always yes. Well, that means the university is going to need more resources beyond state and federal budgets and student tuition to pay competitive salaries and support innovative research.

It is an outrage—not a badge of honor—that Berkeley's outstanding College of Engineering had capacity to accept only 7 percent of its applicants for admission in 2016. Our state and our society urgently need brilliant, well-trained technology specialists to help design and build a better future: more efficient systems and products for energy, water supplies, conservation, transportation, communications, and health care, for example.

The business and investment community, university leaders, state and local government officials, public policy experts, and concerned citizens should be laying plans now to double enrollment in the University of California system to half a million students in another ten years. People say, "Well, where will we get the money?" We may not know all the answers now, but if we don't set the goal and start planning together, we surely never will.

We have a responsibility to future generations to keep great academic centers thriving—as institutions for personal and professional growth, and as avenues to keep our economy competitive and growing. If we don't get it right, our competitive advantage will slip. It will become harder in the decades ahead to create new industries, good jobs, and real hope, especially for the middle class. If you want to deal with the problems of income inequality, stagnant economic conditions, and global business competition, you have to start with education.

Chapter 10

Peace, Democracy, and Development

*"I entered politics young, impatient, and full of
confidence that government could be used to better
people's lives. My faith has not dimmed."*

—Walter F. Mondale

We could hear the sound of guns and rocket blasts from the other
side of Tân Sơn Nhất International Airport. The blasts shook the
floor and rattled the glasses and plates on our dinner table. It
was the fall of 1967, and I was in Saigon for Sutro on assignment
from a company doing USAID work a few days before heading
to Rome for the official closing of our Ringling Bros. deal. Our
job was to have a look at some villages farther north near Da
Nang so we could advise the US Office of Navy Research on
prospects for developing South Vietnam's local economies.

Most American reporters never left Saigon. They just relayed
whatever they were told at the daily briefings. For months US
Army officers, aided by maps and blackboards, had been assuring these journalists and the American people that our military
and the South Vietnamese army were winning against Ho Chi

Minh's forces in the North. But hearing and feeling the booming gunfire and rocket blasts that night, sitting there with a geography professor named Campbell from the University of Arizona who was my partner on the project and a marine captain who was going to show us around the next few days, we had to wonder.

The next morning we flew 375 miles to the air base near Da Nang, and then drove out to villages in an army jeep layered with sandbags to cushion us against anything exploding on the road underneath or in front of us. Da Nang was not far from the hot border with North Vietnam, but we had been told not to worry. Our troops had "won the hearts and minds" of people in the villages we were going to see.

As we drove through Da Nang, we saw people huddled together. They had evacuated villages in the countryside and were just hoping to stay alive. When we passed a bus full of these local Vietnamese, the two marines riding with us suddenly pointed their weapons at them. I was stunned. "Why are you doing that?" I yelled. A few days earlier, one of the marines said, someone in a bus tossed a hand grenade into a jeep that killed a couple of their buddies. These guys weren't taking any chances. If I wasn't convinced the night before, I definitely knew now that I had reason to worry.

From the top of a hill out in the countryside, we could see North Vietnamese fighters attacking a village about a mile away. What mattered most to the local Vietnamese, we learned, was not ideology, but survival—whether their village was being shelled or soldiers were pointing weapons at them. The war was all around them. When shells rained down, they would seek cover wherever they could, even if only in their simple bamboo and thatched-roof homes. On days when combat eased, they would attempt to go back to their daily lives, going to wells for water, working in rice paddies, and so on.

That afternoon, after lunch at the base near Da Nang, we headed out again in the jeep. Suddenly somebody began shooting at us from a rice paddy. I shouted to my companions, "Are we going to see anything different from what we saw this morning?"

"No!" they shouted back.

"In that case," I yelled, "why don't we get the hell out of here!" And we did.

During the most recent wars, when Eisenhower, Truman, and Roosevelt were in the White House, they were trusted. People believed they were trying to do the right thing. At that time, I was still young and optimistic. What I saw in Vietnam, though, was all the evidence I would ever need that what government officials say may have little to do with reality and truth.[1] Their story that a US victory soon would bring a better life to the Vietnamese was a complete lie. We clearly weren't winning.

You can't develop an economy in the midst of all-out warfare, and you absolutely cannot do so if you are on the losing side. That was the basic message in my report to the US government.

After I got back to the States, I was so angry about the government's deception about Vietnam that I changed my registered political affiliation from Republican to the Peace and Freedom Party.[2] I had never actually voted Republican; I registered that way when I was twenty-one because my grandmother was a registered Republican and she was the only one I ever talked politics with. Eventually, I became a Democrat—and I expect all those Eisenhower Republicans of that era by now would be Democrats too—intellectually, and in every other way.

My experiences in Vietnam also prompted me to begin looking seriously at what was happening on the national stage, what our leaders were doing, and what that meant for the world. The United States has incredible influence around the globe. We have some of the greatest minds devoted to solving some of our greatest challenges. But I don't think we're using that influence as well as we could be.

Domestically, we're struggling to make progress because of Washington gridlock. We can't seem to, or aren't willing to, solve the growing income gap that is eventually going to hobble our economic growth and create social instability. Environmentally, although we're making progress, we still produce more CO_2 emissions than any country but China. We produce far more than all the countries in the European Union combined.[3]

People like Jimmy Carter, Bill Clinton, Bill and Melinda Gates, and other dedicated individuals and organizations are making incredible strides to help solve these challenges. We also have some committed leaders in government—those exceptional centrists like Dianne—who genuinely focus on doing what it takes to improve life for all, not just the few, and who are interested in thinking globally. Finally, we have companies and leaders in the private sector who are looking for opportunities to have a positive impact in their communities, local and global.

They couldn't choose more inspirational, challenging paths to follow than those taken by Walter "Fritz" Mondale, a person who has served with great compassion and dedication in all these facets of public life.

My Time with Fritz in the White House

With the exception of my wife, Fritz Mondale is my ideal for the model public official. He is a liberal in the best sense of the word: a guardian of the public trust, an idealist, a believer in the American government's duty to "protect the disadvantaged and advance the rights of ordinary people," as he wrote in his memoir, *The Good Fight: A Life in Liberal Politics*. He is also one of the most gracious, decent men I have known. The son of a Methodist minister, Fritz has a strong spiritual inner core. "My dad preached what might be called the social gospel—that our faith requires good deeds as well as good words," he wrote.[4]

Fritz was one of the new faces in the Democratic Party vanguard after Nixon's landslide defeat of George McGovern in 1972 and then Nixon's resignation as a result of the Watergate scandal in the summer of 1973. Fritz's national prospects surged after his reelection in Minnesota to the Senate in 1972, and he thought he might have a shot at the Democratic nomination for president in 1976. So did I. I was one of his earliest supporters and fund-raisers.

He had denounced the Vietnam War after Nixon took office in 1969 as "a military, a political, and a moral disaster."[5] The war was a tragedy, not only for the fifty-eight thousand US troops and the hundreds of thousands of Vietnamese soldiers on both sides who died, and perhaps as many as two million Vietnamese civilians who lost their lives,[6] but also for the lost potential of progressive social programs in our country just springing to life that could never get traction.

When Lyndon Johnson escalated the war dramatically with 540,000 US troops in Vietnam by the end of 1967, he didn't have the foresight to understand how his surge in military spending was planting the seeds for a disastrous retreat for the progressive agenda. Fritz argued that the war was starving federal funding for many Great Society programs he had helped pass into law in the 1960s. As he noted in his memoir, "We authorized dreams and appropriated peanuts."[7]

"Whenever you have a war, the first casualty is the idea of social progress," Fritz said recently. "People just turn that off. That sure happened during the Vietnam War when I was in the Senate. Many programs couldn't work [with limited funding], which created a sour taste for the public. It still saddens me. Today we've got paralysis in Washington, this train-wreck school of politics . . . that puts pressure on all the progressive things that I want in our society."

Fritz was also wary of extreme wealth being concentrated in the hands of a few. Any of this sound familiar? History does not repeat exactly, as Mark Twain once suggested, but I do believe it rhymes.

We held the first fund-raiser outside Minnesota for a Mondale presidential bid in my home in Marin County, California. My young daughters, Annette, Heidi, and Eileen, then between the ages of twelve and eight, had been watching quietly from the balcony but suddenly jumped up and pelted Fritz with pillows as he was trying to speak. (Whenever I see him, he asks me how the pillow throwers are doing.)

Testing the waters for a presidential campaign is unrelenting, exhausting work, with many parallels, I think, to organizing and leading a business start-up or to framing or executing the recovery of a struggling business. It requires enthusiasm and patience. But you also have to know when to leave the game if the odds are stacked too high against you. As 1974 came to a close, Fritz surprised many people when he abandoned his campaign. But he soon would be back on the national stage.

When Jimmy Carter won the Democratic presidential nomination in 1976, I was excited he had picked Fritz as his running mate. After the president narrowly edged Gerald Ford in the November election, Fritz invited me to meet with him and Jimmy as they vetted people for key positions in their new administration.

Perhaps I would have jumped at the opportunity to work in the White House earlier in my life, but Andrea and I had just gotten divorced. I couldn't see moving to Washington and leaving my daughters behind in California. I also had a pretty good idea of the hectic pace and single-mindedness that comes with working in the White House. "I've thought about it. I just can't do it," I told Fritz the next day.

Instead of taking a White House job, I offered to work pro

bono for the administration. I had an interest in policies that could benefit neglected inner cities. In some cases the scars from racial rioting a decade earlier were still evident. More broadly, inner cities were being starved for resources as millions of people moved to suburbs, and city tax revenues struggled or declined.

One of Vice President Mondale's oversight responsibilities in the White House was urban policy. I was glad to pitch in one week every month in Washington. For a year, we focused on ways to bolster economic activity in inner cities by designing funding from the federal government in a way we thought would attract bigger investments from business. Our group created the Urban Development Action Grant, and the administration distributed more than $1.2 billion to cities over the next three years.[8]

Then as now, I was idealistic enough to think I could contribute something to the common good. On these trips to DC, I often saw my old friend Martin Agronsky, who then was hosting his popular weekly syndicated TV program, a roundtable discussion with political journalists that aired for twenty years on public television.[9] Ever the cynic, Martin said, "You won't get anything done here. They just want to use you." I didn't understand politics all that well then, but I was confident that neither President Carter nor Fritz had that motivation in my case, and I told Martin so.

I was right about that. Even so, by spending time inside the Beltway and hanging around with one of the best journalists of the day, I learned a lot about how things worked in Washington, especially perpetual crosscurrents and cajoling among government agencies, policy think tanks, and NGOs, whose reports so often shape policies enacted from the Oval Office.

A Convergence of Talents

By the millennium, my colleagues and I had—in both the American Himalayan Foundation and the Shanghai–San Francisco sister-city alliance—nearly two decades of evidence on ways that basic management principles enable NGOs to deliver better results for poor people and their communities.

One day, I was chatting about this with Strobe Talbott, a friend and former *Time* magazine journalist, author, and Clinton administration diplomat. Strobe was in his first year as president of the Brookings Institution, the world's most respected think tank then and even more so now. Brookings had always been known for its keen analyses of economics, foreign relations, and government. Strobe was in the process of adding two programs: on cities and on global economics and development.

Here is an opportunity, we thought: Bring together, through Brookings, some of the best scholars and government administrators in Washington with successful people in business, philanthropy, and NGOs. Let them dig into key issues in global development for a few days. Let them ask, what really works? In 2004, we began the Brookings Blum Roundtable on Global Development, now an annual three-day conference hosted by Walter Isaacson's Aspen Institute in Colorado.

These gatherings have examined (among other topics) how the world's poor will cope with climate change, how collaborating can generate more technological breakthroughs, how to frame aid programs that deliver positive results for people, how to understand the role of the private sector in the post-2015 development agenda, and how to jump-start economic growth in the world's poorest nations.

Without question, Blum Roundtable proceedings have helped initiate or energize collaborations among entrepreneurs, NGOs, government, think tanks, and philanthropies on several advances in global development. A few examples follow.

Blended Financing

Development funds traditionally have been provided separately by various sources: private businesses, government agencies, charitable organizations, and so on. This was cumbersome and inefficient, especially for organizations requesting the funds. "If you want to solve a development program, you need to understand the policy environment and you need to put together entrepreneurs, aid agencies, and multilateral banks," said Homi Kharas, a Brookings senior fellow. The blended financing idea didn't originate from the roundtable, but we have helped build awareness among agencies such as USAID.

One example is Power Africa, a program in sub-Saharan Africa, where more than six hundred million people in the region have no access to electricity. Perhaps President Obama's most important development program, it was organized through USAID and partners such as the World Bank, the African Development Bank, and the government of Sweden to help bring electric power for the first time to sixty million homes and businesses in the region.[10]

Big Trends in Development

Before he was elected Afghanistan's president in 2014, Mohammad Ashraf Ghani joined roundtable sessions as an Afghan academic. Other participants have included former and future White House chiefs of staff, secretaries of state, the head of the National Security Council, top administrators of USAID and major private-sector foundations, many ambassadors, and other prominent development specialists from around the world. These public figures recognize that the world's major challenges in combating extreme poverty increasingly will happen in Africa and in states plagued by wars, such as Afghanistan, Syria, Iraq, Sudan, and eastern Congo. The Blum Roundtable has bolstered development agencies by bringing together leaders such as these who understand the difficult, on-the-ground realities in these regions.

Championing Smaller Projects

There are many ways to achieve transformational change in poor countries. Once-favored megaprojects, such as hydroelectric plants or oil-and-gas drilling and production, often require many years and billions of dollars to complete. But smaller projects, such as lower-cost solar power, are easier to finance and can begin operating much faster and in ways local people more easily understand, appreciate, and support. One company at the 2014 roundtable, d.light, says it has reached fifty million people with low-cost, portable solar-power lanterns with a four-hour battery life. And as described in chapter 6, our Latitude Capital Partners, a 2015 roundtable participant, is working to bring hydro and solar energy projects to poor communities without access to efficient power sources.

Philanthropy and Development

There might not have been many people at roundtables a few years ago who believed private philanthropy would be an increasingly important player in global development. But that, of course, has changed. "There are many examples now of philanthropic organizations that started in one country, have exploded out to other countries, and are driving this whole business of social impact investing," Homi Kharas has explained.

The Bill & Melinda Gates Foundation is the world's largest philanthropic organization dedicated to global development and certainly the best known in the United States. Outside of this country, the Aga Khan Development Network (AKDN) and the BRAC are major players. AKDN is a vital supporter of education, economic development, health care, and cultural restoration in Muslim communities in thirty countries. It employs approximately eighty thousand people and has a budget for non-profit activities of approximately $600 million. BRAC (formerly Bangladesh Rural Advancement Committee) has programs in microfinance, education, health care, and other services in eleven countries, reaching 135 million people.

The President's Global Development Council

The purpose of the President's Global Development Council is to help US government development agencies do a better job, borrowing from practices we know are effective in the private sector. We have helped shape ideas for this advisory board, such as the benefits of blended financing, with colleagues at round-table sessions and at Brookings and have advocated for them at the highest levels of the Obama administration. I outlined the concept, among others, in a paper advising the president after he took office in 2009 on how his administration ought to think about global development. When the council was created in 2012, I was one of the founding directors.

Our goal is to focus more US investments in global development on what we know works best, on where government dollars can be a catalyst for innovations benefiting poor people (such as early-stage and midstage financing), and as the council's first report says, on programs backed "by rigorous evidence and demonstrable impact."[11]

The key point of the president's development policy, as outlined in a 2010 White House briefing note, is recognizing that our country's efforts in global development can and should be "a core pillar of American power" and that advancing global development is "a strategic, economic, and moral imperative for the United States."[12] It also is important for our nation's security. As I emphasized in the Introduction, and repeat here: Wherever we are able to make progress in defeating extreme poverty and building economies, we advance prospects for world peace. Wherever poverty and ignorance continue to exist—and access to dangerous weapons is unchecked—the risk of more conflict and a more dangerous world will continue to threaten us all.

Poverty Is a Political Condition

Once you commit to helping people get out of poverty, and if you are serious about this work, it follows that you also want to help them get a political voice, if they don't already have one. Poverty is not only a socioeconomic condition; it is also a political condition. That became obvious to me during my few days touring those Vietnamese villages of terrified peasant families in 1967. The concept is at the heart of the mission of what may be one of the world's least known, most important organizations for advancing the cause of global democracy: the National Democratic Institute for International Affairs (NDI).

Jimmy Carter partnered with NDI on several elections—monitoring projects dating back to Panama in 1989. And Fritz Mondale chaired NDI from 1986 to 1993, advising groups behind the scenes in Poland and Hungary, among others, on their countries' transition to democracy after the collapse of the Soviet Union.

If you care about advancing global democracy, then you care about NDI's work. Building democratic institutions is essential in attracting credible, talented people into government and reducing corruption in countries that succeed in shedding legacies of rigid socialist regimes or dictatorship. I've been honored to be a member of NDI's board for several years and to help Madeleine Albright, President Clinton's first secretary of state and now NDI's chairman, and Ken Wollack, an astute diplomat and NDI's capable president for more than two decades, on many projects.

NDI helps promote fair democratic elections through its global network of trained observers—recently in places such as Myanmar, Nigeria, Honduras, Afghanistan, and Ukraine. NDI and George Soros's Open Society Foundations[13] made important contributions in the legitimate Ukraine elections in 2014 that threw out a corrupt government, strengthened the democracy, and helped stave off Russia's intrusion in eastern Ukraine. I was in Kiev at the time with Madeleine Albright, and I was in Nigeria and Indonesia as part of the election-observing process with Jimmy Carter and Ken Wollack in 1999.

In Nigeria that year, the favored candidate was General Olusegun Obasanjo. Obasanjo had been Nigeria's military ruler from 1976 to 1979 before becoming the country's first head of state to hand over power to an elected civilian government. Jimmy was the US president then, and he admired Obasanjo for leading the transition to a constitutional government.

However, the spirit of democracy didn't last long after Obasanjo stepped down: A series of military coups followed in the 1980s and '90s. By some accounts, the military dictator who ruled Nigeria for six years prior to the 1999 election, General Sani Abacha, looted as much as $5 billion from government accounts with his associates before dying suddenly in 1998.[14]

When we arrived, instead of joining Jimmy's entourage for vote-monitoring in the capital city of Lagos, I went into the sticks with a group of street-smart observers from NDI and The Carter Center, all in their twenties, including Jimmy's grandson, Jason Carter.[15] From what we witnessed, Obasanjo's supporters weren't leaving anything to chance in their effort to regain power. Scenes of open fraud were everywhere.

At one polling place, election workers told us "everyone" had voted a half hour before voting was scheduled to begin. In a place where votes were tallied, the different turnouts for several villages each added up suspiciously to 400—maybe 396 to 4 in one village, and 392 to 8 in another—in favor of Obasanjo, always. In another case, ballots were still in sequential order when they were removed from a ballot box; all were marked by the same fingerprint. The official result was a landslide victory for Obasanjo, with 62.5 percent of the votes.

Obasanjo's lone opponent, a Yale-educated banker named Olu Falae, showed up the next day in our Lagos meeting room claiming to have evidence of massive fraud and saying that the election had been rigged. Every example he gave matched what I had seen, and I thought he was right. Colin Powell, who would become George W. Bush's secretary of state in another two years and was part of our group that night, was less sure. Jimmy decided to wait until after we departed Lagos before announcing The Carter Center's position.

As soon as our plane landed to refuel, Jimmy issued a statement saying there had been too many irregularities—in effect, a rejection of the process. "It is not possible for us to make an accurate judgment about the outcome" of the election, he said. Obasanjo was not pleased. I had also heard that NDI and Carter Center observers who had worked in regions where Falae's party was dominant had witnessed the same kinds of serious irregularities by Falae's supporters that I had seen carried out by Obasanjo's supporters. The center's conclusion was that all parties had engaged in voter fraud. I was told that even if there had been no fraud, Obasanjo probably would have won anyway.

Things didn't improve when Obasanjo ran for reelection four years later. The Carter Center refused to send observers that time, but we heard that the extent of the fraud then was far worse.[16]

NDI also brings together citizens in more than 130 countries who want to create and sustain the basic institutions of democratic government. I have met many of them. Often they are dedicated idealistic thirty- or even twentysomethings who dream of—and are taking action for—a better future for themselves and their families. Opora, Ukraine's largest nonpartisan elections monitoring group, is an example of this.

Secretary Albright and Ken Wollack took several of us NDI board members to Colombia for a few days in the spring of 2015. After four decades of guerrilla war and narcotics-trafficking violence, Colombia has 3.5 million refugees within its borders, and hundreds of thousands more have fled the country altogether. Rebuilding confidence in Colombia's government is a huge challenge. But conditions are improving in part because government leaders, working with NDI, have taken steps to make their institutions more transparent.

As NDI and The Carter Center work to spread democracy and support human rights, they also are campaigning in these ways to reduce extreme poverty. As US citizens we also should take pride in the ways that Presidents Clinton and Carter have dedicated so much of their post–White House years to fighting global poverty and improving health care; and also in the leadership of President George H. W. Bush, who teamed with Clinton to head US relief efforts after a devastating tsunami swept across Indonesia and parts of India in 2004.

Working to reduce extreme poverty is a core mission of many organizations noted in this section—the President's Global Development Council, the Bill & Melinda Gates Foundation, the Soros Foundation, the Aga Khan Development Network, Brookings Blum Roundtable. To be sure, many other pragmatic, well-managed philanthropies, think tanks, and NGOs share this purpose.

Chapter 11

What Can We Learn from China and Tibet?

"We have to accept that Tibet will always
be in the neighborhood of China.
We cannot move it anywhere else."

—His Holiness the Fourteenth Dalai Lama

When Dianne and I first visited China in 1979, I decided to put in a request with the Chinese Mountaineering Association in Beijing for a permit to climb one of the Himalayan peaks from the Tibet side. I knew it was a long shot. My real hope was to get permission to visit Tibet, where foreigners were rarely allowed.

I figured a climbing permit wasn't likely, given my friendship with His Holiness the Dalai Lama, but nothing ventured, nothing gained. I made my pitch to the head of the association. As my words were translated, the man scowled and appeared angry. He told me to put my application in writing. As a formality, I submitted a letter of request, and thought that would be the end of it.

A few months later, though, I was quite surprised—shocked, actually—to receive what appeared to be a clear signal that my proposal might be approved: I was invited back to Beijing. After the Chinese bureaucracy concluded an appropriate number of its functionary fingerprints had been placed on the documents, I was granted permission to lead a Himalayan climbing expedition. And not just on any peak, but on the highest of them all: Mount Everest.

An Unprecedented Expedition on Everest—1981

A Chinese expedition had made it to Everest's summit in the 1960s, but this was the first time the government had given an Everest permit to an American. The only climbing team allowed anywhere in Tibet prior to this was from Iran; otherwise, no foreigners had been allowed anywhere in Tibet for thirty years.

I was thrilled and excited to organize this historic expedition along with lead climber Louis Reichardt, and also to travel to Tibet, where I would have a chance to see how people lived and to experience the Himalaya from the other side. With my friend Bruce McCubbrey, an accomplished mountaineer, we put together a team including some of the world's best: in addition to Louis (who today heads the prestigious Simons Foundation Autism Research Initiative), John Roskelley, Sue Giller, George Lowe, Chris Jones, Dan Reid, Andy Harvard, Jim Morrissey, Eric Perlman, Kim Momb, Geoff Tabin, and Gary Bocarde. All had experience on the world's most difficult peaks.

Kurt Diemberger, world-renowned Himalayan mountaineer from Austria, Michael Reynolds, and David Breashears were with us to film the climb for ABC-TV's *American Sportsman* program. Sir Ed came as well. At age sixty-two, he couldn't pass up the opportunity to see Tibet.

In all, our expedition numbered about twenty people, including climbers, guides and porters at base camp, and a hundred yaks for carrying several weeks' supplies and equipment. Starting from Lhasa, riding in buses and trucks for the better part of a week, then trekking another five days, we were able to set up base camp by the end of August with hardly a wasted moment. Everyone knew the ascent had to be completed by early October, before the onset of potentially extreme blizzard conditions around the summit.

Before we left California, we agreed that climbing the Kangshung Face of Mount Everest, which had never been done, would be our expedition goal. After walking, we arrived at the end of August 1981 and the climbers set up base camp.

Day after day, for weeks on end, the expedition team made progress in fits and starts. They attached ropes and set routes for other climbers to follow to bring up supplies. The rock was poor for climbing, with constant slides. The snow was soft and knee-deep on the ridges. Avalanches were common. One was incredibly thunderous, with snow and ice collapsing more than nine thousand feet after cracking away not far from Everest's peak, tearing through tents, and wreaking havoc in our base camp at 16,000 feet. Luckily, no one was hurt.

Some on our team argued for abandoning Kangshung and heading to the North Face. Sir Ed made a passionate case for continuing. He reasoned that our effort would stand as a triumph of the human spirit and a milestone in international mountaineering whether or not the summit was reached. Everyone voted, and, overwhelmingly, we agreed to keep going. (I felt like a high-altitude bureaucrat, administrator, and political negotiator in the midst of all this.) Yet, slowly, one by one, our numbers dwindled. Some left for medical reasons (intestinal parasites or injuries), and some because they were convinced the climb and conditions were too risky.

Finally, on October 5, Louis radioed back to Jim Morrissey at advanced base camp. "The summit looks so close, you could almost walk there," he said. "But the conditions are terrible. We just have too few people. We're going to get someone killed. We have to give up."

While no one made it to the summit in 1981, our expedition did the heavy work for an ascent, forging a route and fixing ropes on the Kangshung Face. Two years later, another team—including Louis and five others from the '81 effort—completed the ascent, with Louis, Kim Momb, and Carlos Buhler the first people ever to climb Everest directly along the Kangshung Face.

Being part of the team in '81, and awaking each day to the serious concern that we could lose someone as our lead climbers made their way to twenty thousand feet and beyond, made a profound impact on me—in particular, on how I would gauge business situations going forward. After confronting the physical and mental challenges of a Kangshung, your ability to take on risks and not worry about the consequences goes up exponentially.

This historic climbing achievement has never been repeated. Dry weather brought by an El Niño across Tibet had melted away most of the cornices, so it was easier in '83 to find a safe route along the ridges of ice. The team rapidly navigated the buttress, the most difficult part of the climb, in three days rather than battling it in four weeks as the '81 team had. "We knew exactly where to go, and those ropes were a huge deal," Louis said later.

I never learned why the Chinese allowed us to make that first attempt on the Kangshung. Virtually no foreigners had been allowed to travel anywhere in what became the Tibet Autonomous Region since His Holiness the Dalai Lama fled into exile in 1959. Over the years, I wondered if my request might have come at a time when the Chinese wanted to signal an easing of their suppression in Tibet. If so, perhaps I was chosen *because of* my connections with His Holiness, not in spite of them.

Leaders in China were also aware of the sister-city collaborations starting to gather momentum between Shanghai and San Francisco. Deng Xiaoping, who became China's leader in 1978, was experimenting with modern China's first steps toward capitalism in Guangdong province, north of and adjacent to Hong Kong (a citadel of free-market capitalism that would revert from a century of British control to Chinese rule in 1997). Our team at Newbridge Capital would seek and find appealing business opportunities in this and other parts of China some twenty years later, as described in chapter 7. At the time of the Kangshung ascents, however, China was on the verge of opening to outside investment for the first time in more than four decades.

Despite some improvements in creating a more open China in recent years, conditions for people in Tibet have lagged. These people have suffered more than sixty years from the oppressive policies of the Chinese government. At various times in the 1980s and '90s, it seemed the tide might well turn in the Tibetans' favor, but it was not so. Now, in the first years of Xi Jinping's China, Tibetans' prospects within the Tibetan Autonomous Region are as bad as we have ever witnessed.

As I've described, the Himalaya and Asia have been two of the biggest passions of my life now for nearly fifty years. During that time, no nation in the world has done more than China to help its people out of poverty. We should celebrate this. At the same time, no nation in South Asia has suffered more from mistaken Chinese policies than Tibet. We cannot accept this.

For more than thirty years, the people of Tibet and their plight have mattered greatly to me. Tibetans deserve better. And the Chinese deserve better too. Our message to the Chinese government is this: Oppression is never a final solution, and lies don't live forever. If China wants to become a great nation, it needs to become a moral nation, and what goes on in Tibet is immoral.

I have maintained relationships with two of China's most important recent leaders—Jiang Zemin and Zhu Rongji—and a close friendship with Tibet's spiritual leader, His Holiness the Dalai Lama. Does this sound like a contradiction? After all, how could I maintain these friendships, often in parallel, across the past four decades and still have such strong opinions about China's abhorrent policies and actions toward Tibet?

It is a fair question, and I am comfortable with my answer. Our relationships with these men and key people near them over the years have given us unusual insights. I have had the opportunity to engage with Dianne in trying to convince leaders of the Middle Kingdom that it is in the long-term interests of the Chinese government to end oppressive conditions for Tibetans. Perhaps the biggest frustration in my life is this has not happened yet.

But I believe it still can.

The Truth: Brutal Oppression, Marginalization, and Exile

China claims that it liberated Tibet in 1950 from a repressive, centuries-long feudal era and portrays the long line of Dalai Lamas as powerful rulers who enslaved the peasantry. Most Tibetans, however, view China as an invading force that has illegally occupied their country since the 1950 invasion.[1] More than a million Tibetans have died as a result of the Chinese occupation (a figure the Chinese dispute). In truth, it began as a wholesale slaughter. Periodic protests over the years have been violently suppressed by the Chinese military, and often martial law is declared.

During the late 1980s, nearly four decades after the People's Liberation Army's stunning invasion, China's leaders ruthlessly consolidated power in Tibet. They suppressed the Tibetan people and culture while launching various development programs over the next twenty-five years—new roads, airports, high-speed train, hotels, factories, and so on—promised to lift Tibet's economy out of the feudal past. This largely has been achieved—at the macro level. Yet most benefits from a rising economy flowed not to what Tibetan exiles estimate are approximately six million indigenous Tibetans, but to an estimated 7.5 million Han Chinese. Most of the Han Chinese migrated permanently and with the government's blessing into the Tibet Autonomous Region.[2] Mandarin became the dominant language for commerce and education. Development only further marginalized and oppressed Tibetans in their homeland.

In response first to the resurgent occupation, and then to the influx of Mandarin-speaking Han Chinese, many Tibetans fled southward across the border into Nepal. They followed the same routes across the Himalaya that thousands of other Tibetans have taken since the 1950 invasion. Most who survived settled in India and Nepal.

When Vice President Fritz Mondale met Deng Xiaoping during an official state visit in 1979, their talks were more friendly and productive than Fritz had anticipated. But not on the subject of Tibet. As Fritz wrote in *The Good Fight*,

> Deng was prickly on statehood for Tibet and on the Dalai Lama, whom he dismissed as "an insignificant character." I assured him that the Dalai Lama was received in the United States as a religious leader, not a political figure. We also remained concerned about human rights and political freedoms in China, and I touched on that topic during my speech at Beijing University.[3]

Both before the Carter administration and since, most political leaders in the United States, on both sides of the aisle, have agreed about the Chinese mistreatment of Tibetans.

Over the years, Dianne and I have met several hundred Tibetans personally. Most were very poor in material wealth. They were exiles, living in refugee camps in Nepal, in northern India, and elsewhere in South Asia. Most were illiterate, working hard at subsistence farming or as laborers building roads because they had few other options. Even so, for most their inner spirit seemed to carry the gentle wisdom passed down in the teachings and rituals of Tibetan Buddhism. Still, Tibetans living in exile in South Asia, and especially those inside Tibet, are weary. Many are resentful, angry—and for good reason, in my opinion and the opinion of many others.

Tibetans have been deprived of their most basic human rights. Before and during the Cultural Revolution, Mao's army brought to ruin most of Tibet's monasteries, temples, and historic buildings. We passed by some of these sites on our 1981 expedition into Tibet to climb Everest's Kangshung Face. *What a tragedy. What a waste.* By some estimates, Chinese soldiers destroyed more than six thousand monasteries, shattering icons and burning libraries of ancient texts. Fewer than a dozen monasteries remained at the end of the twentieth century. His Holiness has said many times that the survival of the Tibetans' cultural and spiritual heritage continues to be at risk in the wake of this onslaught:

> Without proper teachers and proper training, keeping up a religion is very difficult. Prior to 1959, there were outstanding scholars in Tibet. But most of them were arrested, some were killed, some fled . . . It's not sufficient to ring a bell, you know. Monks have to master the doctrine and the meditation. They need to be good in both. This requires thorough training.[4]

I was visiting Kathmandu in the early 1990s with my daughter Heidi when a Tibetan activist living in Switzerland, Tsultim Tersey, asked for my help. Could I arrange for several monks and nuns who had been part of the 1989 exodus in the wake of a post–Tiananmen Square crackdown by the Chinese to fly to

Zurich? As fellow mountain people, the Swiss shared a kinship with Tibetans, and many Tibetan exiles resettled in Switzerland after China's invasion in 1950. Tsultim explained that these nuns would be welcomed and well cared for if they could arrange passage. Of course I agreed to help.

Before the group left Kathmandu, we asked one nun who could not have been more than twenty years old to tell us her story. What had happened to her before she escaped? In China or the Tibetan Autonomous Region, she explained, anyone who wishes long life to His Holiness is considered an enemy of the state. She was arrested for holding a *puja*, a Buddhist prayer service that included, among the group's rhythmic chanting, an invocation of long life for the Dalai Lama.

The young nun was thrown into jail, beaten, tortured with electric cattle prods, and forced to lie for long periods of time on big blocks of ice in a freezing cell. When her jailers concluded she had no useful information for incriminating others, they pushed her out into the cold. "You don't know anything!" one of her tormenters said.

A few months later, I was in Zurich and called Tsultim to see how the Tibetans were doing. He invited us to meet for dinner with a few of them, including the young woman who had told us her story in Kathmandu. Radiant with an optimism I had not seen before, she told me over dinner that she had woven two yak wool bracelets to focus her mind away from the pain and suffering she had endured in prison. "I want you to have these bracelets," she told me. "One is for you, and one is for your daughter."

Though her experience was a recent one, it reflected the truth of the government-sponsored terrorism that had been happening for decades. As a result, many thousands of Tibetan refugees live in settlement camps in India and Nepal. Some elders in these camps have lived there more than fifty years.

The American Himalayan Foundation supports these refugees in many ways: with homes for elders; a path for education, from day care to college; health clinics; and enterprise funding for improved farming methods and business start-ups. One young refugee from Miao, a refugee camp situated in the most remote jungles of northeast India along what is now the Myanmar (formerly Burmese) border, became the first member of his community to graduate law school, thanks in part to scholarships that AHF funded. A few years ago, we provided a small grant and interest-free loan to young Tibetans starting a cybercafé in Miao. The venture provides services over the Internet and other modern communications that could open opportunities for a better life. The proprietors serve other refugees in many ways, including by taking digital photos, printing health forms, and selling satellite dish subscriptions and cell phone minutes.

Yet life for the vast majority of Tibetan refugees remains difficult. Most Tibetans in Miao, for example, are subsistence farmers. They live just south of the eastern extension of the Himalaya, an isolated region where heavy rains bring summer flooding to farmlands carved from tropical forests. "It is a hostile environment," says Tsedo, AHF's Tibetan field director.

Tsedo himself is the son of Tibetan refugees who fled to Kathmandu in 1959 when the Dalai Lama escaped into exile to Dharamsala in northern India. The region has experienced long-simmering boundary disputes between China and India. Insurgent separatist groups in the area want to secede from India. "The Tibetans there still feel like refugees," Tsedo says. "They are worried for their future, for their children's future, and most important, for the people still living in Tibet."

At the Core of the Dispute

For more than twenty-five years, working with Lodi Gyari, the Dalai Lama's chief envoy in Washington until a few years ago, Dianne and I tried to establish a sensible dialogue between the Chinese leadership and the Tibetans—the same kind of dialogue we've been able to have with those same leaders on many topics. Dianne very much shares my strong views on Tibet. A Chinese official in Beijing once accused me of brainwashing her. "Guilty," I responded, quickly and proudly.

This is the Chinese leaders' reasoning for not budging on the stalemate: Since Mao's ascendance, Tibet has been seen by China's leaders as having great geographic and strategic importance for China, and as a territory rich in natural resources. A land mass of more than 470,000 square miles, the Tibetan Himalaya and high plateau are a strategic buffer against any perceived military threats that might one day arise from India to the south. Furthermore, Tibet is often described as "the roof of the world," with an estimated $100 billion in mineral wealth. It also is a vital source of water supplies for China and South Asia.

Chinese leaders say Tibet has been part of historical China "since antiquity," meaning at least a few thousand years. Tibetans counter that the boundaries of Greater Tibet encompassed much of Sichuan and Qinghai provinces to the east and northeast for several centuries before the current boundaries of the Tibetan Autonomous Region were set in the eighteenth century. An estimated 250 million Buddhists live in China today.[5]

The Chinese government sees His Holiness as a rebel, a secessionist, and a schemer who secretly promotes violence and self-immolations of nuns and monks. This is nonsense. He has stated publicly many times that he does not support independence for Tibet, espouses nonviolence, and is deeply saddened by the self-immolations. His Holiness advocates a Middle Way that would allow China's continued political control of Tibet but give cultural and religious autonomy to all Tibetans living there. His Holiness also seeks to return to his homeland.

In the Tibet Autonomous Region today, local government administrators seem to do what they want; Beijing policies are interpreted differently in different places, which often encourages corruption and brings to mind an old Chinese proverb: *The mountains are high and the emperor is far away.* The region itself is like an armed camp. But if you cross the border into an old Tibetan territory to the north known as Amdo, where millions of ethnic Tibetans live in what now is part of China's Qinghai province, the atmosphere is more relaxed. You see pictures of His Holiness everywhere, and it doesn't seem to matter to Chinese authorities. Many new temples are being built, funded significantly by Chinese Buddhists coming from Taiwan.

Dianne and I have always remarked to Chinese leaders that if they sat down with His Holiness, they would find him to be a man of peace. They could negotiate with trust. While Jiang was China's leader, Bill Clinton and Jimmy Carter (then out of the White House more than ten years) raised with him the issue of Tibet. Lodi even organized nine meetings in Beijing between Chinese officials and Tibetan representatives, but they never led to anything substantial.

Lodi believes Chinese leaders fear that his message could inspire a pro-democracy movement among not just Tibetans but Uighurs (a Muslim ethnic group native to China's far west region of Xinjiang) and hundreds of millions of Chinese citizens. Despite our efforts to mediate between China's leaders and His Holiness, we have not been able to bring them together—yet.[6]

Personal Relationships, Pragmatic Progress

Dianne has long believed that personal relationships are essential for political leaders to govern creatively and effectively, especially in hammering out positive solutions to bridge deep disagreement. When she was mayor of San Francisco, she established a sister-city arrangement with Shanghai. It was a brilliant move, one that seized the moment as China began opening up to the world. Shanghai had been China's center for international commerce before Mao, and San Francisco's large Chinese population had close family and cultural connections there.

The sister-city pact called for each mayor to visit the other city in alternate years. Remarkably, few mayors have missed this opportunity across more than three decades. On several occasions when politicians in Washington and Beijing were in dispute on US–China issues, these friendships forged over the years among participants in the Shanghai–San Francisco alliance endured; we said to each other we wouldn't let them be affected by high-level disputes. The fact that everybody was willing to do this is great. We have toasted our friendships again and again, and pledged that regardless of relations between China and the United States, Shanghai and San Francisco would always be friends.

This collaboration was an important step in China's retreat from isolation and in raising living standards under Deng Xiaoping. "We had fifty different initiatives going at any given time," Dianne has explained, "and a business training program with San Francisco corporations bringing midlevel Chinese managers over. We started a library in Shanghai of American resources. Our program was designed to benefit both cities." We saw the first Chinese ships and planes come to San Francisco. She opened the first Chinese consulate in the United States. And Dianne and I became close to the first ambassador of the People's Republic of China to this country.

Teaching Shanghai's leaders how we do things has included

showing them how we manage San Francisco's operations, including transportation, communications, wastewater treatment, and health care, and sending our experts there to provide assistance. A plan from a lead engineer in San Francisco's Department of Public Works, Jeff Lee, won a competition for a sewage treatment plant to help clean up the polluted Huangpu River that flows through Shanghai. The two cities have hosted scores of banquets, sporting events, trade shows, fashion shows, and other events for each other. We have exchanged business students and arranged meetings with business leaders.

We could not have appreciated at the start of this relationship that two of Shanghai's successive mayors—Jiang Zemin and Zhu Rongji—who were regularly visiting San Francisco in the 1980s and early '90s, would become two of China's paramount leaders. Deng Xiaoping, China's leader from 1978 to 1992, named Jiang general secretary of the Communist Party in 1989, a position Jiang would hold for thirteen years. Four years later Jiang's power expanded when he also became China's president.

Zhu served directly under Jiang as China's vice premier beginning in 1991, pushing reforms that over the next decade made him what many consider a principal architect of China after Deng—the China we know today.[7] Zhu believed in the need for markets in tandem with a strong authoritarian government—a tension he believed would provide checks and balances against excesses in each sector.

After Jiang became president, he elevated Zhu to premier (head of the government) in 1998. During Zhu's five years in that post, China's double-digit economic growth resumed. Zhu overcame skeptics among Communist Party leaders who resisted bringing China into the World Trade Organization in 2001. This bold step opened China to a historic wave of foreign investment.

When Jiang was Shanghai's mayor, he didn't strike me as likely leader material for the world's most populous country. In his

2001 book *On China*, Henry Kissinger, President Nixon's secretary of state and advisor to many other presidents, described the same impression: "I would not have expected him to emerge as the leader who would—as he did—guide his country from disaster to the stunning explosion of energy and creativity that has marked China's rise."[8] Jiang never anticipated becoming China's most powerful leader either.

Jiang is a warm, gregarious man. At a banquet hosted by the sister-city committee marking his first trip to San Francisco in 1985, he waltzed with Dianne and sang the 1930s hit "One Day When We Were Young." His English was pretty good, and he loved San Francisco.

After Jiang had been party secretary for a while, and before Dianne was elected to the US Senate, he invited Dianne and me to visit him in Beijing. We hadn't seen him since he had become party secretary. He indicated he wanted to talk about human rights and Tibet, and we were delighted. We met in a historic fifteenth-century pagoda, a magnificent setting in a grove of willow trees on a little island near the Forbidden City, and dined in a gorgeous Qing dynasty home that had been recently restored. After exchanging friendly greetings, however, things went awry— badly awry. Jiang gave us the standard propaganda that Tibet is a historic part of China and that supporters of the Dalai Lama are separatists seeking to break away. I was more than irritated.

When we sat down to a dinner, I pointed to my right wrist. I was wearing the bracelet the young nun had woven during the time of her brutal captivity in Tibet. "Do you see this?" I asked Jiang. "It was given to me by a Tibetan Buddhist nun living in exile in Switzerland. She could have been your daughter; she could have been my daughter. I just want you to know what the People's Liberation Army did to her."

There were about a dozen of us in the room. Dianne was mortified, and gave me a swift kick under the table. Jiang noticed, laughed, and tried to lighten the mood. "Don't do that," he told her, smiling. Turning to me, he recited a quaint Chinese proverb whose translation is, basically, *Don't believe everything you hear.* But my dark mood cast a pall over the dinner, and we soon went our separate ways out into the night.

A few months later Jiang's son, Jiang Mianheng, came to the Bay Area for a dinner in Palo Alto. A PhD in electrical engineering and an old friend, Mianheng once worked for Hewlett-Packard and lived in the United States for many years before returning home as a high-ranking member of the Chinese Academy of Sciences and a leader in the Chinese space program. I drove down from San Francisco to greet him.

"You should come and see my father," he said.

"I'm not sure your father wants to see me," I replied.

"Why?" he asked.

"Do you know about our Tibet conversation?" I asked.

"Yes," he said. "I know all about it. We Chinese have a saying: *Until you have had a really good argument, you can't be true friends.*"

A few months later I found myself walking into a room in Beijing, at Jiang's invitation, where he was chatting with a mutual friend from Shanghai, a founder of those early sister-city programs, T. M. Chang. When Jiang saw me, he came over and hugged me like a long-lost son. Beaming, the first thing he said was, "We Chinese have an old saying: *Until you have had a really good argument, you can't be true friends.*"

We talked for forty-five minutes about the government's early efforts to sell state-owned enterprises, and he asked questions about the broader Chinese economy. (Jiang didn't understand economics very well and often wanted to talk about it. He had a lot of smart people around him, and I was honored, frankly, that he sought my opinions.) Not a word, though, about Tibet from either of us. I finally asked, "How much more time have you got?"

"A few more minutes," he replied.

"You wouldn't expect me to come all this way and not talk about Tibet," I said.

"Of course not," he said. "Let's talk about Tibet."

A world leader, he could easily have dismissed me as the irritating spouse of a US senator. After my outburst, he never had to see me again. But he continued to hear me out over the years on my strong views about Tibet. "You can say whatever you want," he told me on one occasion. I might not have liked what I heard from him, but he always was willing to have an open discussion with me about Tibet. This is one of many reasons I have great respect for Jiang.

The reason we were able to maintain our relationships with Chinese leaders despite our friendship with His Holiness was that we went with the intention of making friends first and built our relationships over time. I think we may have earned the respect of some Chinese officials because we expressed how we felt, we didn't change our views, and we didn't hide the fact that we were not changing our views. I'm also convinced many people high in the Chinese hierarchy don't necessarily think we're wrong on Tibet, but mostly they keep their thoughts to themselves.

His Holiness

His Holiness the Dalai Lama is a warm and open person with a sharp wit and an easy laugh. He is very bright. He had an excellent education as a child, having been tutored from an early age by several learned monks. He has a curious mind and a special interest in science and mechanical devices.

The Thirteenth Dalai Lama died in 1933. Tenzin Gyatso, the Fourteenth Dalai Lama, was born on July 6, 1935—about three weeks before my birth. His Holiness sometimes jokes about our "karmic connection." One day, when we were both seventy-six, in excellent health, and anticipating many more years in this life, he pointed out that a couple of centuries ago, a Dalai Lama said he, meaning Tenzin Gyatso, would live to be 113. I told him I planned to live to 108, the holy Buddhist number, and then say, "Bye-bye, I'll see you in the next incarnation." His Holiness laughed so hard, I thought he was going to fall on the floor.

It was the practice of the first thirteen Dalai Lamas to never or rarely leave Tibet. Few ever traveled even to neighboring India or China. His Holiness certainly is a man of his time, though. He travels widely. Although certainly not by choice, he has lived most of his life—more than sixty years—in exile in Dharamsala, India, and has visited many countries during the past four decades.

The Dalai Lama's first trip to San Francisco in 1979 was a turning point in efforts to call international attention to China's repressive policies toward the Tibetan people. After that, I began to see His Holiness more frequently and our friendship deepened. I see him at least two or three times a year now, either in the United States or in Dharamsala. I always feel privileged being in his presence.[9]

Buddhists don't spend time with the question of whether there is a prime mover, an almighty power. Buddhists simply say that if your main goal in life is happiness, the most important thing you can do is genuinely care for and help other people. His Holiness teaches that in order to have a happy and meaningful life, money and power should be secondary. The most important quality is having a compassionate mind. "Too much greed brings restlessness," he says. "And too much greed creates environmental and economic crisis."

His Holiness has said that if traditional Buddhist beliefs conflict with science, he will side with science. He is particularly interested in neuroscience and recent studies showing that meditation can alter a person's brainwaves. His Holiness believes that hours and years spent in meditation change the brain so that a person becomes kinder and more compassionate. I think that is essentially correct. I know that older *lamas* (Tibetan Buddhist monks) are among the sweetest, kindest people I have ever met.[10]

I totally agree with what His Holiness teaches, but I do not practice any religion. Although I was raised in a Jewish family, we always had the biggest Christmas tree on the block. I thought of Christmas as a seasonal celebration. San Francisco was a pretty tolerant melting pot, even when I was child. I didn't even know there was such a thing as anti-Semitism until I was twelve and some of my friends joined the city's swanky Olympic Club. One of my friends' fathers told my mother that membership was "restricted," but he could get me in. I didn't think I'd be comfortable, so I didn't join.

I see a lot in Buddhism that is beneficial. I believe that genuinely caring about other people and helping them is a good way to lead a happy life. And I consider myself a spiritual person who tries to do the right thing.

His Holiness has not been the official leader of Tibet's exiled government since he announced in 2011 his intention to hand over his formal political authority to an elected leader. "In order for our process of democratization to be complete, the time has come for me to devolve my formal authority to such an elected leadership," he said in a statement marking the fifty-second anniversary of the 1959 Tibetan uprising.

As planned, His Holiness stepped down later in 2011, when he transferred his political authority to the Tibetan Parliament of the Central Tibetan Administration. I was the one foreign guest invited to Dharamsala for the event—quite an honor. For Tibetans, it was a historic day: the first time in a thousand years that a Dalai Lama would not be their political leader. Many were reluctant to see him make the change, but in reality he had not had a significant role in the administration's functioning. Stepping down was more form over substance. Obviously, he remains Tibetan Buddhists' spiritual leader.

The Chinese government has already staked out plans publicly to identify a Fifteenth Dalai Lama, a shameful ploy to inject state influence into the future of Tibetan Buddhism in China. His Holiness says he does not know when he will be reborn. It could be in a year or perhaps a hundred years. He has said that under the current circumstances, he would not want to be reborn inside Tibet.

Choose Your Moments Carefully

At various times in recent history it has seemed that tensions might ease between China and the Tibetan people. Yet protests such as those in Tiananmen Square in 1989 and leading up to the 2008 Summer Olympics in Beijing were searing setbacks for progress in easing China's position on Tibet. The crackdown in Tiananmen Square was the worst thing that could have happened.

In the early 1980s, Chinese leaders who toured Tibet were shocked by the levels of oppression there, and repercussions in Beijing for a time were favorable. Zhao Ziyang, then a liberal force as China's Communist Party leader, advocated improving cultural and religious freedoms for Tibetans and indicated he might be open to a thaw in relations between Beijing and the Dalai Lama. But he was ousted by Deng after Tiananmen Square, which is when Deng appointed Jiang.[11]

Zhao's last public appearance was to support and warn prodemocracy students staging a hunger strike in Tiananmen Square of imminent military action. "We have come too late," he told the protesters. Within hours of Zhao's warning, hundreds of civilian and student protestors died as Chinese troops opened fire and army tanks rolled through demonstrators' encampments near The Great Hall of the People. Several protest leaders and sympathizers later were executed. (An official death toll was never released by the government.) Deng feared more pro-democracy demonstrations would threaten the Communist Party, a reality far advanced by then in the Soviet Union, which collapsed five months later in November 1989.[12]

Nineteen years later, early in 2008, the Chinese were keeping a close eye on international protests against Chinese policies on Tibet and the Dalai Lama. I had expressed my strong views privately in meetings with Jiang and other Chinese leaders, until deciding to speak openly and candidly at pro-Tibetan rallies and elsewhere during the global Olympic Torch tour ahead of the 2008 Summer Olympic Games in Beijing.

The demonstrators hoped to embarrass the Chinese government in the glare of international media coverage. They disrupted the Olympic Torch relay in Paris, London, Athens, San Francisco, and elsewhere. The demonstrations were a mistake, however, because they antagonized China's political elites and emboldened Communist Party hardliners.

"Every Chinese, including ethnic Chinese around the world, saw the Olympics as a great historical moment for China rising as a global player," Lodi Gyari has said. "People forget that the Chinese wanted to host the Olympic Games and were willing to make some concessions here and there. We *should* demonstrate as Tibetans when our interests are compromised or undermined by China. But the Olympics were about China as a nation. Reacting to the demonstrations, the leaders in Beijing reverted to their policy of no compromises." The protests forced China's leaders to dig in and defend their positions.

Small Successes Matter

Dianne and I hand-carried a third letter from His Holiness to Jiang Zemin in 1997, just before Jiang was to leave China on an official visit to the United States, again asking for direct talks between the two of them. I told Jiang that if he announced before he left that he would meet with the Dalai Lama, he would receive a much warmer welcome in the United States. Otherwise, I said, he could expect to see a lot of protestors.

"When you go to someplace like Harvard," I said, "there will be ten thousand bumper stickers that say, 'Save Tibet.' Do you know how I know that?"

"No," he replied.

"Because I had them printed," I said.

He laughed, but my prediction came true. I still remember the look on his face when he saw the bumper stickers and glanced my way. *Blum! I should have known*, he seemed to be thinking, and I sensed he was amused at some level as much or even more than he was irritated. He did not offer any concessions, however, and he ran into a lot of pro-Tibet protests.

Although we were not aware of this at the time, Jiang in fact had recently removed the Chinese government's corrupt, reactionary administrator in the region's capital city of Lhasa, a step that improved conditions for a while for at least some Tibetans. It was one of a handful of cases I recall where Jiang and other senior Chinese officials displayed a modicum of decency toward Tibet.

A Shanghai banker I knew with high-level Beijing influence for some time before this had been relaying to Jiang and his circle several of my descriptions from sources inside Tibet about state-sponsored terror and discrimination against Tibetans. "I believe Richard Blum. I don't believe the United Front," the banker told them. United Front is the group of hardline Communist Party military and political officials in the Forbidden City.

Of course, most government officials in Beijing who heard the reports were dismissive. They exaggerated their successes in Tibet for party leaders in Beijing and downplayed both how deeply the Tibetan people resented Chinese rule and how immense their devotion and loyalty remained to His Holiness. But Jiang secretly sent two trusted confidants into Tibet, disguised as tourists. Those men validated for Jiang that indeed there was widespread oppression. State police routinely broke into people's houses in the middle of the night, arresting some and breaking artifacts—all for no reason.

"I didn't know about this," Jiang told me later. This was as angry as I had ever seen him. He knew he had been lied to and was embarrassed. "I certainly didn't order this to happen. Sure, we want to keep control of the place, but we didn't need to do this to Tibetans who weren't causing any trouble."

His decision to fire that administrator in Lhasa may be my major accomplishment on the issue of Tibet with the Chinese government. I am sure some officials in Beijing would be upset to read this. The party put out a face-saving statement at the time to mask what was in fact a major demotion. (The announcement said the boss was being transferred from Tibet after five years because of high-altitude discomforts.) The fact is, I had developed a relationship with Jiang, and he occasionally listened to me on Tibet.

A *KHATA* AT THE INAUGURATION

The morning of January 20, 2009, Dianne and I were at the White House to join other members of the official inaugural party for Senator Barack Obama at a breakfast hosted by George W. and Laura Bush, one of their last official acts as president and First Lady.

It is a Tibetan tradition to present a silk scarf, or *khata*, as a sign of greeting when meeting someone. His Holiness had blessed and given me a beautiful white khata on his previous visit to the United States. I said to the president-elect during breakfast that His Holiness had wanted me to convey his congratulations, adding that I thought the khata would be a fitting gift and wanted to give it to him. I figured he would add the khata to the pile of inaugural gifts streaming in. "Who do I give it to?" I asked.

"Let me have it," he said, reaching out. "I'm going to put it in my back pocket and keep it there while I've got my hand on the Bible." And he did.

Not long after Dianne, who was leading the inaugural ceremonies, announced, "It is my great personal honor to present the forty-fourth president of these United States, Barack Obama," word spread on pro-Tibetan websites and elsewhere that the new American president had carried a scarf blessed by the Dalai Lama while taking the oath of office. The White House wanted to avoid antagonizing China in the president's first days in office and declined comment about the khata. I did mention the khata story privately but never confirmed it publicly—until now. My belief is that in reaching out for the khata by his own hand that morning, the incoming president was expressing his respect for the Tibetan people's continuing struggle.

China's Long-Term Interests and Long-Term Plan

China's leaders expect that His Holiness, who turned eighty in 2015, before long will become incapacitated and die. After that, they believe, Tibetan dreams of independence will fade and China then will control, without debate, the process for identifying the Fifteenth Dalai Lama as the leader of Tibetan Buddhism. Game over: The Chinese Communist Party owns the future of Tibetan Buddhism.

This scenario is flawed for at least three reasons. To begin with, Tibetans are not seeking political independence. They want to preserve their culture and way of life, while conceding political sovereignty to China. Next, the Dalai Lama is in excellent physical and mental health. He has an alert mind and a playful sense of humor. His physicians tell him he may live to be one hundred; the Dalai Lama himself says his dreams tell him he will live to be 113. Finally, as a matter of pragmatism and expedience for the Chinese, His Holiness is the best possible negotiating partner they have to avoid escalating social unrest over Tibet.

This last point is important in understanding why a resolution of the Tibetan problem is in the long-term interest of China and the Chinese people. Lodi has explained it well:

> If the Dalai Lama is unable to return to Tibet before he dies or something happens to him, the Tibetan people for generations will not forgive the Chinese. There will be an incurable, untreatable cancer between them. The resentment of the Tibetan people will multiply.
>
> Politicians will try to take over Tibetan leadership. Candidates will compete in making the most provocative statements, such as, "I want complete independence for Tibet" or "I want to start a resistance against the Chinese." If you want to negotiate a settlement, you have to make compromises. In my experience, politicians have difficulty making compromises.
>
> This is my single most important message to China's leaders: When you eventually want to seek a solution, if the Dalai Lama is not living, there will be no one authoritative to deal with. I hope Xi Jinping is intelligent enough to see that the Dalai Lama is not the problem; he can be the solution. But personally I do not think there will be any major shift.

Are Lodi, Dianne, and I hopeful about Xi Jinping agreeing to meet with His Holiness, then permitting him to return to Tibet? Let me put it this way: There is no mission in my life on which I have invested so much time and energy and had so little to show for it.

"The great mystery about China's policy is why it seems to have decided that its best hope lies with the next Dalai Lama, not this one," *The Economist* says.

> Unlike many Tibetans, he has accepted Chinese sovereignty. He has used his enormous prestige to urge Tibetans to refrain from violent resistance . . . To safeguard its internal security, placate its disgruntled Tibetan citizens, and improve its international reputation, common senses suggests China should start talking seriously to the Fourteenth Dalai Lama.[13]

We see plenty of evidence that China's current policy toward Tibet is the harshest in many years. China has tried to stop the flow of refugees fleeing the country, by arresting or shooting anyone they find trying to cross the border. Although Nepal nominally has agreed to continue accepting refugees from Tibet, as it has done for more than fifty years, China has been paying Nepalese soldiers and police for years to round them up and send them back. Chinese soldiers have been on maneuvers near the border with Nepal and even crossed into Nepal near Mustang in recent years, according to Nepalese border guards we spoke with when we were there. Officials in Kathmandu claimed they knew nothing about it, but I am inclined to believe the border guards.

The last time I encountered these deportations personally was back in 2003. I learned then about ten young Tibetans the Nepalese police had arrested. We tried to get them freed and even appealed personally to King Gyanendra for their release. We received assurances that they were not going to be returned to China. But the next day they were driven across the border, where they were no doubt jailed and most likely tortured.

By the summer of 2015, the Chinese were stepping up pressure on foreign leaders quite effectively, too. Pope Francis and heads of state in Norway, Sri Lanka, and South Africa all rejected overtures from His Holiness for private meetings. The Chinese government continues to serve up tired propaganda. In April 2015, the government asserted that His Holiness had a "sentimental attachment to the old theocratic feudal serfdom" and should give up his goals of Tibetan "independence" and "dividing China."[14]

We've heard this too many times over the years. Let me repeat: China's arguments against His Holiness are just nonsense. In the first two of three letters Dianne and I personally delivered to Jiang Zemin, one in 1991 and a second in 1993, His Holiness said outright, "I'm not asking for independence." It made no difference.

Opportunity Not Lost

In 2007 China's ambassador to Washington twice visited Dianne to request that she not carry out her plan to have the Congressional Gold Medal awarded to His Holiness. She told the ambassador she would agree only if the Chinese government said publicly it would meet with the Dalai Lama. China refused, and the award ceremony went ahead as planned in the Capitol rotunda with President George W. Bush and many members of Congress participating.[15]

In her speech honoring His Holiness, Dianne said:

> This world is filled with conflict and strife. But the
> Dalai Lama transcends this world and inspires us with

hope. To know him is to know compassion. To listen to him is to learn wisdom. To be close to him is to feel the presence of something very special . . . I truly believe that if the Chinese leadership were to sit down with the Dalai Lama, they together could work out a solution whereby he would be able to return to his native Tibet, which has long been his hope and dream. This has sadly been a lost opportunity.[16]

No one can say if and when talks with the Chinese about the return of His Holiness will resume. After talks collapsed in 2010, Lodi Gyari stepped down as chief negotiator for His Holiness. "There is nothing to negotiate," Lodi said at the time.

Yet His Holiness and Lodi Gyari do retain a measure of optimism. They note that the initial priorities of Xi Jinping understandably have been fighting Communist Party corruption and consolidating personal power. "The new leader is not someone we should give up on," Lodi has said, noting that Xi likely will remain in power through 2022, when the Dalai Lama would be eighty-seven years old.

His Holiness remains positive. He says that the Chinese leader "has Buddhists in his family. His mother even practices Tibetan Buddhism." Does *he* believe he will return to his Tibetan homeland one day? "Yes, I am sure of that," he told a journalist in 2014.[17]

Before His Holiness and I said good-bye in Dharamsala the day in 2011 that he stepped down from his role as Tibet's leader in exile, he handed me three small gifts. One was a ring for Dianne. Another was a ring for me. The third was a lovely silver Buddhist wheel of life.

Dianne and I still have those rings, and I have kept that silver wheel mounted in my office. It sits next to an honor His

Holiness gave me in 1999 for my work for Tibet, the Light of Truth Award. These gifts are constant reminders of our long friendship, and the sense of urgency I feel to do whatever I can to help Tibetans achieve a better life.

Part 4

Enabling Others to Solve the Problems of Poverty

Chapter 12

Merging Disciplines to Fight Poverty

*"Education is the most powerful weapon which
you can use to change the world."*

—Nelson Mandela

It was the fall of 2004. Robert Birgeneau, chancellor of the Berkeley campus, and I were walking near the Campanile, the landmark bell and clock tower rising more than three hundred feet above the heart of campus. I can't tell you why, but something clicked in my mind, and I asked him, "Is there any kind of global poverty program here?"

"Well, no," he replied. "Not really."

"This place hasn't really changed much in forty years," I said. You could still take an introductory course in art history or music appreciation, but you couldn't take a basic course in global poverty. So we started thinking about how we might change that. The opening idea simply was to start a survey course anyone could take to learn about poverty. That was it.

Once we began exploring that idea with deans and faculty

from different schools and colleges around campus, we realized that courses in business, engineering, public health, and other fields were deeply relevant to the topic. I started to think that establishing a program was a good idea.

Soon we had pulled together a planning group, including academic deans and faculty from the schools of law, business, and engineering and from the Lawrence Berkeley National Laboratory and the UC Davis campus. As I've said before, I feel strongly about including business to teach management of development projects. Then, too, Berkeley Lab was essential for its world-class stature in science research. So was the UC Davis campus, with its excellent programs for improving the health and nutrition of the poor around the globe. All these schools, departments, and people helped take on the challenge of creating a strong curriculum on poverty and income inequality.

A brilliant and lovely man who was dean of the engineering school at the time, Richard Newton, told me one day he thought engineering would be the logical partner for a program in global poverty. I had been thinking the business school would be the right partner, but Richard changed my mind in about ten minutes. You help bring people out of poverty with innovation, he said, adding, "And that means engineering." Sadly, he passed away suddenly from pancreatic cancer only months later and so was not able to see the impact this insight soon would make.

Ananya Roy, a scholar and inspiring lecturer on international poverty and global development, and part of our initial team, reflected on the early discussions: "We had to ask ourselves, what is our competitive advantage? What is our role as a great public research university in these struggles in inequality? What do we do for students who are really passionate about development?"

We had no grand plan—only a goal, a willingness to experiment to figure out what worked best, and a desire to keep things moving. It was very much blue-sky thinking. The answers to the questions we asked helped us develop guiding principles, such as "to teach the ethics of global citizenship."

The deans and faculty members working with me suggested we put together a center. I realized it would take a few years to get it going, and agreed to commit funds to bring our plans to life. It turned out that what we were creating—what would become the Blum Center for Developing Economies—was innovative in many ways.

My work on the Blum Center has been some of the most rewarding in my life. Students from a variety of disciplines come together and talk about global poverty issues and then go out in the field and actually do something about it. Our goal is for them to think and collaborate across disciplines and sectors—an approach I know is necessary to solve these problems.

As far as we knew when we began in 2005, no university had a multidisciplinary center like this for undergraduate students who wanted to take on global poverty issues. Now, many universities do, and our approach has been replicated at universities in the United States and around the world. Nothing could make us more hopeful for real solutions to the complex problems of poverty.

Global Citizens, Cutting-Edge Technologies

We started the Center with a two-pronged approach: enlist Berkeley faculty and students in finding technological solutions to the most pressing needs of the poor, and educate students who are motivated to make a difference in the lives of the poor, through the Global Poverty and Practice (GPP) minor. Our goal is to educate them so they *can* make a difference.

Even though poverty studies could certainly be a major, we decided to offer a minor because knowledge from every field can be a factor in alleviating poverty. We wanted our students to bring what they were learning in a diverse set of majors into our classes and out in the field. Our GPP minor is rigorous: a comprehensive, demanding introductory course followed by two courses bracketing an eight-week field experience. Time in the field is key. Most students volunteer with nonprofits, governments, or community-based organizations in a developing country, but increasing numbers are helping similar groups that serve poor communities in the United States. A few sign on with advocacy groups in Washington, DC, or the Bay Area.

My own study-abroad and travel experiences in Europe and North Africa opened my eyes to global poverty when I was a Berkeley undergraduate. And I learned the value of listening to people many times over in Nepal, starting with Sherpas in the Khumbu. I knew that opportunities to live in the villages alongside local people could show our students how these people usually know better than any "experts" from Western governments or NGOs how to improve their living situation.

Two key priorities at the Center are to educate students to be global citizens and to take cutting-edge technology (which Berkeley is famous for) and put it to work in the service of the poor. We want students to have a better understanding of problems people face in the developing world and of how to find their place as global citizens in a post–Cold War world. In their field practice, students get a Peace Corps–like experience *before* they begin their careers—the sort of real-world education experienced by many volunteers in the twenty-first-century Peace Corps, who are often mid- or late-career individuals recruited for special talents and expertise.

We want students, when they work with poor people, to think of themselves as apprentices. We want students to approach their field experiences with modesty and humility, and to reflect more deeply about their place in the world. That mind-set can only come from living among the poor people we hope to serve. As John Hardman of The Carter Center pointed out (and described in chapter 4), people in poor circumstances know how to improve their living situation. They just lack the resources, training, and tools to do it.

In a speech at the US Naval Academy in 2014, former president Bill Clinton echoed the Dalai Lama's message about the need for empathy in human relations and, in effect, articulated why we at the Blum Center believe field experience is so essential:

> I believe a very important leadership skill in the twenty-first century is the ability to remember that no matter how alien somebody looks to you and no matter how deep the conflict is, they have a story, too. They have their hopes, they have their dreams, they have their disappointments, and they have their nightmares. I think we have undervalued the ability not just to tell stories, but to listen to them. Once you know somebody else's story, it then becomes possible against all the odds to build some measure of trust. For all the high-tech solutions to the world that make us think we can quantify all this in big numbers, personal trust still counts for something, and its absence is devastating.[1]

The course that students take before heading into the field—Ethics, Methods, and Pragmatics—is a deep-dive into the countries and cultures where they are going to work. When they hit the ground, they need to know the sociopolitical situation and to avoid being naïve. Students in that course read widely on all that might be relevant to their experience. They learn how to take a survey; how to document their experience with photos, videos, blogs, and so forth; and how to respect the place they are going and the people with whom they will live and interact.

When students return to campus, they enroll in the Reflection Course Group Seminar. The focus is just as the title suggests:

Students are required through a rigorous process to reflect on what they learned in the field, what mistakes they made, particular circumstances they encountered, and any contradictions they observed. The seminar is important, instructive, and powerful.

We find that after a field experience, students dive into their classes. They say they liked the fieldwork, and want to stay connected somehow while continuing their campus studies. Often, they find a local organization in the Bay Area that provides experiences similar to what they found during their weeks in the field.

A SHORT COURSE ON US POVERTY, WEALTH, AND INCOME INEQUALITY

Since 1975, the number of people living below the poverty line in the United States has been steadily rising, according to statistics from the US Census Bureau.[2] And while the percentage of our population living in poverty hit a low in 2000 of 11.3 percent (about equal to the low seen in the early 1970s), it has been rising fairly steadily ever since. In 2014, the poverty rate was 14.8 percent, which means *46.7 million people in our country are living in poverty.*

The statistics on children living in poverty are more gruesome. In 2012, child poverty in the United States hit a staggering 24.2 percent, according to a UNICEF report.[3] Between 2008 and 2012, when 1.8 million more children fell into poverty in our country, Norway, Australia, Chile, Finland, and Poland reduced child poverty by about 30 percent. Given all these sad statistics, it's not surprising that an increasing percentage of the Blum Center's students are doing their fieldwork in the United States.

Is poverty increasing in our country because of an increasing inequality of wealth and income? And if so, is it really a problem? These are the two core questions Bob Reich explores with students who flock to his Wealth and Poverty lectures.[4] They are the most popular on campus, filling the seven-hundred-seat Wheeler Auditorium to overflowing. Bob's answer to both questions: a resounding yes. A strong middle class is vital for a stable, growing economy and engaging citizens in our democracy, but you won't have a strong middle class if the equality of income and wealth continues to deteriorate.

Bob covers several key themes in his lectures:

- **Unequal distribution of wealth and income**

  - Between the 1970s and 2012, the US economy as measured per capita grew approximately 150 percent, yet median wages declined. We are now at the point that while the United States has one of the world's most robust economies, it also has the most unequal distribution of wealth and income.[5]

  - Most income benefits generated by the recovery since the Great Recession are felt only by those at the very top. The richest four hundred individuals in America have more wealth than the bottom 150 million.

- **Difference in average pay between the typical worker and the top 1 percent**

  - During the 1970s, the typical male worker earned approximately $48,300, and someone fortunate enough to be in the top 1 percent took home around $393,000. By 2010, that typical male worker's income had plunged by approximately $14,000 (adjusted for inflation) to $33,700 a year, but that average person in the top 1 percent of earners was making close to $1.1 million.

  - Three coping mechanisms have helped the middle

class postpone the decline in household purchasing power: Women entered the work force in droves, adding a second family income; most people worked longer hours, sometimes adding a second or even a third job; and many families increased their debt, often by refinancing their home mortgages. Inevitably, as we all know, that mortgage bubble burst.

- **Equal opportunity as an inalienable right**

  - With US economic output doubling in this period, and median income (adjusted for inflation) falling by approximately 30 percent, how can anyone say that economic growth alone is the solution to poverty? Simply adding jobs is not the answer. Individuals on the poorest rungs of the social ladder find themselves working not one but sometimes two or three jobs just to make ends meet.

  - A college degree is more valuable than ever in terms of potential lifetime income, yet it's likely that new college graduates will spend some years in jobs for which they're overqualified.[6] Nongrads are being pushed into ever more menial work, if they can get work at all—a major reason their pay is dropping.

  - The extremes of income inequality are so great that they now threaten our society's foundation of equal opportunity for the pursuit of happiness as an inalienable right.

Real-World Engineering

If you can invent a better metering system for distributing affordable electricity in rural India, or figure out how a smartphone can see and transmit images of tuberculosis cells from a blood smear on a slide taken from a finger prick of someone in rural Vietnam, you can help people in poor, remote areas by the tens of thousands and, over time, maybe millions. In fact, these two innovations are not "ifs." They were both invented by Berkeley faculty and students.

One characteristic that makes the Blum Center unusual is that engineering has been integral from the beginning. "When you involve an engineering school in poverty studies, you appeal to a class of students who want to figure out how to do something," explained our longtime friend George Shultz, former secretary of state.

Exactly.

We encourage and support inventions created in science and engineering research labs at Berkeley that address this imposing challenge of global poverty. Similarly, we fund applied research *in the field* that faculty and research experts believe will improve the lives of poor people. We do this because regular feedback from people on the ground early in the R&D process helps experts in the engineering lab keep the iterations of their inventions practical and accelerates the process. In many development research programs, collaborations among team members in the field and in the lab typically come too late, after prototypes are created. We also fund students' travel to remote areas internationally, where they can and do help researchers connect with poor people during early stages of ambitious R&D projects.

One of my ambitions is to harness the tools and creativity of venture capital investing to rapidly scale these inventions. After the inventions are proven in the field, we help students and faculty pursue funding from government agencies, interested NGOs, private and corporate foundations—and eventually private investors. We want to get these inventions into the hands of millions of people who can benefit from them as fast as we can. This sense of urgency is part of what is required to eliminate extreme poverty.

Smartphone Microscopes, Rapid Diagnostics

By early 2015, among our successes at Berkeley was CellScope, an invention I mentioned at the start of this section. CellScope transforms the camera of a standard smartphone into a diagnostic microscope that can transmit detailed images of blood cells magnified many times. The invention, greatly advanced from the first prototype in 2007, brings the imaging capability of a $150,000 lab microscope to any rural village that can be reached by backpackers, at a cost of less than $1,000 with potential to fall further.

Trained technicians can draw blood samples from villagers with a simple pinprick and then transmit sample images to labs thousands of miles away. A diagnosis of tuberculosis, malaria, or river blindness can be made within hours instead of weeks. Field tests supported by the World Health Organization in health clinics and small hospitals in rural Vietnam and Cameroon proved CellScope's effectiveness.

The CellScope team, led by engineering professor Dan Fletcher, has raised substantial funding from prestigious donors such as the Bill & Melinda Gates Foundation, the Vodafone Americas Foundation, Microsoft Research, and Intel.[7] At my urging, the university filed for patents for CellScope in the United States, Canada, China, India, and the European Union.

THE POLI SCI MAJOR WHO LEARNED TO LOVE THE LAB

As the CellScope team worked through their first year of field tests in Vietnam, they brought on an undergraduate assistant who had studied Vietnamese in high school. Anh-Thi Le, a political science major with no experience in technology or real lab work, had just completed her GPP fieldwork in India, helping a women's organization that aided traditional artisans and connected them to consumers in the US fair-trade community. Anh-Thi had been struck during those months by the myriad ways public health problems held back poor women in India, and she quickly grasped why the CellScope project could be significant. In an essay for the Center's publications, Anh-Thi explained what it was like to make an unexpected leap into the lab from social sciences:

> I remember feeling intimidated during my first meeting with the CellScope team. It was my first time stepping foot in a lab at Berkeley. While I was extremely excited about the opportunity, I was nervous about my qualifications. I was a social sciences student with little experience in global health. I remember being lost when computer programming terms were tossed around, and having to review how to properly wear and take off my latex gloves in the lab (sounds silly, but it's important!).
>
> Yet for many clinicians in the field, working with CellScope would be the first time they had ever used a computer. In many ways, if I could not understand how to use a part of the CellScope device or software, neither would a clinician.
>
> Despite the challenges, I can't remember a time I did not love working in the lab. Neil Switz, a post-doctoral scholar in the Fletcher Lab, and I conducted

weekly Skype calls late at night with physicians in Hà Nôi to troubleshoot the device; spent hours replicating, testing, and solving problems; reviewed hundreds of images to check on quality control; and created countless manuals/instruction guidelines on everything from computer usage to reading sputum slides.

I had never imagined myself working in an engineering lab, let alone collaborating with physicians in Vietnam on a clinical study with the potential to impact thousands of lives, but Neil taught me that I didn't necessarily need to be an expert in global health or engineering to contribute.[8]

Big Ideas@Berkeley

Student projects originating on the Berkeley campus often amaze and inspire us before they are even in the field. Many are vetted, advised, and supported through Big Ideas@Berkeley, a campus-wide competition for interdisciplinary teams of undergraduates and graduates. Big Ideas is an incubator for students to pursue genuine positive change in the world. Two of our trustees, Andrew and Virginia Rudd, provide key funding.

Big Ideas is a brilliant process. Mentors and judges have included leaders from the World Bank, USAID, Google.org, Intel, the Bill & Melinda Gates Foundation, the Hewlett Foundation, and Grameen Bank, and many outstanding Berkeley professors—among them, Dr. Arthur Rosenfeld, emeritus professor of physics at Berkeley Labs and winner of the Enrico Fermi Award for lifetime achievement in energy research. The program demonstrates how a prize competition offering students the barest amount of seed capital can stimulate projects we never would have imagined, such as mentoring high school women in Oakland who are dreaming of a college education, and training staff in rural hospitals with no access to electricity how to use a solar-powered lighting device in their delivery rooms. Project categories have included global poverty alleviation, clean and sustainable energy alternatives, creative expression for social justice, open data, promoting human rights, and scaling up big ideas.

Big Ideas winners are Blum Center heroes. We always fund top-ranking entries. We want winners taking the next steps that in time can lead to amazing benefits for people in poverty *and* attract millions of dollars in private capital to keep building. We push for innovation, field tests, ongoing iterations, and ultimately scaling to dimensions that will bring the results of their genius to help millions of people. Our message to students is they don't have to get a PhD before their ambitious ideas are taken seriously. If they have an idea and a plan, they can get started right away.

Our center is a hybrid. We don't compete with departments for the standard spoils of career-building in academic institutions: research grants, faculty positions, and graduate programs. We offer an array of programs and opportunities, leveraging the resources that already exist within the university and adding some of our own to the mix, to help students and faculty pursue their dreams and apply their talents to alleviating poverty.

Often, It Takes an Outsider

The progress of the Center and the students and faculty involved would not have been possible without the work of some very capable leaders.

Berkeley's College of Engineering dean, Shankar Sastry, has built his career at the intersection of technology and social impact. Shankar studied at the prestigious India Institute of Technology in Bombay before completing two graduate engineering degrees at Berkeley and heading an institute on campus called the Center for Information Technology Research in the Interest of Society (CITRIS). He became the Blum Center's chief academic officer, or faculty director, in 2007.

Shankar led the charge in establishing the new field of academic study for PhD students known as development engineering. In his words, development engineering promotes "high-quality research and development that more reliably advances sustainable social and economic welfare." In 2013, we made him the chief scientist of a new program, the Development Impact Lab.

Laura D'Andrea Tyson headed the Council of Economic Advisors in the Clinton administration and now chairs the Blum Center's board of trustees. Former dean of the London Business School and of Berkeley's Haas School of Business, she is a professor at the Haas School and head of its Institute for Business and Social Impact. Laura has worked with me and the board to build the Blum Center's teaching and research programs. "You almost always find there is an outsider when these things are created, because insiders tend to look at problems from their disciplinary perspective," she has said. In other words, business professors see business problems and solutions, law professors see legal problems and solutions, and few see the bigger picture. What does she think is necessary to break through siloes in thinking? "An outside agitator with capital. It would be very hard to get faculty from different disciplines to come together, hang out, and create an interdisciplinary minor on poverty alleviation unless there were resources to support the research interests of their different disciplines."

My commitment to provide private funding obviously has helped keep the Center's progress on a fast track. Because we are a multidisciplinary center, not a college or school with a specific academic focus, we have more freedom to manage the Center's programs and to be a catalyst of many talents and academic fields that can help people out of poverty. Our center is a *source* of funds for the fourteen schools and colleges across campus.

With two strokes—outside funding and cooperation from Berkeley's Office of the Chancellor—we sidestepped many predictable departmental rivalries. Money for research, for faculty positions, and for graduate students to support research is the currency of major universities. Too often, jockeying among deans within limited university budgets inhibits or blocks interdepartmental collaboration. Collaboration increasingly is necessary.

Great universities must encourage collaboration. Just as businesses do in competitive markets, great universities need to keep pace with and respond to a rapidly changing world. They owe this to their students both to make the college experience more valuable and to better prepare students to take on the major challenges of the twenty-first century.

"In the world college students live in today, problems can't be solved by any one discipline," said Maryanne McCormick, executive director of the Blum Center since 2008. "Students have to understand the social, technical, economic, and cultural aspects of a problem to begin to address it." This is why the Center has a multidisciplinary structure built around new technologies with great potential for the developing world. We aim to bridge gaps that often lie between innovations in the lab and actual effective deployment, to help tens of millions of the more than two billion people who live on less than $2 a day.

Even our trustees—their background, credentials, and areas of expertise—reflect our mission. I have already mentioned Laura Tyson; Steven Chu, President Obama's first energy secretary; and Mark Yudof, president emeritus of the University of California. Two of my valued business partners who helped drive Newbridge Capital's great success in Asia, Dan Carroll and Weijian Shan, also are trustees. So are two humanitarian leaders who have been at my side for many years: Dr. John

Hardman, of The Carter Center, and Erica Stone, of the American Himalayan Foundation.

The diverse backgrounds of our trustees helps ensure that the mission of the Center is fulfilled.

Venture Capital Model for Academia, Government, and NGOs

I always tell people to think of the Center's innovation program, the Development Impact Lab, as a venture capital model adapted to academia. The lab had an impressive start, with fifty projects funded and impacts in twenty-five countries, due in large part to strong backing from Rajiv Shah. In late 2012, USAID committed $20 million to the Center to support Development Impact Lab projects.

Raj and his colleagues at USAID were so impressed by Development Impact Lab that a year later they established a university consortium modeled on the lab, to promote new technologies that improve the lives of poor people. An incubator for start-ups, the Higher Education Solutions Network (HESN) includes seven universities—Berkeley, the Massachusetts Institute of Technology, College of William and Mary, Duke, Michigan State, Texas A&M, and Makerere University in Uganda—plus two research institutions. The universities were chosen from nearly five hundred applications from forty-nine states and thirty-three countries. HESN was funded with $137 million over five years from USAID and matching funds from participating universities. The mission is to leverage great research in universities to address problems of global poverty.

Late in 2014, forty students showcased fascinating technology innovations—all targeted to developing economies—through brief pitches as individuals or small teams before more than four hundred students from these universities as well as speakers and potential investors representing Facebook, Google, Apple, and other Silicon Valley giants and venture capital firms.

The three-day conference, TechCon 2014, was thrilling to watch—absolutely some of my most exciting days ever at the Blum Center. Many teams competing for top honors received standing ovations. Here are a few examples of their work:

- A blood recycling and transfusion device with a simple pump and filter and a sari to filter blood for reuse

- Drone technology to improve forest mapping and monitoring in order to slow deforestation in Indonesia

- Fieldwork in Sudan addressing hepatitis E outbreaks[9] by a PhD postdoctoral expert and in Central America to improve contaminated water systems by a PhD candidate, both of Berkeley and the Blum Center.

It won't be long before promising business ventures emerge from HESN's Global Development Lab. Raj predicted a few years ago that the collaboration will enable the federal government to "recapture the legacy of science, technology, and innovation as core drivers of development."[10] I couldn't agree more. Global leaders in development must embrace the inventors of scalable new technologies—and investors or private foundations willing to back them—if we are serious about continuing to reduce extreme poverty in the next twenty years.

Raj Shah led the way for USAID on this. A former executive at the Bill & Melinda Gates Foundation, where he headed a strategic opportunities effort and managed a $1.5 billion fund for vaccine innovation, Raj markedly improved the focus, senior management, and impact of the agency, opening it up to broader collaborations with entrepreneurs, scientists, inventors, and financiers. In HESN's Global Development Lab alone, these networks extend beyond more than one hundred partner institutions in academia, civil society, and government across thirty-eight countries.

Center students also participate in a nationwide conference each year, organized by the Clinton Global Initiative, that includes potential financial backers—NGOs, government agencies, and other groups—for the students' ideas. The purpose is to spark and then scale innovative solutions to global challenges in education, environment and climate change, peace and human rights, poverty alleviation, or public health.

In 2014, the second year our center sponsored Berkeley's participation in the Clinton Global Initiative, thirty-four Berkeley students from a wide range of majors (biology, math, neuroscience, political science, and business administration, among others) presented on seventeen different projects. Following are a few examples:

- Helping amputees in Jaipur, India, receive and adjust to new prosthetic limbs

- Building and delivering fifty new bicycle ambulances costing $400 each at no charge to villagers in rural Uganda

- Developing and delivering safe, low-cost baby incubators to save lives in rural hospitals in South Asia

Taking Students Seriously

We had no idea how successful the Blum Center for Developing Economies would be—or how fast it would all happen. When Ananya Roy's global poverty lectures were added to the course catalogue in 2005, we expected thirty students to sign up. A hundred came. Just a few years after we officially formed the Center in 2006, Global Poverty and Practice studies became Berkeley's most popular minor. We were drawing more students than some majors. By the close of the spring 2015 semester, more than thirteen thousand Berkeley students had taken our courses and more than six hundred had completed the GPP minor.

All ten campuses in the UC system now have Blum Centers. Most focus on poverty issues in their regions, such as a cross-border initiative at UC San Diego; poverty and health issues in Latin America for students at the UCLA center; and community development at UC Merced, where more than 60 percent of students are the first in their family to attend college and many are sons or daughters of migrant workers.

Oftentimes when you think you are Thinking Big, you really aren't Thinking Big enough. We also vastly underestimated the number of faculty already researching the problems of poverty, in disciplines ranging from engineering to business to architecture, and who were eager to join the Center's network. In the past year, we expanded internationally for the first time with programs at Central European University in Budapest, partnering with investor–philanthropist George Soros, and Hebrew University of Jerusalem, where my daughter Annette Blum was a matchmaker in helping faculty roll out programs tailored for Palestinians as well as Israelis.

Then, just as we were finishing this book, more than twelve hundred students from more than eighty countries came to Berkeley in the spring of 2016 for three days under banners of Clinton Global Initiative University, UC Berkeley, and the Blum Center to showcase and share brilliant inventions and concepts. It was a festival of youthful genius, hope, and commitment, hosted by President Clinton and his daughter Chelsea Clinton. Taking this all in, my thoughts for a moment drifted back to seeing JFK paint his vision for the Peace Corps at the Cow Palace when I was in my twenties decades earlier. How far we have come.

Today our center is organized around three pillars: First, a wide selection of hands-on, interdisciplinary courses in the edgiest (and hardest to fund) areas of engineering and the social sciences. Next, undergraduate and graduate student projects that have the greatest potential for impact and scale. And finally, a network of faculty, staff, and practitioners who serve as mentors.

By the summer of 2016, we had sent 822 students to sixty-nine countries for their field or "practice" experience since 2007. We funded travel and other expenses for nearly half of those practice experiences, with stipends collectively exceeding $700,000.

Eighty percent of our students have been women; many are the first in their family to attend college, qualify for federal Pell Grants because of their family's low income, or both. Half the students enrolled in the College of Engineering's PhD minor in development engineering are women. Their work includes "designing affordable solutions for clean drinking water, inventing medical diagnostic equipment for neglected tropical diseases, and enabling local manufacturing in poor and remote regions," according to Lina Nilsson, the gifted former head of the Development Impact Lab, in her 2015 *New York Times* op-ed article "How to Attract Female Engineers." She added, "Women seem to be drawn to engineering projects that attempt to achieve societal good."[11]

Millennials are truly passionate about social change, particularly around questions of poverty and inequality. Yet until recently, universities had really not helped students channel that enthusiasm. They hadn't given them a better understanding of how to work alongside people in the field on practical problems of public service, planning, and social justice. We were convinced the option to minor in global poverty issues would appeal to many students, especially if they could remain committed to majoring in any other field of study on campus, whether in physical or social sciences. And we were right.

Even for other students on their way to being teachers, business managers, doctors, or lawyers, taking our introductory course, "Global Poverty: Challenges and Hopes in the New Millennium," or attending Bob Reich's Wealth and Poverty lectures might reveal opportunities they otherwise would have overlooked to make a difference in the lives of the poor.

Many young people believe most politicians in Washington, DC, and state capitals obstruct solutions to the big problems millennials care most about, such as climate change and income inequality. Given the gridlock and rhetoric they've observed for years, who can blame them? "Their skepticism toward politics is very high," Bob Reich has said of millennials, "but their desire to get involved in some form of public service is higher still." The center taps and channels this enthusiasm for public service, and according to Bob, "It takes students seriously; it works with students."

Our goal in founding and building the Center was to help educate the next generation of leaders who are passionate about reducing poverty in the world. "We are reaching a whole community of students who feel they are part of a movement," Lina Nilsson once pointed out. "When you think you are part of something bigger, and you can build on past successes, that is really powerful."

As we show through four stories of young alumni in the next chapter, we have every confidence this rising generation of activists in global poverty is off to a great start.

In 2010, when we held dedication ceremonies for the Blum Center's new home—the old Naval Architecture Building, a National Register of Historic Places building that we renovated extensively but delicately—a big crowd of students, faculty, and friends gathered outside the building. In my remarks I said, "I had a dream of a place that could inspire a generation of young people who care about doing something about the world's inequalities. We've achieved more than I ever could have imagined." In many ways, we were just at the beginning.

Blum Center *for* Developing Economies Field Experience Countries, 2007–2016

LATIN AMERICA
Argentina
Barbados
Bolivia
Brazil
Chile
Colombia
Costa Rica
Cuba
Ecuador
El Salvador
Guatemala
Haiti

Honduras
Mexico
Nicaragua
Panama
Peru
Venezuela

OTHERS
United States (North America)
French Polynesia (Asia Pacific)
Samoa (Asia Pacific)

AFRICA
Cameroon
Democratic Republic
of Congo
Egypt
Ethiopia
Ghana
Kenya
Madagascar
Malawi
Morocco
Nigeria
Rwanda
Senegal

Sierra Leone
South Africa
Sudan
Tanzania
Togo
Uganda
Zambia
Zimbabwe

ASIA
Afghanistan
Bangladesh
Cambodia
China

India
Indonesia
Kashmir
Malaysia
Nepal
Pakistan
Philippines
Singapore
South Korea
Sri Lanka
Taiwan
Thailand
Vietnam

EUROPE
France
Greece
Hungary
Spain
Switzerland
Ukraine

MIDDLE EAST
Israel
Jordan
Lebanon
Palestine
Saudi Arabia

Chapter 13

Proof of Progress

"Education is not the filling of a pail,
but the lighting of a fire."

—William Butler Yeats

Every day, more alumni of some program of the Blum Center for Developing Economies are tackling urgent and complex problems in poverty as entrepreneurs, scholars, activists, and global citizens. Following their accomplishments makes me and everybody involved with the Center very grateful and more hopeful. It is proof of progress, proof that we have helped prepare thousands of students to make the developing world—as Jimmy Carter aptly states the challenge—"work better for its people."

For me, the four profiles that follow are emblematic of many remarkable alumni who are touching thousands of lives, and soon, perhaps, millions.

These projects and innovations are helping people now in cities or isolated rural villages recycle waste from landfills, experience the marvel of reliable electric power for the first time, understand consumer rights in microfinance, and use bicycles and bicycle shops to improve their daily lives.

We hope you will agree these four alumni illustrate the power of the Center's multidisciplinary model—and those of other organizations and programs with similar approaches and goals.

Nearly all students come to us before their first class with a passion, energy, and intellectual drive to fight poverty. Our work is to give them the tools and the resources to do this effectively and with compassion. Our mission, in the broadest sense, is enabling them to carry on—in their own unique ways—UC Berkeley's legacy of commitment, innovation, and social impact in the world.

Making Citizenship Mean Something: Pronita Saxena

Pronita Saxena lived in India's capital, New Delhi, for the first ten years of her life. One day, at the age of seven, she was riding in a car when her mother stopped in traffic. A scruffy boy about the same age as Pronita came up to the window, pleading for money. Pronita looked away, grimacing. As they drove on, her mother scolded Pronita, saying, "Don't ever forget; it's sheer luck that you ended up on this side of the window and that boy ended up on the other side."

Be Humble, Ask Questions, Seek Understanding

The haunting image of the boy stayed with Pronita, and as the years passed she began to wonder: If it was just "luck" that that boy was on the other side of the window—or, as we might say—*an accident of geography*, then why shouldn't every child have opportunity as she did? Family wealth or social status shouldn't matter so much.

Pronita's mother, a high school teacher of math, physics, and computer science, comes from generations of activists in

India's struggle for independence and democracy. Over the years she and Pronita's father, a software engineer, inspired in Pronita a deep sense of civic duty. The family moved to southern California, where she learned about the American system of justice in her high school mock trial club and as an intern at a Glendale law firm. Curious about how the law worked in India, she interned one summer with a nonprofit group in Delhi that publishes manuals in Hindi about citizen rights. One project was attempting to simplify the law for prostitutes and girls even younger than Pronita who had been forced into prostitution through trafficking. "The law didn't mean anything to a girl who had been trafficked from Nepal to India, hadn't even been outside the brothel where she was kept, and was raped twenty-five times a day," Pronita explained.

Pronita enrolled at Berkeley in 2005 and a year later found herself among the hundreds of students in our inaugural survey course on global poverty. She was mesmerized and wondered throughout the semester, *How can I create enough impact to improve the lives of millions?* Soon she joined the first wave of students to enroll when we added the Global Poverty and Practice minor to the undergraduate curriculum in 2006.

For her summer field experience, Pronita returned to India. Joining a Berkeley graduate student in public health, she conducted a survey of three hundred households in a Mumbai slum to identify why some households treated their drinking water with inexpensive chlorine tablets stocked in local stores and others did not.

Their findings? Shoppers seemed more interested in buying popular personal-care brands. For example, Garnier Fructis hair conditioner was much preferred by the slum-dwelling shoppers over the Pantene brand even though Garnier Fructis was pricier. And both were preferred over the chlorine tablets. The shoppers often did not understand that adding chlorine tablets to their drinking water would prevent illness. They believed that childhood diarrhea was just a normal part of growing up.

Why would people make these choices? Searching for answers, Pronita encountered the field of behavioral economics and discovered the subject of her honors thesis and field research: barriers to technology adoption.

"The Center taught me to have a lot more humility in any particular environment, to ask questions and seek to understand rather than to impose my own judgments and beliefs," Pronita said. "This attitude of humility is embedded in the courses, how the professors teach and push your thinking, and how you outline your assumptions and actual experience."

After graduating from Berkeley in 2009 with her degree in economics and a minor in Global Poverty and Practice, Pronita launched into a whirlwind of diverse professional adventures. She signed on with MIT's Poverty Action Lab in Bangladesh, where she helped evaluate results of Save the Children's effort to encourage adolescent girls in more than four hundred villages to delay the age of marriage and child rearing. She followed this with stints in policy research at a Washington think tank and as a strategist with a company promoting energy efficiency.

Pronita explained that her career choices were influenced by her experiences with the Center because it

> made you think about the singular impact of your actions in a completely different way. It encouraged you to choose that unconventional path . . . I had this really fancy-sounding job in DC but was uncomfortable about the lack of impact and accountability. One night I was working on a paper on climate financing on a global scale. I just started Googling top clean-energy companies. I found EnerNOC, looked at some positions, and applied at around 9:00 p.m. The next

morning, they called me and asked if I'd like to come in for an interview. I honestly don't know if I would have done that without those conversations in my head from the minor to ask myself those difficult questions about choices and impact.

By the summer of 2013, Pronita was chief growth officer for a start-up in India, Next Drop, which alerts people over their mobile devices to pending deliveries of piped water.

Technology to Bolster Municipal Services

Then, early in 2015, Pronita cofounded her own start-up in Bengaluru (known until 2014 as Bangalore, from early years of British rule) with a real-time platform that makes it easier for citizens to participate in how municipal services are managed. Most of the network's mobile apps require no literacy, numeracy, or language skills to use. Housekeeping staff and garbage collectors enter data each day that helps communities and businesses track how waste is handled from doorsteps to processing centers. Pronita hopes the effort will demonstrate how technology enables citizens to make better choices and improve many services their local governments provide.

India's venture capital community is taking interest: *Inc42*, a magazine for entrepreneurs, named her company, called Citizengage, one of India's top five start-ups for 2016.[1] "Civic engagement is really making citizenship mean something. I would love to make it my life mission to fill that gap," she said, adding:

India is the world's largest democracy. It's high time we innovate and demonstrate what better governance could look like.

If you told me even when I was in college that I

would be a technology entrepreneur, I probably would have laughed in disbelief. The Center showed me how valuable well-designed technology can be in solving deeply rooted social and economic problems. It is arguably more democratic and serves customers better than policy from the top . . . Technology is doing a lot more to create the right kind of ecosystem to reduce extreme poverty now than policy has been able to do for decades. That resonated with me: Just give people the choice, rather than shove some ego-fed proscriptive policy at them.

Citizengage was handling more than 100 tons of waste for customers each month by the spring of 2016 and had diverted more than 500 tons of waste from landfills to biogas plants, composting facilities, and recycling centers.

"Eight-five percent of India's waste is recyclable but ninety percent is sitting in landfills," she told India's *Economic Times*. There is, she added, "a huge opportunity in building a better waste-to-resource management system."[2]

Electricity for Rural Villagers: Yashraj Khaitan

Yashraj Khaitan grew up in the state of Rajasthan, where his family had run businesses for three generations. He knew the politics, the layers of social power and influence, and the extreme poverty that defined how millions of people existed there and in several other regions of India.

When he arrived at Berkeley in 2008 as a freshman engineering major, he worked at the Lawrence Berkeley National Laboratory on advanced designs for solar cells that could store the energy they generated. A trip to rural India the following summer (funded through Berkeley's Engineers Without Borders chapter) gave Yashraj an unexpected education in how the rural poor were deprived of the simplest modern conveniences because they had no electricity. Solar energy, he knew, could change this.

Grant Funds: Seed Capital for Students' Scalable Innovation

Access to electricity can bring villagers into the twenty-first century. It offers light after sundown and on cloudy days, access to the Internet, and the ability to use time-saving small appliances. And it helps reduce the need to burn kerosene, a terrible pollutant. More than seven hundred million Indians live in rural villages, and nearly half use kerosene as a primary lighting source.

Yashraj returned to campus with the goal of designing and building a low-cost system to give tens of millions of people in the developing world access to affordable electricity, starting in India. He didn't waste time.

Yashraj and fellow engineering student Jacob Dickinson invented a small, lightweight device to provide energy for basic lighting and power generation in villages where electricity is unreliable or unavailable. The stackable, portable storage system relied on circuitry they designed for efficient power management. By early 2013, in his article "When E.T. and I.T. Meet ID," *New York Times* columnist Thomas L. Friedman was praising Yashraj for creating "the most exciting" energy innovation Friedman had seen on a trip to India.[3]

Maryanne McCormick and others on the Center staff kept an eye on Yashraj and Jacob's progress and relayed to them well-timed alerts for the Big Ideas@Berkeley and other competitions. Yashraj and Jacob earned $8,000 in grant funding with their initial prototypes, including their award from a Big Ideas competition in spring 2011. USAID was starting its own version of Big Ideas then, a dazzling collaboration with NASA, the State

Department, and Nike known as "LAUNCH: Collective Genius for a Better World." Before the year was out, Yashraj and Jacob's initiative was one of ten winners for energy innovations and the recipient of a $1 million USAID grant. "I had already graduated and was visiting the campus when Maryanne sent me the application for LAUNCH," Yashraj said. "It's always that one thing leads to another."

Gram Power, the start-up company cofounded by Yashraj and Jacob, is in the vanguard of new technologies at the Center with potential to scale rapidly and help fight extreme poverty.

A Revolutionary Electricity Metering System

By mid-2015, Gram Power had raised its sights to help power distribution companies with two major service problems: theft of huge volumes of power and unpaid bills, which annually cost India's power sector $18 billion. The amount is so large, it equals the cost of providing one-third of India's population with electricity.

Helping power distributors sharply pare those losses is one of Gram Power's goals. The money can be used to improve infrastructure, reduce the cost of energy across the country, and even provide free electricity to the poorest populations. Yashraj and Jacob created an advanced microgrid for villages that connects the smart prepaid meters they invented as Berkeley undergrads to the national grid. A total of sixty villages were targeted for installation by the end of 2015, with thirty completed and serving seven thousand people. (Microgrids typically connect to existing power lines but can operate as a separate power source during storms or power outages.)

Gram Power's new system, an integrated metering platform, enables the entire electricity infrastructure to be managed simply, efficiently, and with much lower costs through the Internet, in the cloud. Blackouts should be sharply reduced, with far less energy wasted. Schools and hospitals can be given priority over other customers when supply wanes. Consumers can track their usage and expenses online in real time, spot any power-guzzling appliances, and even avoid overcharging by unscrupulous power suppliers.

"The challenges in the power sector are far different in India from the West," Yashraj explained.

> They include rampant theft, mismanaged infrastructure, inaccurate billing, poor reliability, and consumers who don't pay their bills. We made a lot of design improvements but learned from our field research that the big challenge people had was controlling how much electricity they used and could afford. It was a metering problem, not a power access problem. They needed microgrids with smart meters.
>
> The smart meters can be recharged as easily as cell phones. Customers can track how much money is left on their prepaid meters and which of their appliances are more or less efficient. With our system, they can prepay whatever they can afford, even as little as twenty cents at a time. Plus they don't need to make a trip to a payment center, which before could mean the loss of two days' wages just to pay a bill.
>
> With smart meters, we're giving the utilities an end-to-end solution to manage the entire infrastructure—billing, payments, load balancing, pricing, and planning—across the entire distribution network . . . Utilities see tremendous potential to bring more control, transparency, and efficiency to the power infrastructure. The smart meter has proven to be stable and is being certified to be deployed on the national grid. Our goal is

to work with utilities to have one of these smart meters in every single house in India.

Gram Power is expanding into East Africa next, but with a different product. As Yashraj explained:

> Homes are extremely scattered in a lot of African countries, too far away from each other to connect to a power grid. Even microgrids cannot reach them. We developed a prepaid solar home system for Africa that uses mobile money . . . Our plans are ambitious. Our goal over the next four years with our local partners is to get these systems into a million households in Kenya.

The cost to people in Africa for solar power will be about the same as the monthly cost of kerosene.

Access to affordable, reliable electricity helps raise the living standard for entire populations, and Gram Power's mission is to help make this happen.

Tough Realities in Microfinance: Lauren Herman

When Lauren Herman arrived at Berkeley in 2008, she was a transfer student planning to major in journalism. She had spent the previous year photographing displaced women and children for a nonprofit group in Managua, Nicaragua, and had helped organize a microfinance service for the group to support the local community.

Soon after she arrived on campus, she switched to the Peace and Conflict Studies major, with a particular eye on postconflict development, and then added the Global Poverty and Practice minor. "The minor became more important than my major," she said. "I wanted to better understand the issues of poverty, wealth, and inequality in the United States and abroad. The courses and the faculty challenged me to look beyond what I thought I knew about the world and my role in it."

A student volunteer for a nonprofit that supports microfinance lending in Latin America and Africa, she connected with another microfinance nonprofit organization for her two-month practice experience. This group provided loans to rural women living in the scenic Great Rift Valley in west-central Kenya, a mecca for trekkers and world travelers. "Working in Kenya was a life-changing experience that taught me the importance of community," she said. There she encountered tough realities about the limits and occasional abuse of microfinance practices.

I met Lauren at the opening of the new Center building and again by chance one afternoon when she was walking out the door as I was heading in. She described for me then the problems in Kenya that infuriated her and inspired her to take action:

> It's ridiculous how the microfinance industry works in Kenya. All loan documents are written in English, which well-educated Kenyans in the cities read and speak, but the people I was working with have a limited educational background. Swahili and their native tongue are the common languages. Oral communication is key because most borrowers cannot read Swahili. I thought that if lenders or the government were not protecting consumers, networks of consumer education organizations needed to work in communities where clients lived.

One example Lauren shared was a woman named Mary. She had borrowed $30 to buy materials for her tailoring business but soon became seriously ill and needed expensive medical care. She couldn't work, her business collapsed, and her personal debt soared—needlessly—because she did not know she could have requested a payment deferral.

Instead, facing pressure, resentment, and ultimately isolation from other members of her lending circle who believed they would be responsible for Mary's unpaid debts, she kept up payments as long as she could.

"Mary did not understand the loan agreement, and the NGO was not protecting its clients," Lauren says. Unfortunately, predatory lending is not uncommon in microfinance programs, something Lauren said she discovered in her post-graduate research in Kenya.

While microfinance services broadly have been considered successful in empowering women since they were initiated in the 1970s, Lauren said it is not unusual for micro-lending agencies now to be run by men who prefer dealing with borrowers' husbands. "I am against how microfinance is practiced by many lenders," Lauren said. "It has become commercialized, with the possibility of abuse and fraud. Lending programs too often make repayment rates, not clients' welfare, the priority."

Lauren began a determined journey that within a few years led to her winning a $20,000 Judith Lee Stronach Baccalaureate Prize. After earning her degree, she collaborated with some of the world's leading consumer advocacy groups for microfinance in writing a user's manual published in Swahili and English.[4] She has said:

> You tend as activists to see inequality as just part of your life, part of our world. But [in the Global Poverty and Practice Minor] you learn to be critical, patient, and persistent in your search for a changed world. The Center faculty and staff gave me the tools to do this . . . If you change a few people's lives, that's more than what you came into the world with. Don't overestimate the

power of one, but don't underestimate the power of collective action and collaboration.

Living in Kenya opened Lauren to truths about how social change happens in communities. After graduation, she returned to her home city, Sacramento, and became an advocate for public health and safety, promoting better understanding and use of building codes in California. "Working in Kenya was a life-changing experience," she said. "I realized how much I did not know about the city where I had lived my entire life."

Life Lessons from Rwanda: Jacob Seigel-Boettner

When Jacob Seigel-Boettner was born in Santa Barbara, California, in 1987, his parents brought him home from the hospital in a bicycle trailer. Twenty-one months later, Jacob's newborn brother, Isaac, came home the same way. The two boys grew up taking long bike trips. Their parents, schoolteachers who loved cycling, organized ambitious student bike expeditions every summer in the United States and other countries around the world.

Bicycle as Fun Toy or Deliverance on Pedals?

After his freshman year at Berkeley, Jacob and his father joined a few friends and other members of UC Berkeley's mountain biking team on a road trip in the summer of 2007, pedaling through Rwanda to see firsthand how a nonprofit group called Project Rwanda had built and distributed sturdy cargo bikes to local coffee farmers. The program provided a welcome boost to the coffee farmers' productivity. They now could transport heavy loads on muddy roads during the rainy season. Jacob had read about the project in a biking magazine.

That road trip lasted only three weeks, but it changed Jacob's life. "It was very inspiring, but also forced me to look in the mirror," he later recalled. "I had always seen the bike as this really fun toy . . . but here I saw what a bike could do for people who relied on it for more than just leisure activities." Returning to campus, he declared a major in Peace and Conflict Studies and, just as Lauren Herman did, soon added Global Poverty and Practice as a minor.

What he learned on his second venture in Rwanda, this time through the Center, was unexpected. The nonprofit he picked for his practice requirement had a much smaller on-the-ground presence—essentially a one-man operation run by a student at the University of Rwanda. Jacob soon found himself in a crash course on project management, critical thinking, and the politics of international development.

At times, he knew, he was in way over his head, but he learned fast. And he discovered that, despite the brutal 1994 genocide, Rwandans were much more capable and knowledgeable than he had anticipated. What they lacked, he realized, were resources, institutional support structures, and opportunity. He later said:

> If you don't recognize people's own agency in their own development, then you're failing everyone. Some of the biggest roadblocks I witnessed eventually were solved by a local worker who saw something happening in the field and said, "Look, this is what the people want. This is what they're asking for. We just need to listen."

So he decided to help more people listen.

Sharing Powerful Stories

Instead of writing a field report about the experience to fulfill his course requirement, Jacob created a video telling the story of a coffee farmer named Mudahinyuka Pascal, the first recipient of a cargo bicycle in his region. "I knew that while a forty-page paper has academic merit, my friends would laugh if I asked them to read it," he said with a smile. "The best way I knew to share with them what I experienced was to make a film. Video is how we consume stories and issues in my generation."

His fourteen-minute documentary, *Pascal's Bike*, was screened at the Santa Barbara International Film Festival in 2009, and its enthusiastic reception inspired him to lay plans for a bigger project: a film showing the bicycle as a symbol of mobility and opportunity around the world.

The result was *With My Own Two Wheels*, a forty-two-minute documentary Jacob produced and codirected in 2010 with his brother, Isaac, to much acclaim. A well-timed Stronach Prize, then valued at $25,000, to cover expenses was awarded at a time when Jacob was desperate for money and about to begin shooting in faraway locales. In addition to his brother, then a Berkeley film studies major, the film crew included Ian Wexler, a friend studying cinematography at Emerson College in Boston.

For narratives in the documentary, the trio (collaborating as Pedal Born Pictures) focused on five people: a volunteer HIV/AIDS caregiver in Zambia whose new bike enabled him to visit distant patients more easily; a woman in Ghana who was able to overcome the stigma of being disabled after she learned to repair bicycles; a Guatemalan torture victim who converted the pedals and gears of old bikes to power small farm equipment; a fourteen-year-old girl in rural India who was able to attend high school after receiving a bike; and a young Santa Barbara man who escaped gang life by volunteering at a community-run bike shop.

The film's 2011 premiere at the Santa Barbara International Film Festival filled a 680-seat theater. The response was so enthusiastic that Jacob was invited to screen *With My Own Two*

Wheels more than seventy times over the next year. He found fans at the Mountainfilm festival in Telluride, Lincoln Center in New York City, and the Barbican in London, and at many schools, community groups, and libraries. A screening at a park in São Paulo drew a thousand people.

For Jacob, the lessons from his Rwandan field experience still resonate:

> I stop and pause now before I say I am going somewhere to help people. I may have gone over to Rwanda with that goal, but there is a question of who got more out of my field practice, them or me. A lot of people in the minor would tell you the same thing. People are much more multidimensional than the international development images you see in airport posters or on billboards. Our lives are not so different on a very human level.

If most students are learning this lesson from their work with us, I think we're getting it right.

Being the Change Maker You See in the Mirror

The Center operates with the conviction that today's students want more than sage-on-the-stage pedagogy. Increasing numbers of students see themselves as change makers. They are idealistic, innovative, and civic-minded. They come from every possible major and school. Their family backgrounds are ethnically and economically diverse. Their interests range from clean energy to food security to cellular networks to microfinance. But in one way, they are the same: They want to use their time at the university to get started on projects with social impact, not wait until they are handed a diploma.

We applaud this impatience. In the Center's first ten years, we witnessed a surge in low-cost innovations that are focused on solving basic problems in global poverty moving from engineering and science research laboratories into the field.

We are connecting many students with the new wave of younger philanthropists, many situated in the Bay Area's Silicon Valley, who are committing more talent and financial resources in disruptive, innovative ways to combat global poverty. Other students at the Center consult directly with federal government agencies or international NGOs, or sign on with local government or community-service organizations. We encourage them all to ask these questions: *What can we learn from the past? What should we be focused on now?*

Our hope and our pledge is for the Center to continue to inspire students in whatever career they choose in order to be compassionate throughout their lives. No matter what their major is, no matter what they do later in life, our aim is to help them really think about their place in the world. Many will go on to solve the difficult problems of tomorrow—problems that have not yet made it onto the international agenda or that have not even been identified.

We hope all of them will take action—whether through their day jobs, as volunteers, or as philanthropists—to make a difference in the lives of the poor. We especially want our Global Poverty and Practice students to look back on their field practice and remember the needs of the people they got to know and tried to help in some distant land or right here at home. We intend for the Center's interdisciplinary model to break down traditional academic silos and help transform higher education.

All of us at the Center have committed ourselves to becoming enablers—so that millions more people soon will have the opportunity to be educated, grow in confidence, and improve their lives, their families, their communities, and the wider world.

Conclusion

Finding Your Path

"In a gentle way, you can shake the world."

—Mahatma Gandhi

Too many people still think continued progress in reducing poverty around the world is unlikely, but they haven't been paying attention. The number of people living on less than $1.25 a day—the internationally accepted measure that defines extreme poverty—was cut nearly in half between 1990 and 2010, with the greatest progress in China and India, where more than one-third of the world's population, 2.5 billion people, live.

I may not live long enough to see the day when extreme poverty is cut even more dramatically in the world's poorest countries, but I might. I believe my four daughters and my seven grandchildren will. Regardless, I'll continue to fight poverty, primarily through my work with the American Himalayan Foundation and the Blum Center for Developing Economies, and other interesting projects that come our way. Who knows what ideas next year's Blum Center students will cook up.

And we will continue to encourage people to reach across

those borders and invisible walls that too often stymie progress that could and should be happening. Whether it's a refusal to collaborate, or worse a refusal to acknowledge the intelligence, ability, and capacity of those living in poverty, the barriers have to come down. That's worth fighting for.

It's in all of our best interests to continue the fight against poverty in developing economies. As Alex Dehgan, former chief scientist at USAID and a creator of USAID's Global Development Lab, has pointed out, the biggest opportunities and challenges we face as a country and as a planet are tied to the developing world. By 2050, fifty-one developed countries will *lose* population. "With that decline and the aging of those populations, the importance of those developed nations will shrink," he explained. "On the other hand, the majority of the largest nine countries in population today will continue to grow. This is where the economic development will be."

And this is where the imperatives for fighting against poverty today are most pronounced. I can't not fight. President Clinton framed the basic challenge well in his 2014 speech at the US Naval Academy: "We have to be concerned when half the world's people are still living on barely two dollars a day, when a billion people go to bed hungry every night, and when one in five deaths occur from AIDS, TB, malaria, and infections related to dirty water."[1] Knowing what I know and having access to the resources I have, how could I possibly decide to sit back and do nothing more?

I am now in my ninth decade and will continue to press ahead as long as I am able. My calendar is overflowing, and I'm still curious. My purpose now is to help guide and support in every possible way the extraordinary people in government, the private sector, and NGOs who continue to make progress against extreme poverty.

I have been guided all my life by inspirational people—each

humble yet strongly dedicated to their particular cause. People like Sir Edmund Hillary, His Holiness the Dalai Lama, Jimmy Carter, Mahatma Gandhi, and Nelson Mandela. Their vision, struggles, and achievements captured my imagination and have long fueled my desire to do something, whatever I could. What do the people I admire most have in common? Empathy and altruism, and the ability to get things done. I have endeavored to apply these ideals in deciding how to devote my time, energy, and resources. And I have found that embracing these values has led to a rewarding, fulfilling life. Trust me.

I hope you will find similar influences, possibly from some of the people I've written about. If you're a mountain climber, trekker, or passionate traveler, maybe you'll be inspired by Sir Edmund Hillary to help some of the local communities in which you spend time. If you work with children, maybe you'll be inspired by Dr. Aruna Uprety, who is protecting thousands of girls every year from the horrors of the sex slave trade. If you're an artist, maybe you'll be inspired by Luigi Fieni, who has spent every summer since 1998 in LoMontang restoring ancient Tibetan Buddhist art, and helping revive a community and culture. If you're in finance or private equity, maybe you'll be inspired by Dr. Raj Shah and the work of Latitude Capital Partners to raise capital to fund hydro and solar projects for clean energy in India and Africa. If you're in education, maybe you'll be inspired by the many students and faculty of the University of California system and the Blum Center who are harnessing innovation and new technologies to address major problems in poverty and income inequality.

Or maybe you'll be inspired by a few of my own stories.

Let me leave you with a question: What path will you take? It isn't a challenge. It isn't a demand. But each one of us has a role to play in resolving the great challenges of the day—whether it's within an organization you're already a part of, in your local community, in your career, in your philanthropy, even in how you invest or spend your money. It all matters, and every contribution that helps push us in the right direction makes a difference.

So if you have the time some Saturday afternoon, put your accident of geography to good use. We invite you to find an area among all the places we've discussed in these pages that interests you, and join in. If you continue this work for the rest of your life, you'll be glad you did. I'm certainly glad I have. It has given my life purpose and meaning, and it will do the same for yours.

To learn more about how the Blum Center for Developing Economies is fighting global poverty and inequality, please visit: blumcenter.berkeley.edu, or websites of Blum Centers at each of the nine other University of California campuses.

———

If you want more information about the American Himalayan Foundation, or would like to donate, please visit: www.himalayan-foundation.org

Acknowledgments

I want to begin by expressing special thanks to His Holiness the Dalai Lama and Jimmy Carter. Both have been inspirational for me in their dedication to world peace, human rights, and global development. It has been an honor in these pages to share personal stories and many achievements of these two Nobel Peace Prize winners, and to have President Carter write the Foreword. My dear friends Sir Edmund Hillary and Pasang Kami are no longer with us, but I remain grateful for how both men also influenced and enriched my life.

My wife, Dianne Feinstein, was highly supportive of the project and a source of many recollections for the chapters on the people and politics of San Francisco and China and Tibet. My daughters Annette, Heidi, and Eileen, stepdaughter Katherine and her husband Rick, granddaughter Eileen, and brother Robert all helped to recall, clarify, or add important facts and events.

The people of the Himalaya have great friends and I, gifted, trusted colleagues in the American Himalayan Foundation. Erica Stone, president, has spent endless hours on the book. I am especially grateful to her for adding clarity and key facts in her careful reviews of each chapter. Her team—Norbu Tenzing, Betsy Horan, Bruce Moore, and Tsedo—each contributed significantly to the manuscript, especially part 1. All have my deep thanks for their equanimity and efficiency in getting the most done in our foundation's expanding work, touching the lives of over three hundred thousand people every year. Many thanks also to David Bonderman, Michael Klein, and Barney Osher for their pivotal role in supporting and shaping AHF.

I am grateful to Michael Beschloss, author and presidential historian, and Gillian Tett, author, columnist, and US managing editor of the *Financial Times*. Michael spotted the potential in the book from previous documents, and, along with Gillian, offered wise counsel and encouragement as the manuscript evolved.

Dozens of people graciously gave their time to contribute ideas, insights, and perspectives for this book in interviews. I am indebted to them all. In addition to President Carter, they include Walter F. Mondale, George P. Shultz, Mark Yudof, Sherry Lansing, Robert B. Reich, Laura D'Andrea Tyson, Shankar Sastry, Dr. John Hardman, Lina Nilsson, Dan Fletcher, Ananya Roy, Lawrence H. Summers, David Bonderman, Weijian Shan, Frank Newman, Mickey Kantor, Brett White, Dan Carroll, Gary Wilson, John Dasburg, Michael Klein, Louis Reichardt, Jon Krakauer, Pico Iyer, Siddharth Kara, Bruce McCubbrey, The Scot Macbeth, Conrad Anker, Kit DesLauriers, Lodi Gyari Rinpoche, Dr. Rajiv Shah, Dr. Aruna Uprety, Dr. Ashok Banskota, Raja Jigme Bista, Crown Prince Jigme-Singi Palabar Bista, Luigi Fieni, Alex Dehgan, John Shattuck, Strobe Talbott, Homi Kharas, Kemal Derviş, Kenneth Wollack, Luis Moreno, Phil Fehlen, John De Luca, Jessica Li, Pronita Saxena, Yashraj Khaitan, Lauren Herman, Jacob Seigel-Boettner, and Anh-Thi Le.

Many also graciously sharpened certain passages by their suggestions after reading various chapters. My thanks to them, and to Mary Bowrin, who was among the readers of the final manuscript. I should add, however, that none of the readers is responsible for errors that might have made their way into the finished book. I would appreciate being informed of any should readers spot them.

I am grateful for the steadfast work by my writing collaborator, Thomas C. Hayes, of Finsbury, in framing and bolstering the research and writing. Thanks also to our editors, Lari Bishop, Amy L. D. McIlwaine, Pam Nordberg, and Nathan True, for their deft touch collectively in shaping final drafts. My thanks also to interviewers Victor Geraci, Ann Lage, and Lisa Rubins at the Oral History Center in the Bancroft Library at the University of California, Berkeley, and Richard Paddock, each of whom contributed ideas initially that substantively informed the final work.

The Finsbury-US leadership trio of Michael Gross, Stephen Labaton, and Patrick Gallagher remained committed to this project as months turned to years after Stephen first embraced the potential. I am grateful to all three as well as their enthusiastic team of researchers, especially Melanie Graf, Ben Rosner, Megan Kennedy, and Andrew Carter.

My thanks also to Maryanne McCormick and Heather Lofthouse at the Blum Center; Amy Fowler at the American Himalayan Foundation; Steven H. Hochman, Deanna Congileo, Beth Davis, and Lauren Gay at The Carter Center; and Carole Hall and Kristina Server at the Brookings Institution for their important efforts on research, coordination, and logistics. Stacey Cole and Ivy Elizaga, of my staff at Blum Capital, amiably bore the burdens of long hours and rapid response in helping me focus and stay informed at each step of the process.

I appreciate the work of our production, sales, and marketing team at Greenleaf Book Group: Jen Glynn, Tyler LeBleu, Justin Branch, Steve Elizalde, and Chelsea Richards. Special thanks to

Greenleaf's Neil Gonzalez for his excellent design of the book pages, maps, and cover, to Luigi Fieni for the dramatic photograph that inspired the cover, and to Dawn Schneider for getting the word out as our New York–based publicist.

Above all, I thank my wife, Dianne, and daughters Annette, Heidi, Eileen, and Katherine. This book is dedicated to them, and to my seven grandchildren in the hope that it offers inspiration.

Notes

Chapter 1

1. Nangpa La was the site, in 2006, of a fatal shooting by Chinese border police of a seventeen-year-old nun attempting to escape with seventy-five unarmed Tibetans. According to reports, just more than half of these besieged refugees made their way safely across the border into Nepal and eventually to Dharamsala in northern India. Others were captured, imprisoned, and tortured.

2. According to a *National Geographic* report from Nepal in 2003, most Sherpas "seem able to blend the new with the old as easily as a farmer . . . at a tiny bar in the village of Beni; he was sipping alternatively from a tall bottle of Carslberg and from a shallow cup of *chang*, a thick, home-brewed beer."

3. For the Dalai Lama's explanation of the meaning of *Om Mani Padme Hum*, see http://www.buddhanet.net/e-learning/buddhistworld/tibet-txt.htm. For a more general discussion, see also http://www.dharma-haven.org/tibetan/meaning-of-om-mani-padme-hung.htm.

4. Sir Edmund Hillary, "My Story: Sir Edmund Remembers," *National Geographic*, May 2003, 38–41.

5. Amy Blackwood, Katie Roeger, and Sarah L. Pettijohn, *The Nonprofit Sector in Brief: Public Charities, Giving and Volunteering, 2012*, National Center for Charitable Statistics, October 5, 2012, http://www.urban.org/publications/412674.html.

6. Sir Edmund Hillary, "My Story," 38–40.

Chapter 2

1. Sukey Lewis and Nausheen Husain, "Dalai Lama Visits East Bay, Gives Advice on Achieving Happiness," *Oakland North*, February 24, 2014, https://oaklandnorth.net/2014/02/24/dalai-lama-visits-east-bay-gives-advice-on-achieving-happiness/.

2. John F. Avedon, *In Exile from the Land of Snows: The Dalai Lama and Tibet since the Chinese Conquest* (New York: HarperPerennial, 1994), paperback edition, 125.

3. During the Cold War, Fort Funston became a launch site for Nike missiles, their warheads aimed toward Russia, but for several decades now it has been a beautiful oceanside park. Hang gliders, dog walkers, and others love its stiff winds and spectacular views of the Pacific—a case of turning swords into parklands, not plowshares.

4. About four feet high, with a compact, muscular body and short, bony legs, the Tibetan pony is prized for its strength and stamina despite the thin mountain air. Tibetan ponies can keep a good pace over many miles and sometimes even gallop like the wind.

5. Edward Wong, "Buddhists, Reconstructing Sacred Tibetan Murals, Wield Their Brushes in Nepal," *The New York Times*, February 24, 2013, http://www.nytimes.com/2013/02/24/world/asia/in-nepal-buddhists-reconstruct-tibetan-murals.html. Description of mandala concept is from this article. See also Prayag Raj Sharma, review of *The Mollas of Mustang: Historical, Religious and Oratorical Traditions of the Nepalese-Tibetan Borderland* by David P. Jackson, *CNAS Journal* 13, no. 3 (August 1985): 139.

6. American Himalayan Foundation, "Sharing the Skills of Tibetan Art," *Reports from the Field* (blog), 2009, http://www.himalayan-foundation.org/projects/fieldreport/archives/113018.

7. John Sanday, "Restoring History," in Richard C. Blum, Erica Stone, and Broughton Coburn, eds., *Himalaya: Personal Stories of Grandeur, Challenge, and Hope* (Washington, DC: National Geographic Society, 2006), 194–99.

8. Much of this material is borrowed from the transcript of *Mustang: Journey of Transformation*, a short film about the Mustang restorations produced for the American Himalayan Foundation in 2009.

9. Saransh Sehgal, "Labour of Love: The Villagers Restoring the Sacred, 15th-Century Art of Mustang's Monasteries," *The Independent*, November 4, 2013.

10. Edward Wong, "Buddhists, Reconstructing Sacred Tibetan Murals, Wield Their Brushes in Nepal," *The New York Times*, February 24, 2013, http://www.nytimes.com/2013/02/24/world/asia/in-nepal-buddhists-reconstruct-tibetan-murals.html. Description of mandala concept is from this article.

11. Yangchen Gurung, a young cousin of Raja Jigme Bista, is one of the first Lobas ever to enroll in graduate studies in the United States. I first met Yangchen during the Tiji festival in LoMontang in the spring of 2014. As a young girl she had studied at the Himalayan International Model School in Kathmandu, a school founded in 1994 by monks who wished to pass along Tibetan Buddhist religious and cultural traditions to younger generations in Nepal. Yangchen had just received her bachelor's degree in business management from the University of Minnesota. Five months later, sharing breakfast beneath the Palm Court's towering ceiling at the Plaza Hotel in New York City, we celebrated her success and her dreams for the future. She was four weeks into a two-year master's program in economic policy at Columbia University's prestigious School of International and Public Affairs.

12. In the spring of 2014, on my annual trip to LoMontang, Crown Prince Jigme gave me a big hug and led our group through a festive receiving line with hundreds of people, leading directly to what once was the entrance of the Forbidden City of Lo. The gate there is only about ten feet wide. Inside you can see narrow cobblestone streets—too small and bumpy to drive a vehicle, but tolerable enough for slow-moving yaks hauling carts filled with grain and other food staples. There at the gate, the crown prince placed a stone bearing these words chiseled in English: *In Honor*

of the Contribution of Richard Blum and the American Himalayan Foundation in helping to restore our gompas and revive our ancient culture—May 2014.

13. Maseeh Rahman, "Shepherd Leads Experts to Ancient Buddha Cave Paintings," *The Guardian*, May 4, 2007.

Chapter 3

1. Siddharth Kara, *Sex Trafficking: Inside the Business of Modern Slavery* (New York: Columbia University Press, 2009), 50.

2. The figures were 85 percent and 68 percent, respectively, for fiscal years 2013–14 and 2014–2015, according to Nepal's National Human Rights Commission. The report, by the Commission's Office of the Special Rapporteur on Trafficking in Women and Children, was released in March 2016 and titled, "Trafficking in Persons: National Report 2013–2015," http://www.nhrcnepal. org/nhrc_new/doc/newsletter/Trafficking_in_Persons_National_ Report_2013-15.pdf; accessed April 27, 2016.

3. Kara, 79.

4. Vatican Radio, "UNICEF Reports 7,000 Nepali Women and Girls Trafficked to India Every Year," UN Global Initiative to Fight Human Trafficking, April 9, 2014, http://www.ungift.org/ knowledgehub/en/stories/September2014/unicef-reports-7-000- nepali-women-and-girls-trafficked-to-india-every-year.html.

5. Jimmy Carter, *A Call to Action: Women, Religion, Violence, and Power* (New York: Simon & Schuster, 2014), 130.

6. Kara, 37–38.

7. Katherine Feinstein, "Introduction to Stop Girls Trafficking Evening," American Himalayan Foundation event: Saving girls in the year of the earthquake, St. Regis Hotel, San Francisco, April 14, 2016.

8. World Health Organization, "World Health Statistics 2011" (Geneva: WHO Press, 2011), 96–97.

9. This Swiss humanitarian group is part of the ten-member Terre des hommes International Federation that helps defend and protect children from exploitation in sixty-five mainly poor countries.

10. In Nepal at the time, most hospitals were referred to as "nursing homes," although elder care was not their primary function.

Chapter 4

1. Jimmy Carter, *An Outdoor Journal: Adventures and Reflections*, 2nd ed. (Fayetteville: University of Arkansas Press, 1994), 215.

2. Ibid., 219.

3. Norwegian Nobel Committee, "The Nobel Peace Prize for 2002," press release, October 11, 2002, http://www.nobelprize.org/nobel_prizes/peace/laureates/2002/press.html.

4. "In Memoriam: Norman Borlaug, PhD," The Carter Center, accessed January 21, 2015, http://www.cartercenter.org/news/experts/norman_borlaug.html. For excellent obituaries, see Justin Gillis, "Norman Borlaug, Plant Scientist Who Fought Famine, Dies at 95," *The New York Times*, September 13, 2009, http://www.nytimes.com/2009/09/14/business/energy-environment/14borlaug.html?pagewanted=all&_r=0, and *The Economist*, "Norman Borlaug, Feeder of the World, Died on September 12, Aged 95," September 17, 2009, http://www.economist.com/node/14446742.

5. Diane Cole, "Watch Out, Guinea Worm, Here Comes Jimmy Carter," NPR.org, January 13, 2015, http://ww.npr.org/sections/goatsandsoda/2015/01/13/376966122/watch-out-guinea-worm-here-comes-jimmy-carter.

6. According to the International Monetary Fund, Nepal and Haiti ranked nineteenth and twentieth, respectively, on the list of the world's poorest countries based on gross domestic product. The Dominican Republic was number 117.

7. Office for the Coordination of Humanitarian Affairs, "Haiti Earthquake Response" (New York: Humanitarian Communication Group, 2011), http://www.un.org/en/peacekeeping/missions/ minustah/documents/ocha_haiti_one_year_factsheet.pdf.

8. Bill & Melinda Gates Foundation, "The Carter Center to Receive 2006 Gates Award for Global Health," press release, accessed January 7, 2015, http://www.gatesfoundation.org/Media-Center/ Press-Releases/2006/05/2006-Gates-Award-for-Global-Health.

9. Jimmy Carter described his cancer condition and planned treatment, and responded to several questions from the news media, during a press conference at The Carter Center on August 20, 2015. Highlights and full video of the event are archived on The Carter Center website at http://www.cartercenter.org/news/pr/ carter-press-conference-082015.html.

10. The World Health Organization declared smallpox eradicated in 1980, more than two years after the last naturally occurring case was reported in Somalia. As recently as the mid-1960s, before a global eradication campaign began, smallpox killed an estimated 1.5 million people a year in fifty countries. The disease killed more than three hundred million people in the twentieth century. See Center for Global Development, "Millions Saved, Case 1: Eradicating Smallpox," accessed January 4, 2015, http://www. cgdev.org/page/case-1-eradicating-smallpox.

11. "The Carter Center at 30: Leader in Disease Eradication and Elimination," The Carter Center, April 9, 2012, http://www. cartercenter.org/news/features/anniversary/30-leader-disease.html.

12. The Carter Center, "Carter Center Announces Only 22 People Had Guinea Worm Disease in 2015," press release, January 7, 2016, http://www.cartercenter.org/news/pr/guinea-worm-worldwide- cases-Jan2016.html.

13. The Carter Center, "Carter Center Welcomes Gates Foundation, UAE, CIFF Funding to Achieve Guinea Worm Eradication," press release, January 30, 2012, http://www.cartercenter.org/news/pr/ gw-funding-gates-uae-ciff.html.

14. Jasmine Smith, "Jimmy Carter Tackles Trachoma," *The Borgen Project* (blog), November 19, 2013, http://borgenproject. org/jimmy-carter-tackles-trachoma/. See also Rose Jacobs, "Environmental and Educational Efforts Lead Assault on Trachoma," *Financial Times*, October 9, 2014, http://www. ft.com/intl/cms/s/0/36f3aff0-279b-11e4-ae44-00144feabdc0. html#axzz3OLW1QxV7.

15. The Carter Center, "Lions Clubs International Foundation Announce Expanded Partnership to Pursue Elimination of Blinding Trachoma and River Blindness in Four African Countries," press release, May 16, 2014, http://www.cartercenter.org/news/pr/ trachoma-rb-elimination-051614.html.

16. "The World's Leading Cause of Preventable Blindness," International Trachoma Initiative, accessed March 13, 2015, http://www.trachoma.org/about-trachoma.

17. Richard Fausset and Alan Blinder, "Ailing Jimmy Carter 'at Ease With Whatever Comes.'" *The New York Times,* August 20, 2015, http://www.nytimes.com/2015/08/21/us/jimmy-carter-cancer-health.html?_r=0.

18. Dana-Farber Cancer Institute, "Remission of Jimmy Carter's Melanoma Shows Potential of Immunotherapy for Fighting Cancer," *Insight: Information & Inspiration* (blog), December 11, 2015, http://blog.dana-farber.org/insight/2015/12/remission-of-jimmy-carters-melanoma-shows-potential-of-immunotherapy-for-cancer/.

Chapter 5

1. The Institute for European Studies for many years has operated as IES Abroad (http://www.iesabroad.org/). It works through two hundred colleges and universities in the United States, placing approximately six thousand students a year in thirty-five different global locations.

2. It was a tense summer for Moroccans. A few months after I visited Casablanca, Moroccan soldiers made several armed incursions

southward into what then was known as Spanish West Africa. This area now is Western Sahara, controlled by Moroccans who themselves confront occasional violent clashes with an indigenous nomadic group, the Saharawi, that seeks its own independence.

3. The opening bell signaling the start of trading each day on the New York Stock Exchange was changed to 9:30 a.m. from 10:00 a.m. (Eastern time) in 1985. The trading day was extended to 4:00 p.m. from 3:30 p.m. (Eastern time) in 1974.

4. Here is the full quote as commonly attributed to Mark Twain: "If a cat sits on a hot stove, that cat won't sit on a hot stove again. That cat won't sit on a cold stove either. That cat just don't like stoves."

5. Human Rights Watch, "World Report 2013: Mali," accessed March 15, 2016, http://www.hrw.org/world-report/2013/country-chapters/mali.

6. Jon Krakauer's excellent account of the April 18, 2014, avalanche disaster on Everest, "Death and Anger on Everest," was published online by *New Yorker* magazine three days after the event. See http://www.newyorker.com/news/news-desk/death-and-anger-on-everest.

7. Paul Stanley Ward, "Edmund Hillary: King of the World," *NZEdge*, June 2, 2000, accessed April 4, 2015, http://www.nzedge.com/legends/endurance/edmund-hillary/.

8. Gordon Fairclough, Raymond Zhong, and Krishna Pokharel, "Death at 19,000 Feet: Sherpas, Fate, and the Dangerous Business of Everest," *The Wall Street Journal*, May 22, 2014, http://www.wsj.com/articles/sherpas-fate-and-the-dangerous-business-of-everest-1400780100. This is an excellent multimedia report on the Everest disaster in 2014.

9. Bikash Sangraula, "Sherpas Head Back to Everest, Leaving Bitter Protests Behind," *The Christian Science Monitor*, March 2, 2015, http://www.csmonitor.com/World/Asia-South-Central/2015/0302/Sherpas-head-back-to-Everest-leaving-bitter-protests-behind-video.

10. Grayson Schaffer, "The Disposable Man: A Western History of the Sherpa on Everest," *Outside* magazine, August 2013: 64–71, 98–100, http://www.outsideonline.com/outdoor-adventure/climbing/mountaineering/Disposable-Man-History-of-the-Sherpa-on-Everest.html.

11. Krishnadev Calamur, "Who Are Nepal's Sherpas?" NPR, April 22, 2014, http://www.npr.org/sections/parallels/2014/04/22/305954983/who-are-nepals-sherpas.

12. These points are noted in Norbu Tenzing's excellent commentary a month after the April 2014 catastrophe. Norbu Tenzing Norgay, "Cloudy Days on Everest," *Outside* magazine, May 29, 2014, http://www.outsideonline.com/outdoor-adventure/the-current/events-expeditions/Cloudy-Days-on-Everest.html.

13. Frances B. Cogan, *Captured: The Japanese Internment of American Civilians in the Philippines, 1941–1945* (Athens, GA: University of Georgia Press, 2000), 307.

14. Jon Krakauer, *Three Cups of Deceipt: How Greg Mortensen, Humanitarian Hero, Lost His Way* (New York: Anchor, 2011).

15. Peter Kerr, "Irvin Feld, 66, Circus Operator," Obituaries, *The New York Times*, September 7, 1984.

16. Diana Lambdin Meyer, "The Family Behind Family Entertainment," *American Profile*, October 1, 2009, http://americanprofile.com/articles/the-family-behind-family-entertainment/.

Chapter 6

1. Linda Himelstein, "Reaping the Rewards of Friendly Persuasion," *BusinessWeek*, May 19, 1996, http://www.bloomberg.com/bw/stories/1996-05-19/reaping-the-rewards-of-friendly-persuasion.

2. S. C. Pepper, *World Hypotheses: A Study in Evidence* (Berkeley: University of California Press, 1942).

3. Sari Wahyuni and Luchien Kasten, "How Successful Will the KLM–Air France Partnership Become? Lessons Learned from the KLM–Northwest Alliance," *Problems and Perspective in Management* 1 (2006): 111.

4. The director of the Lawrence Berkeley National Laboratory before joining the Obama administration in 2009, Steven Chu was the first scientist ever to hold a cabinet position. He returned to academia in 2013 as a professor with a joint appointment in Stanford's physics department and medical school.

5. Bjorn Carey, "Q&A: Steven Chu on Returning to Stanford, His Time as US Energy Secretary," *Stanford Report*, May 15, 2013.

6. Aniruddh Mohan, "The Time for a 'New Deal' for Climate Change Is Now," *PlanetPolicy: The Intersection of Energy and Climate Policy* (blog), September 21, 2015, http://www.brookings.edu/blogs/planetpolicy/ posts/2015/09/21-new-deal-climate-change-mohan.

7. Carey, "Q&A: Steven Chu on Returning to Stanford."

8. Shawn Donnan, "Poverty: Vulnerable to Change," The Big Read, *Financial Times*, September 23, 2015, http://www. ft.com/intl/cms/s/0/f599b75c-6042-11e5-a28b-50226830d644. html#axzz3oJAudjbo.

Chapter 7

1. His Holiness the Dalai Lama and Howard C. Cutler, MD, *The Art of Happiness: A Handbook for Living* (New York: Riverhead Books, 1998), 137, 142.

2. Andrew L. Yarrow, "Freedom Bank's Failure Hits Harlem Like a Death in the Family," *The New York Times*, November 12, 1990.

3. Michael Idov, "The Stench of '89: The Last Great New York Recession Was Prolonged and Deep—and It Is Eerily Familiar," *New York Magazine*, February 4, 2008.

4. Mark L. Clifford, "Banking's Great Wall," *Business Week*, June 1, 2003, http://www.businessweek.com/stories/2003-06-01/bankings-great-wall.

5. Professor Keun S. Lee, "The Korean Crisis and the IMF Bailout" (Crisis in Asia: Analysis and Perspectives seminar, Hofstra University, Hempstead, NY, February 28, 1998), http://www.hofstra.edu/pdf/biz_MLC_Lee3.pdf.

6. "China's patient crusader: Weijian Shan is fighting to make Chinese business more normal," *The Economist*, May 12, 2005, http://www.economist.com/node/3960876.

7. Li Liming, Yanchun Wang, and Chaoge Shi, "Banking Tycoon Weijian Shan Enters the Chinese Banking Industry" (in Chinese), *The Economic Observer*, December 30, 2002, http://finance.sina.com.cn/roll/20021230/1114296285.shtml.

8. Stephanie Strom, "US Firm Has Control of Korea First Bank," *The New York Times*, September 17, 1999, http://www.nytimes.com/1999/09/18/business/international-business-us-firm-has-control-of-korea-first-bank.html.

9. These and many other details noted in this section on China's banking industry, Shenzhen's condition in 2003, and difficulties Newbridge confronted after a year of negotiations to acquire Shenzhen are described in the Harvard Business School Case 210-020, "Shenzhen Development Bank," by Li Jin, Yuhai Xuan, and Xiaobing Bai (Harvard Business School Publishing, revised March 2011, http://www.hbs.edu/faculty/Pages/item.aspx?num=37769).

10. Clifford, "Banking's Great Wall."

Chapter 8

1. Western bureaucracies evolved in the nineteenth century to impose structure, stability, and consistency amid perceived chaos as organizations grew larger, especially in military and civic administration. Leaders of the first corporations to emerge in the twentieth century, such as Ford Motor and General

Motors, borrowed heavily from the military in creating top-down, command-and-control organizations. German sociologist Max Weber identified benefits of bureaucratic principles in the 1920s, but also cautioned wisely against bureaucracy's limits on individual freedoms and human progress.

2. Irvin Molotsky, "Joseph Alioto, 81, Dies; Antitrust Lawyer Was San Francisco's Mayor in Boom Years," *The New York Times*, January 30, 1999, http://www.nytimes.com/1998/01/30/us/joseph-alioto-81-dies-antitrust-lawyer-was-san-francisco-s-mayor-in-boom-years.html.

3. John Burton's brother, Phil, was a powerful congressman for two decades who nearly became House majority leader, losing by one vote in 1976 to Representative Jim Wright of Texas. Phil gerrymandered several California districts, including the one for John where I lived in Marin County, so they would be more favorable for Democrats. These and other details of Phil's outsized life as a force in progressive politics are covered in the excellent biography by John Jacobs, *A Rage for Justice: The Passion and Politics of Phil Burton* (Berkeley: University of California Press, 1996). For highlights of Phil Burton's career, see also "Rep. Philip Burton, Democratic Liberal, Dies on Visit to California," Obituaries, *The New York Times*, April 11, 1983, http://www.nytimes.com/1983/04/11/obituaries/rep-phillip-burton-democratic-liberal-dies-on-visit-to-california.html.

4. David Talbot, *Season of the Witch: Enchantment, Terror, and Deliverance in the City of Love* (New York: Free Press, 2012), 257.

5. Dianne Feinstein et al., with Catherine Whitney, *Nine and Counting: The Women of the Senate* (New York: William Morrow, 2000).

6. Jerry Roberts, *Dianne Feinstein: Never Let Them See You Cry* (New York: HarperCollins Publishers, 1994), 35.

7. Ibid.

8. Thirty years later, Dianne talked publicly and at length with reporters about the assassinations. For a full account of that session with reporters, see Rachel Gordon, "Feinstein Recalls S.F.'s 'Day of Infamy,'" *San Francisco Chronicle*, November 26, 2008. For a ten-minute video segment from that session, see "Dianne Feinstein on Moscone, Milk Deaths," YouTube video, 9:59, from an interview conducted November 25, 2009, posted by SuchIsLifeVideos, July 19, 2010, https://www.youtube.com/watch?v=_4051pdMlnQ.

9. Talbot, *Season of the Witch*, 339.

10. Ibid., 335.

Chapter 9

1. University of California, "Statistical Summary of Students and Staff," fall 2002, http://legacy-its.ucop.edu/uwnews/stat/statsum/fall2002/statsumm2002.pdf.

2. "Berkeley Ranked No. 1 Public University by US News," UC Berkeley News Center, September 9, 2014, http://newscenter.berkeley.edu/2014/09/09/berkeley-ranked-1-public-university-by-us-news/. See also "Best Global Universities Rankings," *US News & World Report*, accessed May 6, 2015, http://www.usnews.com/education/best-global-universities/rankings.

3. After taking maternity leave for a few years, Betsy joined the American Himalayan Foundation as head of finance and budgeting. Her story is an example of a skilled executive with experience in business and academia shifting careers and further strengthening programs of a well-managed charitable organization.

4. Robert Birgeneau, "What the Energy Biosciences Institute Means for UC Berkeley—and the World," Bear in Mind: Conversations with the Chancellor, March 2, 2007, http://www.berkeley.edu/news/chancellor/bim/mar07_transcript.shtml.

5. Financial assets in the Harvard Endowment were valued
    at $36.4 billion in 2014, according to Dan Fitzpatrick,
    "Harvard Endowment Earns 15.4% Return for 2014," *The
    Wall Street Journal*, September 23, 2014, http://www.wsj.
    com/articles/harvard-endowment-earns-15-4-return-for-
    fiscal-2014-1411506002. The fund distributed $1.5 billion to
    research, professorship, and financial aid in the 2013 academic
    year, or approximately 5 percent of fund assets and one-third of
    the university's annual operating budget. For more details on how
    the Harvard Endowment is managed and its role in supporting
    university programs, see http://www.harvard.edu/about-harvard/
    harvard-glance/endowment.

6. "UC Day 2015," University of California, March 10, 2015, http://
    www.universityofcalifornia.edu/sites/default/files/ucday2015_
    economic_impact.pdf.

7. Nanette Asimov, "Mark Yudof, UC President, to Step Down,"
    San Francisco Chronicle, January 18, 2013, http://www.sfgate.
    com/education/article/Mark-Yudof-UC-president-to-step-
    down-4206304.php.

Chapter 10

1. Millions more Americans lost faith in President Lyndon Johnson's
    conduct of the war a few months after my trip to Da Nang when,
    beginning January 30, 1968, forces of the North Vietnamese and
    Vietcong mounted the largest orchestrated attacks yet across
    South Vietnam. Known as the Tet Offensive, coinciding with the
    Vietnamese "Tet" New Year holiday, the attacks stunned both
    the US and South Vietnamese armies and the American people.
    Americans had been assured after a massive buildup of US troops
    in 1965 and 1966 that the enemy was not capable of executing
    such large-scale attacks against military and civilian command
    posts in South Vietnam. On March 31, 1968, with his credibility
    and popularity waning, President Johnson announced to the
    country at the end of a speech about the war that he would not
    seek reelection. See Walter F. Mondale, with David Hage, *The*

Good Fight: A Life in Liberal Politics (New York: Scribner, 2010), 69–71.

2. Then an incipient civil rights and antiwar organization based in California, the Peace and Freedom Party is still active today, fielding candidates with a broad socialist agenda. I was audited regularly for many years by the Internal Revenue Service after filing my report. I was led to believe, but could never confirm, that my report and subsequent affiliation with the Peace and Freedom Party earned me a spot on Richard Nixon's infamous "enemies list." If I was on the list, I'm proud of it. In any event, it has been twenty-five years or more since I last was audited by the IRS.

3. "Global Greenhouse Gas Emissions Data," United States Environmental Protection Agency, 2011, accessed March 21, 2016, http://www3.epa.gov/climatechange/ghgemissions/global.html.

4. Mondale and Hage, 6, 71.

5. "Walter F. Mondale, 42nd Vice President (1977–1981)," US Senate, accessed June 25, 2015, http://www.senate.gov/artandhistory/history/common/generic/VP_Walter_Mondale.htm.

6. Estimates of Vietnamese military and civilian deaths during the war vary. In 1995, the Hanoi government's official report put civilian deaths at more than two million—four times higher than estimates by others outside Vietnam—and estimated that 1.1 million soldiers died in the war. Ku Bia, "How Many People died in the Vietnam War?" *Vietnam War*, April 11, 2014, http://thevietnamwar.info/how-many-people-died-in-the-vietnam-war/.

7. Mondale and Hage, 46.

8. Ingrid W. Reed, "The Life and Death of UDAG: An Assessment Based on Eight Projects in Five New Jersey Cities," *Publius: The Journal of Federalism,* Oxford Journals, 19, no. 3 (1989): 93–109, http://publius.oxfordjournals.org/content/19/3/93.abstract. In her abstract of this academic report, the author writes, "The federal Urban Development Action Grant program, begun in 1977, provided $5 billion over eleven years revitalizing severely

distressed urban places through the encouragement of private sector investment. Designed to assist commercial, industrial, and housing projects that 'but for' the federal grant would not be built, the program was characterized by a streamlined grant-making process administered by finance and development experts . . . During the Reagan years, the administration sought to end the program. Congress supported it, but reduced the funding each year" and shut down UDAG in 1988.

9. Martin Agronsky is widely credited with creating the format in broadcast news with prominent journalists reviewing and commenting on current events. His initial program, *Agronsky & Company*, began in 1969, and introduced the format as a program segment. A shorter-lived program, *Agronsky at Large*, used the format entirely. Earlier in his career Agronsky hosted the CBS Sunday public affairs program, *Face the Nation*, was a political correspondent for all three major commercial broadcast networks, and was honored with a George Foster Peabody Award in 1952 for first exposing in radio reports the excesses of Senator Joseph McCarthy in McCarthy's pursuit of communist conspirators among government officials and private citizens. For highlights of Agronsky's career, see "Martin Agronsky; Political Talk Show Host," Obituaries, *Washington Post*, July 26, 1999, http://articles.latimes.com/1999/jul/26/news/mn-59706.

10. More details on Power Africa are available on the USAID program's microsite at http://www.usaid.gov/powerafrica.

11. The first report of the President's Global Development Council was published on April 14, 2014, two years after the council was established by the White House and four years after President Obama released his US Global Development Policy in 2010. See President's Global Development Council, "Beyond Business as Usual," April 14, 2014, http://www.usaid.gov/sites/default/files/gdc_memo_for_the_president_final.pdf. A second report was published the following year; see President's Global Development Council, "Modernizing Development," May 15,

2015, https://www.usaid.gov/sites/default/files/documents/1872/
GlobalDevelopmentCouncilReportModernizingDevelopment.pdf.

12. White House Fact Sheet, 2010, https://www.whitehouse.gov
/the-press-office/2010/09/22/fact-sheet-us-global-development-
policy.

13. Investor–philanthropist George Soros established the Open
Society Foundations to help countries make the transition
from communism to democracy. The Soros Foundation's Open
Society Foundations have supported grassroots efforts for self-
determination and creation of a civil society in Ukraine since
1990. See https://www.opensocietyfoundations.org/explainers/
understanding-ukraine.

14. Reuters, "U.S. Takes Control of $480 Million Stolen by
Nigerian Dictator Abacha," August 14, 2014, http://www.reuters
.com/article/2014/08/07/us-usa-nigeria-assets-
idUSKBN0G72BO20140807.

15. Jason Carter, also a Carter Center trustee, ran unsuccessfully
for Georgia governor in 2014 against the Republican
incumbent, Nathan Deal, receiving 45 percent of the
vote. For Jason Carter's postmortem on the defeat, see
Greg Bluestein, "Jason Carter on a Potential Comeback:
'I'm Not Ruling It Out,'" *Atlanta Journal-Constitution*,
November 18, 2014, http://politics.blog.ajc.com/2014/11/18/
jason-carter-on-a-potential-comeback-im-not-ruling-it-out/.

16. Obasanjo left office when his second term ended in 2007. Late
in 2014, he was publicly critical of his successor as president,
Goodluck Jonathan, accusing Jonathan of squandering billions
in the government's oil-revenue savings. See Dimeji Kayode-
Adedej, "Obasanjo Attacks Jonathan Again, Accuses President
of Squandering Oil Savings," *Premium Times*, January 5, 2015,
http://www.premiumtimesng.com/news/headlines/174294-
obasanjo-attacks-jonathan-accuses-president-squandering-oil-
savings.html.

Chapter 11

1. According to the first official census of the People's Republic of China, in 2010, there were 2.7 million Tibetans living in all of China, and 1.2 million within Tibet.

2. See Tibet Support Group UK, "Chinese Presence in Tibet: Population Transfer," Tibet Online, accessed March 21, 2016, http://www.tibet.org/Activism/Rights/poptransfer.html, and "Beijing Sends a New Flood of Han Migrants to Lhasa: Tibetans Risk Disappearing," AsiaNews.it, January 27, 2015, http://www.asianews.it/news-en/Beijing-sends-a-new-flood-of-Han-migrants-to-Lhasa:-Tibetans-risk-disappearing-33294.html.

3. Walter F. Mondale, with David Hage, *The Good Fight: A Life in Liberal Politics* (New York: Scribner, 2010), 331.

4. Jorg Eigendorf, "The Dalai Lama Talks Chinese Reforms, Tibetan Challenges," NPR, October 4, 2014, http://www.npr.org/sections/parallels/2014/10/04/353570578/the-dalai-lama-talks-chinese-reforms-tibetan-challenges.

5. "The Global Religious Landscape: Buddhists," Pew Research Center, December 18, 2012, accessed June 29, 2015, http://www.pewforum.org/2012/12/18/global-religious-landscape-buddhist/. A study by the Pew Research Center estimated the total 2010 world population of Buddhists at 488 million—approximately 250 million of whom lived in China—based on 2010 census figures.

6. When Lodi Gyari stepped down as leader of the International Campaign for Tibet in 2014, he wrote an eloquent summation of the campaign's work with leaders in Congress and the White House over the prior twenty-five years. Lodi graciously singled out Dianne and me for helping elevate the Tibetan cause beyond a human rights and humanitarian concern, which it absolutely is, to an important geopolitical issue. Lodi wrote, "Senator Dianne Feinstein and her husband, Richard Blum, deserve special mention. They were relentless in this endeavor and even made special trips to China carrying personal communications from His Holiness the

Dalai Lama to President Jiang Zemin." See Lodi Gyaltsen Gyari, "My Personal Words of Gratitude," International Campaign for Tibet, December 31, 2014, http://www.savetibet.org/my-personal-words-of-gratitude/#sthash.8fAEo3bl.dpuf.

7. Barry Naughton, "Zhu Rongji: The Twilight of a Brilliant Career," *China Leadership Monitor* (Winter 2002) no. 1, http://media. hoover.org/sites/default/files/documents/clm1_BN.pdf.

8. Henry Kissinger, *On China* (New York: Penguin Books, 2001), 447.

9. When I introduce His Holiness at speaking engagements, I often say, "We know who His Holiness was in his last life. He was the Thirteenth Dalai Lama. What we don't know is who I was in my last life. I must have done something really terrible to be reincarnated as an investment banker."

10. Susan Begley, "Scans of Monks' Brains Show Meditation Alters Structure, Functioning," *The Wall Street Journal*, November 5, 2004, http://www.wsj.com/articles/SB109959818932165108.

11. A. Tom Grunfeld, *The Making of Modern Tibet* (New York: Routledge, 1996), Kindle edition, location 5909.

12. "Son of Purged Reformer Zhao Ziyang Tells of China's 'Shame', 25 years after Tiananmen," *South China Morning Post*, May 19, 2014, http://www.scmp.com/news/china/article/1515862/son-purged-liberal-leader-zhao-ziyang-tells-chinas-shame-25-years-after?page=all.

13. "The Golden Urn: Even China Accepts That Only the Dalai Lama Can Legitimize Its Rule in Tibet," Banyan column, *The Economist*, March 19, 2015, http://www.economist.com/news/china/21646795-even-china-accepts-only-dalai-lama-can-legitimise-its-rule-tibet-golden-urn.

14. Reuters, "China Calls on Dalai Lama to 'Put Aside Illusions' about Talks," April 15, 2015, http://www.reuters.com/article/2015/04/15/us-china-tibet-idUSKBN0N608720150415.

15. Brian Knowlton, "Bush and Congress Honor Dalai Lama," *The New York Times*, October 18, 2007, http://www.nytimes. com/2007/10/18/washington/18lama.html.

16. "Congress Awards the Congressional Gold Medal to His Holiness, the Dalai Lama," website of Dianne Feinstein, United States Senator for California, October 17, 2007, http://www.feinstein.senate.gov/public/index.cfm/ press-releases?ID=af6d24ef-ff69-4302-ebc1-e74997171713.

17. Eigendorf, "The Dalai Lama Talks Chinese Reforms."

Chapter 12

1. Bill Clinton, Forrestal Lecture Series, US Naval Academy, April 8, 2014, in William Jefferson Clinton, *Select Remarks: 2014* (New York: The Clinton Foundation, 2014), 20.

2. For full data on income and poverty in the United States, see www. census.gov/hhes/www/poverty/data/.

3. UNICEF, "Innocenti Report Card 12, Children of the Recession: The Impact of the Economic Crisis on Child Well-Being in Rich Countries," October 2014, www.unicef-irc.org/publications/733.

4. Most material in a 2013 documentary narrated by Bob Reich, *Inequality for All*, is drawn from Bob's Wealth and Poverty lectures and his thirteenth book, *Beyond Outrage: What Has Gone Wrong with Our Economy and Our Democracy, and How to Fix It*.

5. Emmanuel Saez, a UC Berkeley economics professor who tracks income distribution in the United States, reported in his white paper "Striking It Richer: The Evolution of Top Incomes in the United States (Updated with 2014 Preliminary Estimates)" (June 25, 2015, http://eml.berkeley.edu/~saez/saez-UStopincomes-2014. pdf) that a "significant fraction of the surge" in incomes of the top 1 percentile of wage earners since 1970 "is due to an explosion of top wages and salaries" for that segment. The top 1 percentile

earned 12.4 percent of total wages and salaries paid in the United States in 2007, up from 5.1 percent in 1970.

6. Robert Reich, "Why College Is Necessary but Gets You Nowhere," *Huffington Post*, November 24, 2014, http://www.huffingtonpost.com/robert-reich/why-college-is-necessary_b_6215668.html?utm_hp_ref=email_share.

7. The alliance in Vietnam, known as the Vietnam National Tuberculosis Control Programme, featured world-class medical scientists from UC San Francisco's biomedical research campus, the US Agency for International Development, and the World Health Organization, among several other organizations. For more details on CellScope, see Tamara Straus, "A Device That Could Change Healthcare," accessed March 22, 2016, http://blumcenter.berkeley.edu/news-posts/a-device-that-could-change-healthcare/.

8. This excerpt from Anh-Thi Le's essay is adapted with permission.

9. The US Centers for Disease Control and Prevention says hepatitis E, a liver disease, "is widespread in the developing world, with major epidemics reported in Asia, the Middle East, Africa, and Central America. People living in refugee camps or overcrowded temporary housing after natural disasters can be particularly at risk." Inadequate water supply and sanitation often are reasons for outbreaks. For more information, see "Viral Hepatitis—Hepatitis E Information," Centers for Disease Control and Prevention, accessed December 23, 2014, http://www.cdc.gov/hepatitis/HEV/HEVfaq.htm.

10. Dr. Rajiv Shah, "Remarks . . . at the University of California Berkeley," US Agency for International Development, October 10, 2012, https://www.usaid.gov/news-information/speeches/remarks-usaid-administrator-rajiv-shah-university-california-berkeley.

11. Lina Nilsson, "How to Attract Female Engineers," *The New York Times*, April 27, 2015, http://www.nytimes.com/2015/04/27/opinion/how-to-attract-female-engineers.html?_r=0.

Chapter *13*

1. "My Vote Today Wins 'Art of Start' Pitch Session
   at LetsIgnite 2016," *Inc42*, March 11, 2016,
   accessed April 3, 2016, http://inc42.com/buzz/
   my-vote-today-wins-art-of-start-pitch-session-at-letsignite-2016/.

2. J. Vignesh, "How Citizengage Is Engaging Citizens to Make
   Bengaluru Cleaner," *Economic Times*, March 18, 2016, accessed
   April 3, 2016, http://tech.economictimes.indiatimes.com/news/
   startups/how-citizengage-is-engaging-citizens-to-make-bengaluru-
   cleaner/51451158.

3. Thomas L. Friedman, "When E.T. and I.T. Meet ID," *The
   New York Times*, February 12, 2013, http://www.nytimes.
   com/2013/02/13/opinion/friedman-when-et-and-it-meet-id.html
   Accessed December 12, 2014.

4. Lauren Herman's manual is available at http://www.
   microfinancegateway.org/library/my-guide-microfinace-lending,
   the website of Microfinance Gateway (part of the World Bank's
   Consultative Group to Assist the Poor) and at http://www.
   smartcampaign.org/, the website of The Smart Campaign (part of
   ACCION International, a global nonprofit organization that for
   more than fifty years has supported microfinance institutions in
   providing financial services to low-income clients).

Conclusion

1. Bill Clinton, Forrestal Lecture, US Naval Academy, April 8, 2014,
   published in William Jefferson Clinton, *Select Remarks: 2014*
   (New York: The Clinton Foundation, 2014), 20.

Bibliography and Resources

Avedon, John F. *In Exile from the Land of Snows: The Dalai Lama and Tibet since the Chinese Conquest.* New York: Harper Perennial, 1994.

Bernstein, Peter L. *Against the Gods: The Remarkable Story of Risk.* New York: John Wiley & Sons, 1996.

Beschloss, Michael. *The Conquerors: Roosevelt, Truman and the Destruction of Hitler's Germany, 1941–1945.* New York: Simon & Schuster, 2002.

———. *Presidential Courage: Brave Leaders and How they Changed America, 1789–1989.* New York: Simon & Schuster, 2007.

Blum, Richard C., Erica Stone, and Broughton Coburn, eds. *Himalaya: Personal Stories of Grandeur, Challenge, and Hope.* Washington, DC: National Geographic Society, 2006.

Boo, Katherine. *Behind the Beautiful Forevers: Life, Death, and Hope in a Mumbai Undercity.* New York: Random House, 2012.

Breyer, Stephen. *The Court and the World: American Law and the New Global Realities.* New York: Alfred A. Knopf, 2015.

Carter, Jimmy. *A Call to Action: Women, Religion, Violence, and Power.* New York: Simon & Schuster, 2014.

———. *A Full Life: Reflections at Ninety.* New York: Simon & Schuster, 2015.

———. *An Outdoor Journal: Adventures and Reflections*. 2nd edition. Fayetteville, AR: University of Arkansas Press, 1994.

Chandy, Laurence, Hiroshi Kato, Homi Kharas, eds. *The Last Mile in Ending Extreme Poverty*. Washington, DC: Brookings Institution Press, 2015.

Clifford, Mark L. *The Greening of Asia: The Business Case for Solving Asia's Environmental Emergency*. New York: Columbia Business School Publishing, 2015.

Clinton, Bill. *Back to Work: Why We Need Smart Government for a Strong Economy*. New York: Alfred A. Knopf, 2011.

———. *Giving: How Each of Us Can Change the World*. New York: Alfred A. Knopf, 2007.

Clinton, Hillary Rodham. *It Takes a Village: And Other Lessons Children Teach Us*. New York: Simon & Schuster, 2006.

Coburn, Broughton. *The Vast Unknown: America's First Ascent of Everest*. New York: Crown Publishers, 2013.

Collins, Daryl, Jonathan Morduch, Stuart Rutherford, and Orlanda Ruthven. *Portfolios of the Poor: How the World's Poor Live on $2 a Day*. Princeton, NJ: Princeton University Press, 2009.

Dalai Lama, His Holiness. *My Land and My People: The Original Autobiography of His Holiness the Dalai Lama of Tibet*. New York: Grand Central Publishing, 1997.

Dalai Lama, His Holiness and Victor Chan. *The Wisdom of Compassion: Stories of Remarkable Encounters and Timeless Insights*. New York: Riverhead Books, 2012.

Dalai Lama, His Holiness and Howard C. Cutler, MD. *The Art of Happiness: a Handbook for Living*. New York: Riverhead Books, 1998.

Dalai Lama, His Holiness and Alexander Norman. *Beyond Religion: Ethics for a Whole World*. New York: Houghton Mifflin Harcourt, 2011.

Easterly, William. *The White Man's Burden: Why the West's Efforts to Aid the Rest Have Done So Much Ill and So Little Good*. New York: Penguin, 2006.

Friedman, Thomas L. *Hot, Flat and Crowded: Why We Need a Green Revolution—and How It Can Renew America*. New York: Farrar, Strauss and Giroux, 2008.

Goleman, Daniel. *A Force for Good: The Dalai Lama's Vision for Our World*. New York: Bantam Books, 2015.

Grunfeld, A. Tom. *The Making of Modern Tibet*. New York: Routledge, 1996.

Halliburton, Richard. *Richard Halliburton's Complete Book of Marvels*. New York: The Bobbs-Merrill Company, 1948.

Hillary, Sir Edmund. *Ascent: Two Lives Explored: The Autobiographies of Sir Edmund and Peter Hillary*. New York: Doubleday, 1986.

———. *High Adventure: Our Ascent of the Everest*. BCL Press, 2003.

———. *Schoolhouse in the Clouds*. New York: Doubleday, 1964.

———. *View from the Summit: The Remarkable Memoir by the First Person to Conquer Everest*. New York: Doubleday, 1999.

Iyer, Pico. *The Open Road: The Global Journey of the Fourteenth Dalai Lama*. New York: Alfred A. Knopf, 2008.

———. *Video Night in Kathmandu and Other Reports from the Not-so-far-East*. New York: Alfred A. Knopf, 1988.

Jinpa, Thupten. *A Fearless Heart: How the Courage to Be Compassionate Can Transform Our Lives*. New York: Hudson Street Press, 2015.

Kara, Siddharth. *Sex Trafficking: Inside the Business of Modern Slavery*. New York: Columbia University Press, 2009.

Kidder, Tracy. *Mountains by Mountains: The Quest of Dr. Paul Farmer, A Man Who Would Cure the World*. New York: Random House, 2003.

Kissinger, Henry. *World Order*. New York: Penguin Press, 2014.

———. *On China*. New York: Penguin Books, 2011.

Krakauer, Jon. *Three Cups of Deceit: How Greg Mortenson, Humanitarian Hero, Lost His Way*. New York: Anchor Books, 2011.

———. *Into Thin Air: A Personal Account of the Mt. Everest Disaster*. New York: Villard Books, 1997.

Kristof, Nicholas D. and Sheryl WuDunn. *A Path Appears: Transforming Lives, Creating Opportunity*. New York: Alfred A. Knopf, 2014.

———. *Half the Sky: Turning Oppression into Opportunity for Women Worldwide*. New York: Alfred. A. Knopf, 2009.

Matthews, Chris. *Hardball: How Politics Is Played, Told by One Who Knows the Game*. New York: Simon & Schuster, 1999.

Mondale, Walter F. *The Good Fight: A Life in Liberal Politics*. New York: Scribner, 2010.

Reich, Robert B. *Beyond Outrage: What Has Gone Wrong with Our Economy and Our Democracy, and How to Fix It*. New York: Vintage Books, 2012.

———. *Saving Capitalism: For the Many, Not the Few*. New York: Alfred A. Knopf, 2015.

———. *Supercapitalism: The Transformation of Business, Democracy, and Everyday Life*. New York: Alfred A. Knopf, 2007.

Ricard, Matthieu. *Altruism: The Power of Compassion to Change Yourself and the World*. New York: Little Brown, 2015.

Rubin, Robert E. and Jacob Weisberg. *In an Uncertain World: Tough Choices from Wall Street to Washington*. New York: Random House, 2003.

Shultz, George P. *Turmoil and Triumph: My Years as Secretary of State*. New York: Scribner, 1993.

Soros, George. *George Soros on Globalization*. New York: PublicAffairs, 2005.

———. *Open Society: Reforming Global Capitalism*. New York: PublicAffairs, 1998.

———. *The Soros Lectures: At the Central European University*. New York: PublicAffairs, 2010.

Talbot, David. *Season of the Witch: Enchantment, Terror, and Deliverance in the City of Love*. New York: Free Press, 2012.

Tett, Gillian. *Fool's Gold: How Unrestrained Greed Corrupted a Dream, Shattered Global Markets and Unleashed a Catastrophe*. New York: Free Press, 2009.

———. *The Silo Effect: The Peril of Expertise and the Promise of Breaking Down Barriers*. New York: Simon & Schuster, 2015.

Wolf, Martin. *Fixing Global Finance*. Baltimore, MD: Johns Hopkins University Press, 2009.

———. *The Shifts and the Shocks: What We've Learned—and Have Still to Learn—from the Financial Crisis*. New York: Penguin Press, 2014.

Zakaria, Fareed. *In Defense of a Liberal Education*. New York: W.W. Norton & Company, 2015.

———. *The Post-American World: Release 2.0*. New York: W.W. Norton & Company, 2011.

Index

About the Authors

Richard C. Blum

Richard C. Blum is the founder of the University of California's Blum Center for Developing Economies, founder and chairman of the American Himalayan Foundation, Honorary Consul of Nepal, emeritus trustee of the Brookings Institution, and founder of the Brookings Blum Roundtable on Global Poverty. A private-equity investor, he is founding partner and chairman of San Francisco–based Blum Capital Partners and its affiliate partners. He is former chairman of CBRE Group, and was a long-serving director of Northwest Airlines, and vice chairman of URS Corporation. He was cofounder and partner in Newbridge Capital, an investment group focused on Asia.

Richard has been a regent of the University of California since 2002, and chairman emeritus after serving more than two years as chairman. He earned his undergraduate and master's degrees at UC Berkeley's School of Business. He is married to US Senator Dianne Feinstein, of California, and serves on the boards of The Carter Center, the National Democratic Institute for International Affairs, the President's Global Development Council, Central European University, and The Wilderness Society, among others.

Thomas C. Hayes

Thomas C. Hayes is a principal with Finsbury, a global consulting firm in strategic communications, and a former award-winning *New York Times* economic correspondent. This is his fourth book, collaborating on each as writer with authors in business, investing, management, technology, and philanthropy. He and his wife live in Bethel, Connecticut.